TOUR DE FRANCE

TOUR DE FRANCE

THE HISTORY, THE LEGEND, THE RIDERS

GRAEME FIFE

MAINSTREAM
PUBLISHING

EDINBURGH AND LONDON

For Lucy

First published in Great Britain in 1999 by
MAINSTREAM PUBLISHING COMPANY (EDINBURGH) LTD
7 Albany Street
Edinburgh EH1 3UG

ISBN 1 84018 806 5

Revised and reprinted 1999, 2000, 2001, 2002, 2004

This edition, 2003

A catalogue record for this book is available from the British Library

Typeset in Sabon and Garamond
Printed and bound in Great Britain by Creative Print and Design Wales

CONTENTS

AUTHOR'S NOTE

Wherever possible I have based this account of the Tour de France on original testimony: the riders' memoirs – Bidot, Anquetil, Merckx, Hinault, Robic, Maertens, Lemond, Simpson and others; the specialist French journals, magazines and books; and my own recollection garnered over a period of some 25 years of addiction to this unique event. It is not a comprehensive history. Such a tome would probably be unreadable and certainly too heavy to read other than from a lectern. My aim, rather, was to get inside the mystique of the Tour.

I have checked and cross-checked information but am aware that factual errors may have strayed into the text – sources tend to be contradictory. I cheerfully acknowledge the sterling help of two fellow enthusiasts and friends of mine, John Partington and Nick Flanagan, who have helped me with statistics, sharpened my knowledge of the more arcane workings of Tour methodology and given unflagging support in the enterprise, not least in fielding my opinions on and joining discussion of tactics, the evaluation of riders and exploring the peculiar allure of the race itself. If any errors have survived a painstaking scrutiny, the fault is mine alone.

Anthony Wood, as ever, gave me invaluable help in shaping the text; and John Partington's editorial advice in streamlining the original manuscript was as spot-on as his wheelbuilding.

Henri Desgrange, the 'father of the Tour', was all for simplicity. Set aside the Byzantine complexity of his rules, his undimmable idealism, his fanatical resistance to technological innovation, his misogyny – sex and cycling in his view did not mix – his restless search for more arduous challenges, and the imperative was direct: to win the Tour, he said, requires two things – *tête et jambes* . . . head and legs.

This book has much to do with both.

Here are the stories, epic, tragic, comic, bizarre, incredible, fascinating, of the riders who have won, lost or simply ridden the Tour de France.

FOREWORD

BY CHRIS BOARDMAN OBE

When I first entered the Tour I didn't really know what to expect. I had no idea what I was going into. It was our plan for me only to ride the first ten days, up to the Pyrenees, to see how I went and as preparation for future rides. Winning the Prologue was something I'd thought about, obviously – it's my specialist event – but I was so new and inexperienced I hardly knew it had happened. Even standing on the podium, receiving the yellow jersey that every cyclist dreams of wearing, I could hardly grasp the importance of it. I was really hyped but it felt as if that victory had just landed on my plate. It was only later that it really dawned on me just how big the event was, how important, and riding the other Prologues, knowing what it took to win, trying to emulate that first win, was much harder than anything else I had ever done. That first year I went to see the finish in Paris; it was thrilling to see the *peloton* ride the final lap. It was when the manager drove me up the Champs-Elysées that morning that I fell in love with the Tour. I don't take my Prologue wins for granted in the least as they are only part of my goal, a goal I am pursuing as hard as I can.

The Tour is, without doubt, the biggest single sporting event in the world. You have to see it in person – standing at the side of the road, behind the barriers at the *Arrivée*, perched by the side of the mountains – to believe the impact it has. When the Tour comes to town it's like the Olympics arriving. There simply is nothing else like it. And, as a test of physical and mental endurance it has no equal. Other sports may be as intense, as pressurised, as hard for short periods: but the Tour goes on day after day after day. They say it's the only race in the world where you have to have a haircut halfway through.

Graeme has written a terrific account of this amazing race, from the early days. It's a book tailor-made for bike fans as well as for the casual fans who see the Tour on Channel 4 every year. The Tour de France *is* a legendary race and here is a great read to go with it.

PREFACE

Millau, 15 July 1995

The Tour de France is due to pass through here around noon. Metal barriers lining the streets have been in position since 9 a.m. Last night, the town was *en fête* for Bastille Day: fireworks, accordion bands, thronging crowds and dancing in the town square. The same crowds are beginning to flock into town now. The accordion band, eight-strong, is back on the makeshift stage in the Place de Ville, zipping through a medley of boulevardier tunes, quintessentially French. Mid-morning, the municipal brass band, in maroon uniform with silver brocades and swagging, struts and oompahs its repertoire up and down the main street – cornets, trumpets and euphoniums, cymbals, tubas and drums . . . *Allons enfants de la Patrie, Le jour de gloire est arrivé.*

We stroll round the shops, but everyone is at the same game this morning in Millau: filling in time. There's an air of expectancy as if the whole town was waiting with bated breath, and sudden silences pervade the streets and pavements. We wait, nerves taut, listening for the whisper from way off that the Tour has hit the outskirts; but it is a false alarm. The low murmur of meandering citizens at leisure and desultory business resumes, Saturday-morning errands, window-shopping and rendezvous. The cafés and bars do slick trade in the lazy sunshine.

By 11 a.m. the barriers are pretty well lined with spectators, there's some good-humoured jostling for a better view: on the cusp of a bend, maybe, or with a long view of the straight, even if slightly obscured by plane trees to either side. Some old hands keep their seats at the pavement tables, time enough to move in before the action proper begins. A flurry of applause, cheers, laughter, as a young bride in white silk and lace, hoisting her dress up round her calves, is tiptoeing across the street and through a gap in the hurdles, picking her way to the church to be married. The Tour rules: thou shalt walk to thy wedding. She beams with mirth at the public congratulation on this doubly auspicious day.

At 11.30 a.m, a raucous fanfare of klaxons in the distance heralds the Tour vanguard: radio and television cars, Commissariat, publicity cavalcade – soda cans on wheels, motorised Coca-Cola bottles, petrol-driven bonbons – team wagons topped with serried ranks of spare wheels spinning fast in the slipstream. A maroon saloon draws up alongside the barriers where I'm standing. Out steps Raymond Poulidor. Blimey. The great Poupou, suntanned, fit, smiling. Poupou, the 'eternal second', still in the Tour promoting Poulain chocolate. He never promoted himself half as successfully; one reason, perhaps, why he never won the Tour, never even wore the *maillot jaune*, albeit he had the class, and class to spare. His *bête noire*, Anquetil, was the first to win five times, and when he retired Poulidor met another *bête noire*, Merckx, the second man to win five times. What luck. Poulidor came to terms with defeat; Anquetil never could. But here is Poulidor while Anquetil is eight years dead, mourned by none more than his old adversary. Someone taps him on the arm; he scrambles back into the car. Apparently a break of five riders has jumped clear of the main field and will be through 15 minutes ahead of schedule. The chocolate saloon roars off. I remark to a bystander, a local: 'Poulidor, eh? Such a pity he never won.'

'Yes; still, he's got more money than he can spend, and he's still alive. Anquetil had no heart; he was always for himself. Poulidor? A gentleman; too much a gentleman, maybe, but that's past and he's as popular now as he ever was.'

Anquetil enjoyed not an iota of that: indubitably the best, but he never won their hearts.

Hush again like a blast of heat. They must be close and, in a sudden intense silky hiss of ultra-lightweight racing tyres on hot tarmac, a windrush of whirring spokes, a flash of colour, the escapers are there and past us. The American Lance Armstrong, ex-World Champion, the prime mover, evidently. He's controlling things from the middle to the side, gesticulating urgently with his right arm, wagging a finger at the road, glancing over his shoulder at his *directeur sportif* (team manager), maybe, but why? Food? Drink? An update on the lead time? Mechanical adjustment to the bike while on the move? Such tiny snippets of drama; the Tour is replete with them. But, most of all, 'escape' sums it up. These fugitives are riding as if they were aristocrats and the bunch were a Jacobin mob howling for their blood.

Ten minutes later, the Tour is on us; the *peloton, en masse*, a multicoloured polycycle, 150 rider-strong express engine moving at such a lick you can't believe the attack will ever have the speed and stamina to hold them off. The sensation of raw power makes you shiver; the thrill of the colour; the noise of the generator whirring – wheels, cranks, chains – is abrupt but exhilarating. Spotting faces in the pack is well-nigh impossible: too dense, they're riding tyre to tyre, elbow to elbow; and too many splashes of yellow in the team jerseys to pick out *the* yellow. But wait, there he is, Indurain, six feet plus of him, crouched like a big cat on the bike; effortless power, fluid action, ball-bearing-smooth tempo. Not all of them have that, the supple grace that only changes as the stage finish approaches and the break is still out and they charge up to crisis acceleration. Merckx was a bruiser in style.

And, like a daytime comet blazing across France by small ways and highways in garish pageant, they are gone, west. Millau's sudden moment of regal blessing has passed. *Ville d'étape*, a singular honour the town has enjoyed before. Within 15 minutes all the cordons have been dismantled, cars and pedestrians are soft-shoeing the market-day shuffle in the four roads leading to the central roundabout, and we head for lunch in a tiny restaurant down the road leading north which the Tour did not touch. It is markedly darker, cooler, quieter, lonelier without that heat of the race and the elation of the crowd when the leading bikes burst out of the mirage. I commiserate with the *patronne* who couldn't watch the race go by because she was busy serving lunch. And who, please, was eating *lunch* when the Tour came by? French who didn't *care*? Tourists who didn't *know*? *Imagine.*

One and a half hours later and the pack of eastbound traffic, which concertina-ed up along the Gorges du Tarn till the Tour had passed on closed roads, is still overheating on the outskirts of town. We drive past the jam in the opposite direction; I scan the verges for sight of a discarded water bottle, but they've all been snapped up. And as we wind up the twists of the gorge roads which the riders flew down, I wish I were on a bike, not cooped up in a car. The rest of the day's action we'll see on television. Armstrong missed out by a few wheel lengths. He had his victory later.

The Tour de France is, and always has been, one of the hardest endurance events in the professional sporting calendar. And the roads of France are free, year round, to be ridden in the wake of the Tour itself. For the fanatic, special tours allow amateur riders to cover the route of the day's race, starting long before the Tour rolls out; and the *Tour Routier*, an event for club cyclists, ghosts the race a month or so after the final *Arrivée* in Paris. Organised sallies apart, France is a fine country beckoning to any cyclist. While there may be no real feel of the race, the long flat coast roads in the Landes of the Atlantic coast beckon us, or the brutal cobbles of the 'Hell of the north' which may simply amount to masochism on a grand scale, as unkind to the metal frame as to the human. Spin the twisting lanes of Champagne, follow the sweep of the big rivers – Loire and its châteaux, the rocky defiles of the Gorges du Tarn, the baking hot ups and downs of the lower Rhône – and you will be tracing the route, this way or that, of one Grande Boucle or another. But the one place you will get as close as any non-participant can to the emotion, the physical stress and distress, the elation, the frustration and the punishing effort of will which animates the still photos and the moving pictures of the Tour de France riders, at one extreme or another, joy or despair, is in the mountains. The mountains almost invariably form the crucial battlefield of the Tour.

Many images of the Tour, caught in still photos, encapsulate the drama, the forum of its rivalries, its cruelty, its essential magic and the peculiar fascination of cycling and might, perhaps, appeal to few other than cyclists. However, there is a generosity about cycling rooted, I believe, in its very equality. Where high-performance machines are in competition, their drivers will always have to concede some of their triumph to the machine; or ought to; there are some disagreeable exceptions. But the bicycle can never make so much difference that we will all call 'Foul' because one rider has a demonstrably, an intrinsically, superior machine to another. On the road, at any rate.

SNAPSHOT: Coppi and Bartali, big rivals in their day (the duel between them talked up, of course, by journalists to sell newspapers, but neither was disposed to do the other any favours in the pursuit of victory), are here, riding a mountain road. The sun is evidently beating down, not a breath of wind, air burning hot, both of them sweating profusely, both wearing that gaunt expression which portrays effort at the limit. Coppi, slightly in front, Bartali stuck to his wheel, stares fixedly ahead and reaches behind to take the drinking bottle his adversary is handing him.

I want to see the mountains the Tour crosses, to ride them, to seek out the compulsion of this majestic, crazy, perdurable, inspiring, heroic cycle race which started as a publicity stunt, was written off as a grotesque absurdity almost as soon as its first edition ended and yet has continued to astonish ever since.

They call the high mountains *les juges de paix*: 'conciliation magistrates'. In the mountains, the man who weakens will be eliminated; men who were in command one day may falter the next and sustain crippling losses, even abandon the race. The mountains preside without pity.

Above all, this is a record of courage: the courage of all the riders who have ridden the Tour, every rider in the bunch. And, ever present, surging through the mêlée, the metronomic, unyielding momentum of the strongest men who devour punishing mileage and competition day after day – in French the *train-train* – the ceaseless treadmill of stage racing; the men of herculean constitution and will, those who somehow find the wherewithal, mental and physical, to launch an all-out attack when they're at their limit, ill with fatigue, knowing that even if their rivals aren't suffering as badly yet, they soon will be. The Tour is a test of nerve, audacity, stamina, competitive instinct and generosity without equal. Three weeks of punishment and nowhere to hide. Everyone has a bad day; it's the mark of the champions that not only can they keep their bad days secret from the others but even ride through them at cruel speed. Hinault said it: 'When I feel bad, I attack; that way no one can find out just how bad I do feel.'

Naturally, there comes a day when the champion can't do it any more; when, however strong the mind is, the legs are not capable. So often that fatal onset of weakness, *défaillance*, can be pinpointed to a moment when the young wolves cast off the old Akela: 1990, on the Tourmalet, when Lemond watched the leading group move ineluctably ahead of him; he had nothing to counter with and Indurain rode to his first victory. Six years later, Big Mig took his own long stare into defeat's same telescope as the leaders vanished into the distance without him.

Marcel Bidot, a pro during the '20s and '30s and, later, manager of the French national team, said: 'In this business you cannot afford sentiment or else you'll be flattened.' You need mental and physical toughness, plus the supereminent courage that surpasses both, and courage day after day after day. Bravery, as the Spanish say, must be judged again and again on performance, not reputation.

In 1893 the French government imposed a yearly tax on bicycles and official census figures show that by the close of the century over a million cyclists were paying it. Men and women clamoured to own the new freedom machine: it was relatively cheap, it was fast – *vélocipède*: 'fast walker'. The basic 'ordinary', nicknamed penny-farthing, had been superseded by vital technological advances, in particular, the invention of the chain which made efficient transmission possible and pneumatic tyres for a smoother ride. The new bike with its diamond frame was called a safety. Penny-farthings were ungainly and perilous, especially downhill: no brakes, feet off the fixed pedals. Accidents, some fatal, were frequent.

It was an age of astonishing ingenuity and invention: the steam engine, telephone, telegraph; advances in science of major significance. But two revolutionary machines actually paved the way for the great social upheaval of the twentieth century: the 'pernicious sewing-machine', as one apopleptic male diehard called it, emancipated women from the domestic prison of the needleroom where not the sneakiest devil would find idle hands. And the bicycle gave all who could afford it – and large numbers of a hitherto disadvantaged populace could – independent transport, the freedom of the road. From the start, it was a clean machine, in contrast to the railway (whose impact on towns and landscape was roundly rebuked by Dickens in England and Zola in France). On bicycles, anyone could ride out from town to countryside to partake of *la vie au grand air* – a phrase used to publicise the first Tours.

The French army saw another more sinister potential. Obsessed since 1870 with the idea of reclaiming Alsace-Lorraine from the Germans, to whom it had been ceded in the Franco-Prussian war, the military Staff formed a regiment of bicycle soldiers – *pioupious à bécane* – stationed at Longchamp, in 1901. They would head the dash across the border:

> *Les cyclistes nouveaux soldats*
> *S'ront les premiers aux combats,*
> *Pour nous votre baïonette*
> *Sera sera sera la bicyclette.*

> Knights on horses,
> soldiers on bicycles,
> first into battle,
> the bike as bayonet.

In a blatant gesture of patriotism, the first time the Tour crossed the border out of France it was into German-occupied Alsace, on stages to Metz in 1907–10.

The army insisted, however, on an optimum weight for the bike of 10.5kg; this was, at the time, beyond reach. The average for a racing machine at the time was 13kg.

The bicycle wasn't universally popular. Combining practical usefulness with the benefit of exercise, it drove many gymnasiums, riding schools and swimming-pools into bankruptcy. Sales of bikes soared and the publicity campaigns to sell them often featured sportsmen – track-racers, male and female, and long-distance men. Popular sport was comparatively recent, anyway, and a proletarian sports machine was a wonder. Athletic prowess, sporting celebrity and commercial sponsorship joined hands vigorously, as manufacturers scrambled for a share of the exploding bicycle market. Many factories which had already converted from rifle and pistol manufacture to the production of sewing-machines (the light-engineering plant being fairly adaptable to components for both – swords into ploughshares, indeed) were soon turning out bicycles, too. This survived many years in the famous BSA acronym, originally the British Small Arms company.

One of the biggest nineteenth-century French industrialists with diverse interests, besides his bike factory, was Comte Dion. His main outlet for advertising was in the pages of *Le Vélo*, a sports journal owned by Pierre Giffard. In 1899 an event occurred which made them implacable enemies and gave birth to the Tour de France.

Five years earlier, an officer in the French army, Alfred Dreyfus, an Alsatian Jew from the vexed territory conterminous with Germany, had been found guilty of passing military secrets to the German attaché in Paris and sentenced to life imprisonment at the Devil's Island penal colony off the coast of French Guyana. The process of the trial had been far from regular; the outcry against the transparent injustice of the verdict was vociferous and a powerful lobby of liberal intellectual opinion demanded his release and the exposure of his false accusers. This was as much an exercise in radical politics as in libertarian support for (it must be said) a singularly uninspiring scapegoat: Dreyfus himself was entirely unlikeable. But the Dreyfus Affair split France: socialist, pro-republican, anti-clerical Dreyfusards, among them Pierre Giffard, versus Catholic, imperialist, anti-semitic, pro-establishment anti-Dreyfusards, including Comte Dion.

Zola's famous diatribe, *J'Accuse*, rang with indignation, fired up the opposition and the campaign of protest succeeded, to a degree – in 1899 Dreyfus was retried and, though once again found guilty, his sentence was reduced to ten years. However, the second trial, as summary and flawed as the first, provoked a violent outcry which exploded into civil strife. The Third Republic was tottering and it seemed in grave danger of collapse, and so the President stepped in to calm matters with an offer of clemency, which Dreyfus accepted. (He wasn't legally exonerated until 1906, after a third trial.)

On 3 June 1899, on Auteuil race-course a hostile mob of anti-Dreyfusards, mingling with the punters, greeted the President of the Republic, Emile Loubet, with chants of 'Resign. Long live the Army'. A bunch of them scrambled up on to the President's tribunal and one, a baron, clumped Loubet with his cane. Comte Dion was among those arrested and taken to the Sainté prison. Giffard visited him in gaol and the two of them quarrelled. Giffard, never shy of mixing sport with politics, had run a fervent, pugnaciously moralistic account of the anti-Dreyfusard demonstration in the green pages of *Le Vélo*.

Dion took exception to Giffard's partisan encomium and (versions differ), Dion either withdrew or Giffard refused to accept any more advertising for the Dion products. So, needing a new source of publicity, Dion gathered a syndicate of other manufacturers – including Adolphe Clément and Edouard Michelin – and set up and financed a rival journal, *L'Auto Vélo*, to be printed on *yellow* paper under the editorship of one Henri Desgrange, former holder of the World Hour Bicycle record. The circulation war was on. At the time *Le Vélo* sold 80,000 issues daily; it had no rival and its network of contacts with bike clubs and commercial interests was very wide, its influence on popular opinion immense. 'The bicycle,' said Giffard, in a statement of policy, 'is more than a sport and a means of transport, it is a social benefit.' He had, though, fatefully antagonised his new rival editor. When Desgrange created the Parc des Princes *vélodrome* 'the green paper' hardly commented, save to say that it was 'too big, too far . . .' – from the centre of Paris, that is.

Giffard demanded that Dion drop *Vélo* from his title; Dion

refused; Giffard took him to court and, in 1902, the new journal became *L'Auto*, reporting on cycle and automobile sport, fencing, gymnastics, alpinism, weight-lifting, horse-racing, athletics and ballooning.

While the principal source of interest in cycle-sport was the track – the famous Parisian *vélodromes* d'Hiver, de L'Est, de Clignancourt, Parc des Princes – which provided an avid public with a continuous spectacle, road-races had begun to establish themselves. Their drama unfolded more slowly, but they were a gift to journalists with flair for telling a good adventure story *and* to rival manufacturers eager to vaunt the reliability and speediness of their bikes. (In one poster, a park-keeper nabs a pair of trespassing lovers who'd outridden him before: 'Ha, now *I* have a Gladiator bike, too: you couldn't get away *this* time.')

Long-distance races gained popularity and caught the imagination of the legions of bike fans. *Le Vélo* had sponsored a race from Bordeaux to Paris in 1891, the doyenne of the classic marathon races, the Paris–Roubaix (263km) in 1896 and, in 1901 as a publicity stunt to boost sales, a second edition of a race from Paris to Brest and back. The possibility of extending sales across the whole of France was irresistible; it matched precisely the trend for commercial backing of professional riders attempting new endurance records. In 1891, Charles Terront (sponsored by Giffard, then of *Le Petit Journal*) covered the 1,185km of Paris–Brest–Paris in 71 hours on a one-brake Humber weighing 21kg. His pneumatic tyres – a novelty – punctured five times. In 1901, Maurice Garin bettered Terront's time by 19 hours, riding a La Française machine, brand name 'Diamond'. Other races proliferated, most of them centring on the main hub: Paris – to Tours, Clermont-Ferrand, Nantes, Brussels, Ostend, St Petersburg via Vienna – as well as to Paris from Marseille, Liège and back, Lyon and back, Rome . . . Stéphane completed the 572km from Bordeaux on a Clément bike in 25 hours and 37 minutes, and in 1895, Terront, by now a celebrity, proposed to ride all the way around France on a motorbike. His arch-rival (another eternal second) Corre went one better: he'd do it on a pushbike, but was pipped by Théophile Joyeux who, in May of that year, covered 4,429km in 19 days at an average of 235km per day. The first *boucle* (loop) around the six sides of France had been forged. In September, Corre took 25 days to ride his solo journey of 5,012km, and an idea for a race had been germinated. Mooting ways and means to publicise *L'Auto*, and thereby shut Giffard up, Desgrange's assistant, the 26-year-old Géo Lefèvre, remarked: 'What about a race around France?' Except that for the first time he uttered the magic words: Tour de France.

Being a good Frenchman, Desgrange proposed that they eat and drink on it.

Desgrange discussed Lefèvre's idea of a big new race with him over lunch at the Paris office of *L'Auto* at 10 Faubourg, Montmartre. Desgrange needed some persuading. His first objection was to the vast distance that the riders would have to cover over chancy roads in extremes of weather.

'You want to kill them?' he said.

'It's okay. We'll split it into *étapes* (stages).'

'You know how much it would cost? What's Goddet going to say?'

Victor Goddet, father of the future Tour director, Jacques, was the financial administrator of *L'Auto*; he kept the keys to the safe.

However, as an undoubtedly bibulous lunch progressed, Desgrange got fired up with Lefèvre's crazy wheeze. 'The more I thought about it the more I thought we could do it.' The French say that red wine cures almost everything; it's certainly a potent remedy for natural scepticism and a replete Desgrange agreed to approach Goddet.

Goddet listened, cheerfully threw open the door of his safe and said: 'Help yourself. This Tour of yours will buy me a bigger safe.'

Desgrange's sterner motive must have been to outdo his rival Giffard: 'He'll go as green as his paper.' But he was a man of quixotic idealism and remarkable vision; unabashed romantic and steely ascetic in one. Writing his last article before he died in 1940, he described the day, 11 May 1893, when he took the world hour record on the open track of the Buffalo Vélodrome in Paris, built to his specification with funds from the Folies-Bergères:

> Under a blue sky, I mounted a bicycle weighing a
> good 25kg with tyres an outrageous 500mm in

diameter ['balloons'], a multiplication of 4.70m [the distance covered at each full revolution of the cranks] . . . As a measure of prudence, I slung a bottle of milk from my handlebars, in case of bonk.*

When I got off the machine at the end of the 60 minutes, I wasn't only the world recordman for the hour on a bicycle, I was an object of horror to the people who took care of me after my 35,325km. I was filthy, streaked with oil and snot, covered with dust; in short, nobody would touch me with a pair of tongs. My director bought me lunch at La Porte Maillot, a sumptuous meal, 2.50 francs a head; he also offered me several bank notes which I could cash for gold louis; because of my amateur status I refused instantly. But my God! How happy I was.

The rage to be a track-racer never left him; he transmuted it into championing cycle-sport.

This Tour would become, for him and all France, '*la grande croisade morale du sport cycliste*' – the great moral crusade of cycle-sport. But not yet.

In January 1903 *L'Auto* announced: A cycle race to cover 2,428km in six stages, between 31 May and 5 July. No trainers or physios for the first five stages so that all riders will compete on equal terms.

('Equal terms' refers both to a distinction between professional team riders with commercial sponsorship and freelance solitaries riding for prizes and, more significantly, to the fact that most back-up men were emphatically *not* Corinthian in spirit, but hard-nosed cynics, ready to do anything to ensure victory and its profits: any sharp practice or skullduggery for their men; barefaced mischief and finagling to obstruct their rivals.)

A week before the closing date, only 15 riders had signed on: the conditions were too severe. Press reaction to the proposed race explains why: 'A monster' one paper called it; 'colossal . . .

*(Bonk is old cyclist's slang for ravenous hunger, total depletion of blood sugar.)

grandiose . . . gigantic . . . an enormity' chimed in the others. Desgrange softened his stipulations: the race to be staged between 1 and 19 July; entry fee reduced from 20 to ten francs; five francs-per-day expenses to be paid to the first 50 finishers, provided that they had won no more than 200 francs in prizes; total prize money on offer – 20,000 francs.

(Yearly subscription for the daily *L'Auto* in 1903 was 20 francs, while five cents bought a postage stamp or also the eight-page weekly *National Illustrated*. A new Clément bike sold for 450 francs.)

At 3.16 p.m. on 1 July, 21 sponsored men – plus 39 others – rode away from the Réveil Matin ('Morning Call') inn at Villeneuve-St Georges, a suburb 18km south of Paris, headed for Lyon, 467km distant. Desgrange stayed in Paris; Lefèvre accompanied the race – intermittently on his bike – along with other controllers to clock riders through checkpoints and curb cheating; some were at secret locations, some driving the route. The French stars, Maurice Garin, aged 32 – 'The Little Chimney-sweep', Edmond 'Pioupiou' Jacquelin – the demon sprinter whose star was waning; Léon 'the Brute' Georget – who stoked himself with gargantuan quantities of strawberries, rough red wine ('brutal' in French) and biscuits; René Pothier, the taciturn unknown, riding for Garin; and Hippolyte Acouturier (one of several riders who openly admitted he was competing only for stage wins, an oddity of the first Tours: each day's stage being a discrete entity). They were racing against provincial French as well as Swiss, Belgian and German riders.

Garin won the first stage in 17 hours 45 minutes 13.2seconds (Desgrange was nothing if not a stickler for detail) on a La Française bike and wore the first yellow armband as stage victor, also the first green *brassard* as leader of the overall classification. Acouturier, riding a Crescent, took Lyon to Marseille, 374km in 14 hours 28 minutes 53.2 seconds and Marseille to Toulouse, 423km in 17 hours 55 minutes 4.6 seconds; the Swiss, Laeser, another stage-victory man, won Toulouse to Bordeaux on a La Française, 268km in 8 hours 46 minutes 0.8 seconds; the fifth went to Garin, Bordeaux to Nantes, 425km in 16 hours 26 minutes 31 seconds and, on 19 July he headed the leading group of 21 race survivors (the last man two days behind) along roads lined with what the German champion described as 'a hedge of fans opening out in front of us' – 100,000 according to estimates – and through Ville d'Avray, by Versailles, and at last on to the 666m of new concrete cycle track at the Parc des Princes in Paris where a crowd of 20,000 spectators was waiting to cheer them in. Seven minutes after the *Arrivée*, a special edition of *L'Auto*, 130,000 copies, went to press.

The impact of the race on popular attention was nothing short of phenomenal; everywhere it went it was a veritable *succès fou*. Casual cyclists even joined the race for the last few kilometres into Bordeaux. Most important for Desgrange, sales of his paper rocketed and the interest in the commercial backing of cycle manufacturers' for the enterprise was thoroughly whetted.

The first laureate, Garin, weighing 64kg as he had at the start, rode a machine of just under 20kg at an average speed of 26.450kph, pocketed 6,125 gold louis and landed a substantial fee for promoting a weekly magazine *The Fresh Air Life*. He led home 20 survivors from the original field. Crowds had lined sleepy roads in the backwaters of France – even at 2 a.m. – to see the Little Sweep's ghost-white face go by, caught in the glow of the officials' green car's headlights. The same officials were regularly passing food out to Garin and the other La Française team men; but when Pothier gave up his bike to Garin there was no spare for him on hand. Even so, he eventually came in second, with a deficit of nearly three hours. Further on in the race, Garin gave a spectator 100 francs not to lend his bike to a rival, Augureau, who had just punctured. Cyclotourists, seeing these men ride past pushing a gear, six-metres multiplication, said: 'They're bulls, not men.' They had endured a torrid 30°C in the Marseille shade; pelting rain that turned the roads into slurries of mud; shivering-cold night departures, 'dark as an oven'; riders pitching off as wheels caught in tramlines; Fischer and Samson, 80km from the arrival in Nantes, rode into a scree of broken glass – bottles discarded purposely by the leaders – and punctured five and six times; on the first stage Acouturier, going well, took a drink from a bystander – 'lemonade made from sulphuric acid' he said – which turned his legs and arms to jelly; he had to abandon the stage. He recovered, rejoined next

23

day to win that and the third stage. Georget fell out with his La Française boss during the race and refused to rejoin the team, even after the chief mechanic decked him. No penalty, no disqualification, followed: Desgrange needed the high-profile, strong La Française team with its champion Garin; he needed publicity for *L'Auto*. He turned a blind eye. During the Tour, circulation of *L'Auto* rose from 20–30,000 to 65,000 daily and *Le Vélo* did not survive. Desgrange wrote that this race provided the 'best way of exciting wonder among the people of France, of encouraging emulation, energy, willpower on a wide scale' – he linked this Tour of his to national morale, no less – and concluded his report: 'We are satisfied, for this year we have given cycle-sport its finest, its greatest competitive event at a time when know-alls were saying it was impossible to better what was already on offer.' After the 1904 race he was saying: 'The Tour is finished and I am very afraid that its second edition will be its last. It will have been killed by its own success, driven out of control by blind passion, by violence and filthy suspicions worthy only of ignorant and dishonourable men.'

The second Tour was marred by blatant sabotage of the meanest kind: powdered emery and itching dust in riders' shorts; fouled drinks, spiked drinks; a bike frame filed through which collapsed and pitched off its rider in a heavy fall; obstacles flung into the road; composite nails like anti-cavalry coltrops which always point upwards; there seemed no end to the thuggery of envious rivals trying to dish each other and fanatical supporters ('fans') getting out of hand.

At Nemours, local gendarmes, instructed to keep the crowds in order, planted themselves across the road on horseback: the *peloton* swept round the corner straight into them and there was a huge pile-up. (Some 90 years later, a lone policeman stepped out in front of the bunch sprinting for the line at a stage finish to take a picture on his instant camera with similar disastrous effect. In 1958, Darrigade was brought down in the Parc des Princes by a race marshall who leaned out too far at the edge of the track. Darrigade was carried off on a stretcher; the official died.)

Acouturier and Samson took tows by way of a string attached to a cork which each gripped in his teeth. On stage two, the leaders Garin and Pothier – now christened 'the fierce butcher of Sens' – found themselves flanked by an open car full of men in goggles, telling the two La Française men to give their man, Faure, the stage victory. La Française was having it too easy. Harrassed, the leaders were caught by Faure. Past St Etienne, Faure's home town, on the col de la République, (1,161m) at three in the morning, the riders were confronted by a large mob, some hundred-strong, brandishing cudgels. They let Faure through then blocked Garin and his four team-mates and set about them. Géo Lefèvre drove up firing a revolver into the air to disperse the mob. Garin and others were bruised but carried on; the Italian, Gerbi, had to retire hurt. Even so, Faure didn't win and was disqualified in Marseille. The next stage, riding into the control at Nîmes, the local man, Payan, was disqualified for taking shelter behind a car. There was a riot: 2,000 locals versus police, officials and riders. Payan was not reinstated. His supporters took silent revenge by strewing the road with nails and broken glass: the riders punctured in droves. Lefèvre did all he could to avoid trouble: altered the route, set new start times, called in more police; to no avail. Malcontents blocked the road into Paris with logs and farm wagons. Eventually Garin got through, the *de facto* leader but, inevitably, a furore ensued.

Three months later an official enquiry under the aegis of the *Union Vélocipédique de France* found Garin guilty of various 'irregularities' (taking car rides, for instance, had been a staple method of cheating in long-distance races). He was banned for life and his win annulled, along with Pothier, second, César Garin (Maurice's brother), third, and Acouturier, fourth. The fifth man, Cornet, nicknamed 'Rigolo' (which means, appropriately enough, 'joker' or 'revolver') found himself the winner, the youngest ever, at 20 years old. He rode seven more Tours. Garin, who belonged to the old century more than the new, protested his innocence till he died aged 86 in 1957, and it's by no means sure that he was guilty of any misdemeanour; he probably had no need to cheat. However, the Tour was already bigger than the men who rode it. Garin did return to bike racing in 1911, aged 40, to come tenth in the third Paris–Brest–Paris race, beating his 1901 victory time by six hours. It was a riposte of sorts, if too late.

The disqualifications purged Desgrange of his pessimism; and, it must be said, scandal sold newspapers. He had, for the moment at least, won the circulation war. Giffard was declared bankrupt and his *Vélo* left the stands. Desgrange generously hired him as a reporter for *L'Auto* and wasted little time in announcing a third even tougher course for his nascent Tour, and this time the mountains were in 11 stages including the Vosges, côte de Laffrey, col Bayard and the famous Ballon d'Alsace, some 10km of climbing to 1,247m at the summit, whence could be seen magnificent vistas across the Vosges, the Jura and the Black Forest. The classification for overall victory was changed to a points system to obviate cheating on times. This applied for the next seven editions.

On the first stage between Paris and Nancy there were nails strewed across the road. Puncturing right, left and centre, the field of 60 dwindled to a mere 15, the last man arrived five and a half hours after the stage winner, Trousselier. The organisers, outraged, cancelled the race then relented and reinstated all those riders who'd managed to reach Nancy, whether by bike or train. Over the Ballon d'Alsace, Pothier in his trademark linen cap changed bikes and rode up at 20kph. The mountains were an instant hit and Pothier was dubbed 'first king of the climbers'.

Trousselier, on leave from the family flowershop in Paris, won overall, though robbed of a fifth stage win, he broke the inkstands at one checkpoint so that his pursuers couldn't sign on and after the race he stomped off back to his sprays and bouquets.

Desgrange had his dander up now; if the public wanted tough he could be tough. For 1906 he proposed 13 stages, 4,637km, and when a friend of his, Alphonse Steinès, suggested taking the Tour across the Pyrenees, he said: 'Fine. Go and scout them out.'

Steinès drove his car to within 4km of the Tourmalet in worsening conditions till snow forced him to abandon his car and make for safety on foot. He slogged some 12km down the exposed southern slopes through the night, frozen, feverish and scared and stumbled into the gendarme post in Barèges. From there he sent a telegraph to Desgrange:

HAVE CROSSED THE TOURMALET ON FOOT BY NIGHT.
ROAD PASSABLE FOR VEHICLES. NO SNOW.

From 1906 the high mountains were in, though not till 1910 the Tourmalet, loftiest peak in the Pyrenees at 2,114m, a monster, the original *juge de paix*. (The Tour has crossed it 67 times, a record.) 'The mountain is the legend of the Tour.'

Firstly the 11, and now 13, stages made the Tour resemble more closely the hexagon that is France. It crossed the great Alpine massif of la Grande Chartreuse in 1907 and established the big climbs as a feature of the race: the desolate wastes of the mountain tops, the wilderness where the first Carthusian monks built their austere monastery, the forbidding landscape of rock swathed in mist or blizzard. In what locals called the 'circle of death' in the Pyrenees, bears roamed. As late as 1946, Apo Lazaridès, ahead by a street on the mighty Izoard, stopped in that bleak wilderness to allow the rest to catch him up because he feared attack from wild bears.

Alert to the cheating of riders whose first loyalty was to their sponsors – the bike manufacturers – not the purist Henri Desgrange (HD) who made the vaunted English insistence on fair play sound rather mealy-mouthed, Desgrange imposed new, more stringent rules. Each rider's bike was taken, in secret, to the offices of *L'Auto* where officials hallmarked the crankshafts and the head of the forks with a stamp. And, to be doubly sure that the rider rode in on the same machine as he'd ridden at the start, they planted a secret cipher somewhere else on the bike.

The 1907 winner, Lucien Mazan, known as 'Petit-Breton', also took the first double, in 1908, and circulation of *L'Auto* nearly doubled, too: 140,000 to 250,000. The Luxemburgeois François Faber rode through snow, gales and rain, over roads prickling with flints and scored with ruts, to a final victory in 1909; between Roubaix and Nice he won all five stages on the trot, and when his chain broke in Lyon he shouldered his bike and ran to the line.

In 1910, the race produced a ding-dong battle between Faber and Octave Lapize. Desgrange watched his circulation soar as 300,000 readers read the epic tale of Lapize and Faber racing, elbow-to-elbow, as the French say, on the tenth stage over the stupendous Pyrenean chains, Peyresourde, Aspin, Tourmalet. Garrigou was the first man ever to cross the Tourmalet for a handsome prize; Lapize, tiring, was down on the regional rider Lafourcade over the Aubisque and very nearly abandoned from exhaustion – this was the year the broom wagon made its début, sweeping up riders who'd had enough – but he hung on and retained his four-points margin over Faber into Paris.

Apparently mountains didn't kill cyclists and the 1911 Tour (won by Garrigou), the longest so far, 5,344km, crossed the monsters of the Alps, including the Galibier of which, in an Act of Adoration the Father of the Tour wrote: 'In the history of human affairs, does not this ascent of the Galibier on bicycles constitute the first triumph of mortal intelligence over the laws of gravity?' Never short of purple ink, HD.

For the 1912 Tour, no fewer than 131 riders started the race. The Belgian competitors formed a coalition which demoralised Lapize and even the danger man, Christophe, could not dent their power. Odile Defraye won overall and they placed six others of their men in the first ten. In 1913, classification on points having proved unjust, Desgrange restored the fairer system of time difference and, for the first time, sent the Tour around France in an anticlockwise direction. (Since then, tradition sends it vice-versa in alternate years. Tradition has been flouted, notably in 1998.)

Petit-Breton was well-placed behind Thys but fell, broke his kneecap and had to withdraw on the last-but-one stage. Then Thys fell, yet managed to stagger in to take the win.

On 28 June 1914, at 3 a.m, the Tour set out. Later that same day the Archduke Franz Ferdinand of Austria was assassinated in Sarajevo; the Tour finished nearly a month later, shortly before the Austro–Hungarian Empire declared war on Serbia on 28 July. Five days later France was at war and these very Alps became a front-line war zone with mountain regiments from Italy and Austria entrenched across the valley chasms.

JERSEYS OF THE
TOUR DE FRANCE

Yellow jersey (*maillot jaune*).

Maillot: a theatre costume designer's original *maillot* was a skin-tight dancer's outfit.

The *maillot jaune* is worn by the rider with the shortest-accumulated time overall. In 1997, for the first eight stages of the race, to incite competition, time bonuses were awarded to winners of the stage and intermediate sprint competitions along the route. Thus Boardman, who wore the first yellow jersey of the 1997 Tour, lost it to Cipollini, the stage winner, although he finished in the same bunch at the final sprint. Any rider not deemed to be separate from a group by a significant distance is given the same finishing time as the front man.

The yellow is worth a daily £210. The final yellow currently earns its wearer £242,000, a sum which traditionally he shares out amongst the members of his team who have co-operated to work for his victory. Their leader will make up for that generosity amply with appearance fees in the year following his win. Second place overall is worth £121,000; third £66,000; even the man as far down as 150th place earns around £250.

Polka dot jersey (*maillot blanc à pois rouges*). The King of the Mountains Prize.

Points are awarded for the first 12 men over the non-category and first-category climbs: 20 down to 1 and successively fewer points for second, third and fourth category, where a mere three points goes to the first man over. In addition, every major col carries a *prime* – a cash prize for the first man to cross – *hors catégorie* climbs yield £520; fourth category £105. Every day in the polka dots earns £210 and eventual victory in the competition £15,600.

The rules for assigning categories are arcane, depending on altitude, steepness of gradient, quality of road surface – the Pyrenean climbs tend to be less well paved than those in the Alps – and the position of the climb in the day's racing (nearer the end an otherwise second category might be designated a first, and l'Alpe d'Huez, though relatively low for a *hors catégorie*, but steep for an Alpine ascent – nine degrees average – being a cul-de-sac, always features at the end of the stage.)

You may see, painted on the road up to a col: GPM 10km. This means *Grand Prix de Montagnes 10km ahead*.

Green jersey (*maillot vert*). The Points Prize.

Points are awarded for the first finishers on every stage; more points for the flat stages – to encourage the sprinters – so that the eventual winner will be the rider who has been most consistent over the whole Tour. Sprinters amass points from Hot Spot sprints at intermediate points along the route – £520 on offer for the first three men – as well as on stage finishes. A day in green earns £210 and the Points Competition is worth some £96,000 spread out over the whole tour; the winner taking £15,000-plus.

CHAPTER ONE

L'ALPE D'HUEZ

Fear, Moral Strength and Eddie Merckx

Monday.
We ride 32km east from our overnight stop in Vizille, most of the way in placid sun, along the Gorges de la Romanche which sidle up a mild gradient from about 250m to 750m, a gentle loosener, no great strain; vista of skyscraper mountains all round. They call it the Valley of the Dead because the mountains crowd in so close very little sun gets in. And a signpost right indicates the ominously named village La Morte ('the Dead Woman'), as if we need any warning. We're heading for l'Alpe d'Huez, which has a reputation as daunting as its own gigantic bulk. It *looks* horrible on the map: like a squat concertina of diseased yellow worm. The raw statistics aren't sociable, either: a climb of 1,000m in 14km, corkscrewing round 21 snap-comb hairpin bends. It *sounds* gruesome: it must *be* gruesome. I'm thinking: 'L'Alpe d'Huez, today we cycle l'Alpe d'Huez,' as if jingling the name alone can make the prospect somehow less unhomely, more my size.

The climb was introduced to the Tour de France in 1952, when many of the remoter Alpine roads were still little more than minimally improved cart-tracks: rough, narrow, littered with scree, split, potholed and rutted from arctic cold in winter and the oven heat of summer, titubating up and down the mountains in what looks, from old photos, like a trance of fatigue and asthma. Or traversing perilously narrow corniche paths no better than rude shelves cut in to the rock, the precipice edges bare and unprotected: one lapse of concentration and you're over. And at night?

In those early days, the Huez road extended to 1,495m, stopping short at the village which christens the Alp. It was eventually driven on to the deep snow line at 1,860m, giving cul-de-sac access to the modern ski station, and has been a fixture of the Tour ever since; dreaded by many riders. A mountain-top finish is especially punishing after two or three major climbs already the same day: an hour or more for many of them, racing the steep flights of the road against a merciless clock and dwindling strength and stamina, gasping at thinning air in thick July heat. Mountains are classified, by length and gradient, in three categories, the monsters are *hors catégorie*. They epitomise the stark challenge of the Tour; on them it is so often won or lost, even today when a multiplicity of gears equalises the riders in a way that the pre-*dérailleur* machines could not. In those days, the chasm between the best climbers and the worst yawned wide. One thing hasn't changed: the awe that the high mountains inspire. When the Englishman Bill Nickson, winner of the Milk Race, riding for the Raleigh team, first saw l'Alpe d'Huez from this same valley approach he voiced what many riders think: as knackered as he then was, he simply couldn't believe he'd ever get up the mountain; it would have to be an act of faith heavily larded with luck. Freddy Maertens, the Belgian speed-merchant, *flahoute* in the slang, chose this very alp on which to quell his dread of the mountains. He fancied his chances in the Tour overall, a class sprinter keenly aware that he faced possible disaster on the high climbs. Sean Kelly, the great Irish rider who holds the record of wins in the Points competition – four green jerseys in Paris – has been known to dismount and rest on the climbs. The pace up these ascents is ferocious, the toll severe.

No rider, not even the strongest, can match the natural fluency of the gifted climbers. When the pace accelerates on to the mountain and the high-flyers mount like weightless creatures and leave the rest of the field trailing with shaky legs and bursting lungs, the men with any ambition have to hang on by raw power and unshakeable self-belief; or lose. Winning the Tour generally demands a complete rider, one who can contend sprints, climbs, time-trials with the best, but with a consistency that outstrips them all. Few pure climbers have taken overall victory. Federico Bahamontes, the Eagle of Toledo, won the mountains prize six times between 1954 and 1964, the Tour only once, and Van Impe was five times king of the mountains, though interestingly not in the year he won overall.

As to the biochemistry of fear; it is as fundamental as the instinct for survival and the competitive spirit, both of which it fuels *and* thrives on. Fear originally meant 'ambush, a sudden fright or threat'; and there is no shame in being startled. The compelling lure of sport is to observe contestants face their fear and conquer it: as in the boxing ring, the 'four corners of truth', so on the pitiless roads of the Tour de France. We are witness to a supreme test of nerve; an inspiration to face challenge. We all nurse fear inside us. Fear is one of those sewer beasts in the mind's bilge that has to be ruthlessly cleaned out, time after time. Fear lives on indecision, self-doubt, prevarication: go in hard, ride it into the ground. If you see the mountain and say 'No way' and ditch the bike, you'll never know if you would have made it, if you had it in you; and your demons will multiply. Demons are the killer dogs prowling the grounds of self-knowledge. To face them is to follow aspiration.

In the 1976 Tour, Maertens wore the leader's yellow jersey for nine days and eventually took the green points jersey in Paris by a distance. He also won eight stages overall, a record shared by Charles Pélissier (1930) and Merckx (1970 and 1974), then crowned a glorious season by winning the World's Road Championship. The December before, Maertens, a redoubtable sprinter with no stomach for mountains, came to l'Alpe d'Huez with his friend and team-mate, Michel Pollentier, to steel himself for the ordeal ahead, by wrestling with and taming this savage climb that rears up zigzag, zigzag, like the ramps flanking a sacrificial Inca ziggurat. All mountains are gruelling; what makes this climb so hard – at an average nine degrees, unduly steep for an alp – is the absence of natural flow, a disregard for contour; it is a road hacked out of the bare rock without finesse, like a firebreak. Many Alpine cols, even first category, run smoothly over good surface, dawdling bends and steady gradient.

The two Belgians rode up and down l'Alpe d'Huez, over and over again, till Maertens had quelled his panic, even if he hadn't beaten the jinx. On the ninth stage of the Tour, 4 July, he set off for l'Alpe d'Huez in yellow, with two minutes and four seconds advantage over his lieutenant Pollentier. At the end of that day, he had dropped to third overall, with a deficit of 54 seconds on the eventual winner, the diminutive Belgian climber, Van Impe. Who can say where he'd have been without that winter's psychological toughening? He finished the Tour in eighth, 16 minutes down. Poulidor, over 40 by now, came third. Incidentally, Maertens, in his autobiography, claims that the Belgian public never supported him because he was born in proletarian Ostend, whereas the great and favoured Merckx – who, he swears, cynically dished him in the Worlds to secure the title for Gimondi – came from posh Brussels. (The reason? Gimondi and Merckx had a contract deal with Campagnolo.)

Maertens also says that often, during the final kilometres of a long race, he had his team car pass him a bottle containing champagne: a booster shot for the sprint. It's not unknown.

His friend Pollentier was a considerable rider. In the 1974 Tour he beat Merckx in a time-trial – almost unheard of – and in 1978 took the yellow jersey when he trounced Hinault on the stage to l'Alpe d'Huez; only to be disqualified for supplying a false urine sample.

As we near l'Alpe d'Huez, the temptation is to wonder: 'What's it like? Will I be all right?' Comparisons won't work; seductive, but no more than a way of dodging the issue. Like self-help manuals: largely useless, unless you're prepared to undergo the same trials that went into writing them; these High Alps have to be taken as they come; each has to be ridden into temporary submission; each presides over its own judgement and nothing you have ever done before matches up to the first encounter.

The summer's daydream poring over maps is about to meet solid reality. We are no better acquainted with the solid reality of l'Alpe d'Huez than with television miniatures of it, ten-minute cameos from successive Tours: vivid images of Sermon on the Mount-size crowds; shimmering heat haze thickened by exhaust fumes; coruscant spokes; *perpetuum mobile* of bicycles; riders on form, riders flagging, riders dropped, sweat-drenched, emptying water bottles over their heads; ardent fans running alongside their heroes and dowsing them, even if their heroes don't always want to be. Torrid heat going up the mountain; fierce cold going down: watch the riders take newspapers from fans on the cols to stuff up their vests against the wind on the descent. (Anquetil took an unsolicited soaking in 1966, caught a chill at the top of the next col, the Great St Bernard, and abandoned next day.) The riders plough on through a cacophony of klaxons yodelling like a jamboree of deranged Tyroleans, exhaust pipes snort plumes of carbon monoxide, the whole circus parade of team cars, service cars, official race cars, motorbikes with and without cameramen perched on the pillion seat, broom waggon snaking up the mountain – as fast as the leader at the front, as slow as the stragglers at the tail – through a jungle of spectators crammed so deep by the road's edge they leave no more than a single file path down their middle and then bulge shut again over the riders as they pass, like a python consuming its lunch. The July sun blazing on full joules, the Alpe d'Huez stage drama played out metre by metre on the one in six . . . vital minutes lost, saved, gained. But television has virtually no real emotional power; it's a peepshow. The closeups from the motorbike cameras are as close as most people get; better than nothing but they are only a cartoon of the enormous strain involved: the habitual pain-streaked rictus of some riders, the impassive introspection – or icy control – of others; the blank, frayed, drained mask of the men whose will and physical resource has been pared down to the quick but won't give in; the hunched, bobbing, shoulders, pushing their bit of extra weight to the tired legs, the pistons driving the pedals; the extremes of physical and mental stress written in a sort of enigma: the restless twist of fingers round the handle bars . . .

SNAPSHOT: The Spanish ace Ocaña, dead to the world, on his way to a high col, index finger of his right hand extended to touch the brake cable, as if it were his pulse, telling him he's still functioning, earthing the whole force of his concentration through that single contact.

The slack gape of the mouth, the dip and lift of the chest pumping the lungs to capacity, the sea-deck swaying gait of a rider dropped by the leaders, heaving his own leaden frame out of the saddle to flog the bike frame that gets heavier than Christ on St Christopher's shoulders, through oxygen-depleted air and the deadening drag of gravity, dredging up scraps of acceleration, a semblance of fluency, more *rhythm*, to catch the leaders again. He can still see them a hundred metres ahead, still within reach, tied on by the unravelling thread of possibility which links him to them, *don't give up*, dig, dig into the reserves, if there are any in such extremes, to keep the pursuit alive until the incomparable relief or despair of the *Arrivée* line shuts pursuit off.

We are soon to adjudge the inadequacy of television to tell the truth about the gradient. Any frailties will be routinely exposed, though failure, it goes without saying, is unthinkable; maybe succeeding isn't possible, either. I am riding incautiously big gears, and recall the remark made by Bernard 'Nanard' Thévenet, shrinking at the size of the gear Merckx was pushing round in the Alps: '*un méchant braquet pour les montagnes*'; (*méchant*, of a dog: 'it bites', a vicious gear for the mountains.)

We ride the last bit of level road to the bend that broaches the climb, wheel 45 degrees and nose on to the first ramp. It's horrible: a long, wide section of road as steep as Highgate West Hill, which I climb every day. No, it looks steeper in this ungiving prospect, us at the bottom of an ugly concrete slab of wicked uphill. I think: 'This is going to be a bastard.' Two days earlier I had ridden Highgate West Hill, the same kit loaded as I carried now, in a sly drizzle, not warmed up and tired, but I struggled and, as I struggled, I said to myself, 'And you're going to ride in the Alps?'

And now my heart taps out messages far too urgent, quite at odds with the even tempo I should be aiming for. Pulse and nerves are performing a double act of frantic percussion. A sudden fragility. 14km? 1,000m? Yet if pro riders dread the mountains, no matter how often they climb them, at the foot of l'Alpe d'Huez I have a macabre advantage over them: I don't know what's coming. I push the forebodings aside. Patience. And forget the pros: they do nothing all year but ride a bike, and get paid for it, they're decades younger. Besides, they have a less flexible incentive – their *directeur sportif* barking at them from the team car and the need to put on enough show to win a contract for the following year; all that plus the ticking of the clock and the threat of elimination on time.

The 21 hairpins are numbered from 20 in descending order as you climb. Number 21, the first, isn't marked for some reason. I was relieved that they count down as you go up. Somehow, piling the total up would make the ride psychologically harder. A new assistant in the Moscow department store Gum was set to work on the dry goods counter. Several customers complained that she was giving short measure of sugar and rice which were weighed and sold loose. The girl protested innocence; a supervisor observed her at work. The measures were exact; but instead of putting too little into the pan to start with and *adding* more to make up the weight, she was pouring in too much and *subtracting* the surplus. The customers felt cheated; she was robbing them before their eyes. I was glad to see the hairpin numbers getting slowly lighter in weight.

Small comfort: the hairpins on l'Alpe d'Huez are unlike any others. They come every 700m or so, ugly as sin, hoisting you roughly 50m nearer the top. Every inch of the way there is no escaping a sense of the mountain's massive, intimidating bulk.

And here you are, playing at it. What keeps you going? Mostly the fact that you set out to do the climb and, barring accident or misadventure, bodily or mechanical, climb it you will and must. *So far so good.*

Boardman has admitted that he doesn't really enjoy the business – it's dangerous, painful and exhausting – but he does derive huge satisfaction from it, and the satisfaction is what we can all indulge in, and be grateful we don't have to race up this rotten steep seemingly endless road.

The early Tour traversed the mountains by way of tracks familiar to mules and smugglers but only recently made passable to cars. The first ever Pyrenean stage quit Luchon for Bayonne at 3.30 a.m. and when Lapize, near-spent, struggled to the top of the Tourmalet, he rounded on two of the race marshalls posted on the col to check the riders through and screamed: '*Vous êtes tous des assassins!*' – You're all murderers. Sure, he went on to win, but the vehemence of his reaction gives the lie to any cosy dilettante idea that the Tour was some kind of play up, play up, play the game, all good chaps, taking part's the thing. These were hard men in a hard *métier*, unromanced by fey illusions about what they were being asked to endure or notably reluctant to voice protest. One of them, Emile Georget, the very first Tour rider to vanquish the Galibier, 10 July 1911, arrived in a filthy state; his moustache clogged with bits of snot and food from the last control point, his jersey filthy with mud, soaking wet from the last stream he'd pitched in to. He vaulted off his bike – he must have been an absolute fright to look at – gathered up some dignity and said to the official observers: '*Ça vous met un coin dans la bouche.*' (That's given you something to think about.) Then rode on.

Those early *coureurs* crossed the high mountains in conditions unthinkable to the riders of today, and even with the material support they enjoy, it's never anything but a hard, hard ride. The Dog Days heat they face is the same, the bitter cold, the rain, the fog. The overwhelming physical fatigue and mental strain. And the persistent danger. Boardman, riding down the first category col du Soulor through dense fog in 1997 told how he followed another rider who shot off, apparently well acquainted with the descent. Suddenly the road turned green and they were riding up an embankment. Boardman nearly held on but couldn't, and fell heavily, damaging vertebrae in his back and neck. He rode on, even managed another cruel day in the Pyrenees and a 55km mountain time-trial, but the pain became so intense that he was forced to abandon on the Alpe d'Huez stage.

The pioneers had to carry their own food, repair kit, spare tyres, water, extra clothing, lights, and could only call on two gears. No wonder they became heroes to sports fans eager to own the brand of bike ridden by a Tour rider. They were demigods, muscles of steel, apparently indomitable, survivors of the amazing adventures described in *L'Auto*. For strength, physical and mental, willpower and apparent immunity to the combined onslaught of natural obstacles and human malevolence, they matched the great heroes of antiquity, pound for pound, exploit for exploit.

The epic has changed as little in essence since its inauguration as the basic road-racing bike: two wheels, chain, a frame. Technical innovation has crucially reduced the weight of materials and increased mechanical efficiency (even gear-changing is automatic these days – another manual skill lost, when riders would jump an attack on hearing a rival's clumsy shift of gears). Modern cyclists are mollycoddled by comparison with the *forçats de la route* (the convict labourers) of the early Tours, but the *Grande Boucle* – the Big Loop – of France (with occasional excursions into bordering countries) was, and remains, bike and rider against himself, the road, the other riders. It is the most uncompromising test of stamina, willpower and athletic prowess for any pro cyclist, perhaps any sportsman. They climb l'Alpe d'Huez after a hundred miles or more of mountain roads; they race up its exposed flanks knowing that if they crack, or even look like cracking, their rivals will pounce on the weakness ruthlessly. Seconds lost, minutes lost and tomorrow's mountain will seem twice as steep, twice as long, twice as back-breaking, twice as disheartening. Sure they get paid, sure the rivalry spurs them. That doesn't level the mountain, and they're as prone to fear of it as any of us who ride a bike: the greater the talent, the greater the dread and the penalty of falling short.

Lance Armstrong, the strong man, on his début Tour won a flat stage – joy – then came to the Alps (cols du Glandon and Galibier in one day) and barely had the strength to finish; he collapsed in his hotel room, wanting only to abandon. His team persuaded him to start next day, helped him all they could, but he was empty and quit that night. Such wretched depths is the spirit forced to. Learning to cope with the misery and the elation is at the root of all challenge.

★

And now, at hairpin 15, six to go, the road glares at me like the Gorgon. Age pants at my heels and they are no longer what could be called in athletic terms a clean pair. Nonetheless, I *am* grinding on and the kilometres recede beneath my tyres.

The nearer you get to the top, the tougher the mental battle gets. Stamping behind the fences of your self-control lurks a greyhound of impatience, straining to cut loose, make a dash, get it over, sprint up there and across the line whatever the cost. The cost will be spontaneous combustion of lungs, a flood of lactic acid into the muscles and you gasping at the side of the road like a beached fish. Rhythm and a clear head, self-belief and arithmetic, these are reliable. Undue haste is a plausible liar. Impatience reminds me that, on the Tour, the run-in to the *Arrivée* is flat if not marginally downhill. Well, praise be.

At last, the hairpin is the precious *numéro un*: gate to the city. My spirits lift. Any minute now the steep up will tilt forward in my favour like a seesaw as my weight crosses the fulcrum. But it doesn't. Never rely. Anything not the top is not the top. You can't argue with fact. Fact is the old pro with all the tricks up his sleeve. The Tour actually takes a fork to the right, skirting the steep bluff below the ski station centre. I ride straight on, up the bluff, the last snarling ramp of this 14km to cap the climb. I sprint it in a real *haka* of defiance, wringing out the last ounces. I'd ridden l'Alpe d'Huez in one and a quarter hours.

As destinations go it has all the innate charm of a ski resort out of season: none. A hotchpotch of purpose-built hotels, souvenir shops, bars and restaurants designed by a stripped-pine vulgarian certificated in architectural tat. As a totem of cycling achievement, however, it's pretty fair wampum.

A placard informs me that the *Maire* will gladly sign a diploma officialising my ascent of the mountain after his siesta at 2.30 p.m.

It's barely 2 p.m. and I don't need proof or ratification. I drink from the water fountain; a couple of English cyclists rest in the shade. We exchange laconic greetings. The view from the top is all the better for the sight of those tortuous snake-and-ladder hairpins, silver as snail trails in the sun. The valley is a long way off, the girdling mountains, too; but retracing the hard path at downhill speed makes a splendid feast of self-indulgence.

'Who would you like to be?' a friend asked me at home before I set out. I demurred: I couldn't *be* any of them, so I didn't want to be – the great *géants de la route* were far beyond me. This is why I came: to prise open my imagination, to get closer, to root round in my fascination. 'But which of them do you most admire?' she said.

No hesitation: Eddy Merckx. In 1964 he won the World Road Race Championship for amateurs, having been first refused permission to ride by the Belgian Federation's doctor because 'his heart was too small'. His own doctor went crazy and scotched that. Contracted to an Italian team, he scored his first major win in the 1966 Milan–San Remo: *La Primavera.* Next year a second *Primavera,* plus a hatful of classics and the second of his four World Road Race titles. He won the 1968 Giro d'Italia and was strongly placed to win the 1969 edition when a random dope test eliminated him. Two flasks of his urine sample had gone missing from the mini laboratory set up in a following car and the doctor told him, sorrowfully:

'I know you're innocent, but the test was positive.' Years later a rumour circulated that he had been offered a considerable bribe to hand the race to Gimondi. Unthinkable.

The rigged disqualification – a Belgian winning the great Italian stage race *again* – might have dealt a devastating blow to his morale. Instead, he came to his first Tour a month or so later, smarting and parched for revenge and did what no rider has ever done before or since: he won all three jerseys – leader's yellow, mountains, points. On one stage, over the Aubisque and

Tourmalet, he made a breathtaking solo break of 140km. He pulverised the opposition and won the Tour by 17 minutes 54 seconds, a margin that hasn't been approached in recent years. At Luchon, a journalist sighed: 'My friend, you're squeezing the race to death; it's not funny.' Another wrote: 'Merckx was like a gaoler with absolute power, each day ragging his prisoners in the *peloton* with another rough joke.' He went on to win the next three Tours and was victorious in five altogether, in succession to Anquetil; add to that five Giro d'Italia, Vuelta a España, four road-race titles, some 50 one-day classics, countless other victories, World Hour record . . . On 13 July 1975, the 15th stage Tour de France, Nice–Pra Loup, wearing yellow, he appeared to be on the verge of an unprecedented sixth victory.

After a rest day, at the beginning of this tough stage – 135 miles in all, across five cols and a vicious four and a half miles' climb to the finish – Merckx led the Frenchman Thévenet by a minute and 58 seconds. However, Thévenet had looked strong in the Pyrenees and, more worryingly, imperturbable. Like Poulidor and many outstanding French cyclists, he'd been a farmboy; his muscles and sinews toughened by gruelling labour on the land; his mind inured to the grind of long days in the saddle. He attacked on the col des Champs, 1,000m in 16km of climbing, his team-mate, Delisle, supporting him. It was his first show of open challenge. Merckx, flanked or paced by his men Janssen and de Schoenmaecker (ready to ride themselves to a standstill for their boss), stayed in touch and, 45 miles from the finish, went out on his own, as it was always his style to do. He headed the leading group over the col, class riders every one, no wheel-suckers keeping the shade of the men doing the work. 'Never gets a tan', they say of the slipstreamers. Thévenet said: 'Merckx went so fast to take the col, he had 50 or 60m on me before I realised I was at the back of the group.'

From the tiny perch of the summit at 2,095m, Merckx attacked again; rocketed at breakneck speed down a tortuous descent no more than three metres wide, slippery with melting ice, into Colmar, 740m below. He was a famously audacious descender and Thévenet notably cautious: it's not only climbs where minutes can be gained. 'You have to switch your brain off and let it roll,' one gravity-surfer replied after a particularly hair-raising descent at speed, trying to explain what can't be explained. Merckx may have been no great stylist, all bunched strength, but going downhill he embodied panache. Tomba on a bicycle. Behind him, Thévenet and the Italian ace, Moser, had punctured; a hurried wheel change and a frantic pursuit for them to regain the leading group. Merckx was riding with the uncalculating fury of a man betting every scraping of his reserves on the attack. Some way down, he nearly careered into a group of press cars. The press usually ride way ahead of the race, gleaning material for their columns from Tour radio; they rarely *see* any of the action live, save start and arrival. This day, they had the scent of a bitter, perhaps decisive, duel being fought; an elbow-to-elbow between the two men going for yellow. They wanted to catch some of the bloodletting live and stopped to watch the race, their cars parked loosely off the verges. Merckx shot down nearly straight into them, just managed to swerve past, screaming blue murder. He'd lost time, precious seconds, momentum and cool. He was never a man to show excessive emotion, never winced in defeat or glowed overmuch in victory – beyond the ecstatic grin all winners crack wide when they cross the line and there's no more stupid bike for a while.

As he flew on, the Italian Gimondi's Bianchi team car swerved at the same obstacle, but too late, and went over the edge; driver and manager spilled out, slid 40 feet, clutched hold of the undergrowth and watched their vehicle somersault down the mountainside, bouncing off the spare bikes on the roof-rack.

Merckx hurtled on, hotly pursued by Gimondi, at 50 mph. Behind them, Zoetemelk, Van Impe and Thévenet squeezed the brakes more circumspectly. From Colmars in the valley, 24km to the col d'Allos, 2,240m, Merckx head down, all out, never frugal with his effort. With only 24km, plus the short finishing climb to Pra-Loup, the stage and the race overall seemed to be his.

But, 20km from home, he lost everything, his power went, he cracked. Two days before, in the closing metres of the climb to the Puy de Dôme, a crazed French fan had leapt out of the crowd and punched him heavily in the kidneys. He held on to his bike and came in third behind Van Impe and Thévenet. (Months later the miscreant was fined a hefty sum of which Merckx claimed a token one franc in damages.) The medication he'd been given almost certainly upset his system. It is scarcely conceivable for a man of his class not to have eaten enough and got hit by the bonk, the wolfish hunger that afflicts cyclists. Perhaps there was even some jealous dragon of Destiny guarding the unprecedented sixth victory. Whatever happened he went to pieces. He struggled on, driven by what tatters of willpower he had left.

Gimondi (winner 1965) caught him, offered Merckx his wheel, but Merckx was in a wretched state and couldn't raise himself. Gimondi, riding for a rival team, had to press on.

Thévenet caught Merckx, by now almost delirious, 3km from the finish, and rode by. The pictures show Merckx's face torn with anguish, eyes hollow, body slumped, arms locked shut on the bars, shoulders a clenched ridge of exertion and distress. Thévenet, mouth gaping to gulp more oxygen, looks pretty well at the limit, too, but his effort is gaining; he's out of the saddle, eyes fixed on the road. He said he could see that one side of the road had turned to liquid tar in the baking heat and Merckx was tyre-deep in it. Behind Thévenet came the Dutchman Zoetemelk (winner 1980) and Van Impe (winner 1976). Both overtook Merckx.

Thévenet surged on, caught Gimondi, sat on his wheel a while to recoup, changed gear and rode on to the stage victory. When Merckx eventually crawled in, he trailed Thévenet by a minute and 56 seconds; he had ceded nearly four minutes on the day. Thévenet was in yellow.

The following day, Bernard 'Nanard' Thévenet suffused with a new confidence, stormed away from Merckx on the infamous col d'Izoard, a brilliant solo exploit, to win, alone, at Serre Chevalier, valuable minutes added to his lead. 'Ah . . . the last 3km,' he said, 'cutting through the crowd, pressing right on my front wheel, even though there was a motorbike *gendarme* escorting me. They were going crazy.' Bastille Day ended sweetly in France.

Next morning, in the neutralised zone which precedes the start of the racing proper, Merckx touched wheels with the Danish champion Olé Ritter and came off; his face hit the road and he was stunned. The doctor diagnosed a broken maxilla and perforated sinus bone and advised him to abandon. Merckx was in considerable pain, his jaw wired so he could take only liquid or liquidised nourishment, but he wouldn't give up the race into Paris, five days away. The doctor disowned responsibility. Merckx even regained some time from Thévenet in a mountain time-trial.

The race finished on the Champs-Elysées for the first time. 'Nanarchy' reigned in France, and by mounting the podium next to the first man to beat him in the Tour, Merckx afforded him unimpeachable triumph. As the old pro used to ask when a rider bragged of winning a race: 'Who came second?' Merckx came second . . . hell of a victory. Anquetil, when asked how he felt about Poulidor, his arch rival, winning the Tour, replied: 'Of course I'd like him to win it, in my absence. His victory would only enhance my reputation.'

Merckx's all-out gesture was heroic, generous, typical of a peerless champion; even if he later called it an unthinking mistake. The fact is, if Merckx was still in the saddle he could never be discounted. In 1971, for instance.

The following is partly based on Merckx's own account.

The winter before the Tour, there had been a mounting hate campaign levelled at Merckx in the French press. His domination of 'their' Tour had become repugnant. He chewed up all the French riders and spat out the pieces. The man wouldn't even smile. *Paris-Match* put it bluntly: 'Is Merckx going to kill the Tour de France?' Of course the organisers of the Tour knew that Merckx was vital to the race: he was, without question, the man to beat.

The classy Spanish champion Ocaña assembled a strong team round him – including the Dane Mortensen – and came to the Tour in cracking form. Merckx had missed the Giro because of a bad knee, his preparation had been nowhere near as thorough as usual and Ocaña fancied his chances. Anquetil advised him: 'Keep your nerve, wait for the mountains and when you strike, make it count.' This he did. On the descent of the col du Cucheron, 30km from the finish in Grenoble, the col de Porte still to climb, Merckx, riding with a lead group which included Ocaña, punctured. His director, Driessens, in the team car, was giving help to Wagtmans and doling out *bidons* (water bottles) to Van Springel. Merckx, fuming, lost 40 seconds waiting for a bike change, and then had to mount a team machine not set up to his own exacting size specifications. Hurtling down the descent in pursuit of the leaders, one tyre rolled off the rim and, unable to control the bike, Merckx ricocheted some way along the roadside safety rail before managing to stop. Another repair, another delay: the Driessens Peugeot 404 was having trouble keeping pace with their man on the bike.

Merckx shrugged off the trauma of the crash and flew on to the bottom of the col de Porte where he launched into nearly 500m of ascent to 1,326m in 8.5km. The climb seemed interminable; he could find no rhythm, the effect, surely, of that punishing chase on an unfamiliar bike. When he was 300m from the summit, he caught Aghostino and three Spanish riders behind a procession of cars following the break ahead. In the race director's words, Merckx made a 'ferocious effort' to get through the jam of vehicles to his own car at the front of the cavalcade. Here he came level with Ocaña's team rider, Mortensen. Tour rules permitted a rider who was behind because of accident or mechanical failure to ride past the leading team cars. A rider who had simply been dropped, however, was required to let the cars through to catch up with the leaders. Mortensen had, very conveniently, slipped off the back of the leading group when word came that Merckx was on them; the cars were overtaking him even as Merckx was chasing up on to his wheel and, 80m from the summit, the organiser Goddet, reluctantly enforced the barrier. The drama heightened: '80 derisory metres,' said Goddet, which 'the man who dominated modern cycling, probably the greatest rider of all time' could not, for the moment, ride across. When he eventually emerged on to clear road, Merckx fought and fought, livid with fury, but for a long time could make no inroad into the two-minute advance the leaders – working together at maximum effort – had over him. The effort left him breathless. A frenzied descent recouped a few seconds and in Grenoble he was a minute and 38 seconds down.

After a fitful night's sleep 'hatched like a zebra's skin' – waking, sleeping, waking, sleeping – Merckx came to the start next morning. A few miles out, on the col du Laffrey, Ocaña, gambling on Merckx being weary and heavy-legged from the previous day's exertions, launched an all-out attack. This was bold: the stage had 177km to run. At the top of the col, Merckx was already two minutes down on Ocaña, Zoetemelk, Aghostino and Van Impe, pedigree climbers every one. Supported only by Wagtmans and Huysmans, Merckx had to pursue virtually alone, neither of his *domestiques* (the servants, watercarriers, of the *peloton*) being equal to the fierce pace he set. He rode the whole distance to the finish in Orcières-Merlette with a hostile *peloton* champing at his heels; a bitter struggle, flogging himself 'like a madman'. The temptation to abandon was strong; he very nearly capitulated but tottered in at last, eight minutes and four seconds down. He said: 'My morale was crushed.'

He had been jeered at and insulted by French crowds over the preceding days; the hated Mossieu Merckx, finally getting a taste of his own medicine. 'Mossieu' the contemptuous form of Monsieur. But now the French press, shamed by his enormous courage, rallied to him:

> In defeat, the Belgian champion has revealed an unknown and admirable side of his character. He showed himself to be a man of iron through a long, terrible and, yes, in the greater context, catastrophic day. A day which bankrupted him . . . For four hours, the former wearer of the yellow jersey expended superhuman energy, demonstrating how justly he merited the glory his victories have brought him, a glory that is untarnished. As for those who whistled at and booed him, their only excuse is ignorance of his real worth and the blindness of chauvinism. In truth, Merckx's behaviour in defeat offers us an exalted, a solemn, lesson in the conduct of sport as well as in dignity.

Merckx offered his own tribute to the hammer blow Ocaña had delivered: the Spaniard had despatched the rest of them as the great matador Cordobès dealing with a bull.

In the modern Tour, such a huge deficit as Ocaña had imposed on Merckx is nearly impossible to make up but Merckx set out to do it. A criticism levelled at him constantly was that he did too much, overstretched himself, expended energy unnecessarily in the drive to stamp his authority on the racing field. When other riders were sheltering from arctic conditions in the 1968 Giro, Merckx rode on, apparently impervious. Sure, he felt the cold: he just didn't let it get to him. They kept telling him to ease up; the words weren't in his vocabulary. He was the sort of rider who'd read a SLOW sign as an insult, a speed limit as a challenge.

The day after his trouncing, he went off from the start and, in sweltering heat on an extremely hilly course, with Wagtmans, Huysman and others, 14 in all, and, as they peeled off, with four survivors, rode himself and the rest of his team into the ground all day. A break of 250km, average an amazing 45.351kph, for the paltry lead over an increasingly frantic *peloton* of never more than two minutes ten seconds.* They reached the finish in Marseille so far ahead of race schedule no one was around: it was siesta time. Merckx had clawed back a mere one minute 56 seconds on Ocaña.

This riposte was characteristic, though it made neither sound tactical or common sense; as a psychological blow it can have had very limited impact on the man who had more or less crushed him the day before. It stemmed, finally, from pride and phenomenal moral strength. Merckx, forced into a hopeless position, fought back with everything he'd got. They all say that of him: he'd never give up, even when he was off-form and riding for someone else. A *jusqu'auboutiste* (whole hogger), winning from the front, not the shelter of the bunch.

Two days after Marseille, 12 July, a cold, drenched ride towards St Béat descending the col de Menté in the Pyrenees – torrential rain, night in day, thunder tearing the sky in ruins – a small group, Merckx at the front, Ocaña sticking as close as he dared, led the race. Suddenly Merckx aquaplaned and careered into a parapet; Ocaña tried to avoid him, slid and crashed. He got up, tried to remount but Zoetemelk coming behind ran into him and then Aghostino. Ocaña was out, his legs and shoulder badly wrenched

---

*Other sources record a lead of one minute and 56 seconds at the finish, the advance never exceeding two minutes ten seconds.

and contused. On arrival at Bagnères de Luchon, Merckx refused the yellow jersey as reinstated race leader – he hadn't earned it nor would he wear it till he'd done so at the end of the following stage. Four days later, he found time at the end of the day's racing to visit Ocaña at home, laid up in bed. A visit of friendship. (Ocaña eventually won the Tour, in Merckx's absence, 1973.)

The day after Ocaña's crash, Thévenet also fell, this time on a treacherously wet descent on the Aubisque, in the Pyrenees. He did what most pro riders do instinctively, remounted and set off. His *directeur sportif* drove up alongside him to check that he was all right and Thévenet said: '*Où sommes nous? Qu'est-ce que je fais ici?*' 'Where are we? What am I doing here?')

Merckx said that the only time he experienced any real physical pleasure in a race was when he passed the finishing line. That momentary joy over, he could start worrying about whether someone was going to damage his bike or else clap him on the back and exacerbate the constant pain he endured after a heavy fall on the track one autumn that nearly wrecked his career. Riding on the *vélodrome* in Blois, a race paced by Derny motorbikes, Merckx fell and was badly hurt. He didn't race for three months and suffered extreme depression. His pelvis had been displaced and he never recovered his true efficiency in the mountains; moreover, he was never free of pain in his back. That he achieved all he did following that misadventure is astonishing.

I join John and Angela, my cycling companions, at Huez. We cycle off around the back of the mountain to find our lunch spot on a patch of grass whence we gaze out across a chasm to the mighty, folded flanks of the Châine de Belledonne, where the Romans mined copper and lead, their workings still in evidence near the Lac Blanc. There were anthracite mines, too, till the pits were swamped by avalanche in 1952.

From the map, the col du Glandon presents little problem: 10km down into the valley, then a 29km ride from 720m to

1,924m, with a couple of steep sections marked. If not easy then manageable, and from the col a 22km glide all the way downhill to La Chambre, an apt place for an overnight stop. So much for maps. Clouds begin to accumulate in the sky ahead and the air grows damp while the breeze becomes cold. Here's Virgil on the brewing of storms which portend trouble:

> *interea magno misceri murmure*
> *magno incipit; insequitur commixta*
> *grandine nimbus*

> The sky rumbled, deep, thundrous
> borborygmus, and clouds rolled
> in, loaded with hail.

A portent of just how ugly the mountains can be.

We set out at 4 p.m. and scooted down to the valley floor, in freshening temperatures, on past a village called Oz, blithely unaware.

CHAPTER TWO

COL DU GLANDON

Hinault and Fighting Spirit

Bernard Hinault, nickname *le Blaireau* (the Badger), five-time winner of the Tour and now its technical director, has complained in recent years – during the Indurain stranglehold – that riders have lost, if they ever had, what ought to be central to their trade: fighting instinct. It's the kind of complaint that the old pro might be expected to unleash on the new bunch, the men who have no idea how hard things used to be. But, the simple countryboy Spaniard with the freakish lung capacity and a heart-rate so low even some doctors disbelieve it, commands such baffled awe yet such affection, too – no one can find a hard word to say of him as a man – that his invincibility was underwritten by even those riders with the talent to stretch him. They shied away from attacking him as if he were just too nice to be given a hard time. But, as Merckx said once: 'You can't *like* a rival.' Not when he's on the bike, at least. And the fact is, Indurain rarely had to drive himself hard against real threat.

Pantani made him suffer one memorable day in the Pyrenees on the 1995 Tour, leaving Big Mig and the rest trailing in his wake when he launched a scorching solo attack, dancing over the col d'Agnès to 1,527m and on up the slopes of Guzet Neige at unremitting pace. Indurain, in yellow, had to heave himself out of the saddle again and again just to survive, and came in over three minutes down on the Italian climber. But, such challenges were rare and Pantani had not the reserves to convert one day's gains into a longer siege. The rest of the would-be heirs to victory behaved as if it were a kind of *lèse-majesté*, treason, to call out the amiable, dull-witted Spaniard's lingering superiority.

I believe the Badger has a point. He was a formidably aggressive attacker; a man who'd announce to his team-mates that he was going to win that day and win he would. If he got beaten one day – as Hinault was, against all prediction in the time-trial up the Puy de Dôme on the 1978 Tour – he went out and crushed the rest the following day, which he did in the sprint into St Etienne. He'd ignore the day's predetermined team plan if he thought it propitious to do so, observing what his rivals were doing, and seizing on the mistakes and frailties of the moment rather than following a tactical blueprint. That ability to adapt, to change rhythm, to ditch the agreed tactics and ride as circumstances, or instinct, or just plain fire in the belly, dictate, is what all the great champions possess.

On the 1979 Tour of Lombardy, for instance, the Italian stars, Moser amongst them, were sitting on Hinault's team-mates, so Hinault went off on his own, with 150km still to ride. Cyrille Guimard drove up in the team car. 'You must be mad,' he said, 'you'll crack way before the finish.'

Hinault replied: 'Give it a rest.' Held out and won.

Like the Badger, most dangerous when cornered, he, like Coppi and Anquetil and Merckx, possessed what the French call *le coup de maître*, the master-stroke, which combines supreme physical strength and durability, moral power and a need to win that nobody can match. That need the French call *rage*, also their word for rabies. One of Merckx's ploys was to spring repeated flat-out sprints to pulp the rest of the field into submission. He used it to effect in the Milan–San Remo one-day classic, which he won an unequalled seven times. Nearing the finish, he'd fly off the front and take a hundred metres; the pack clawed their way back up to him; then he went again and again until they were spent. Anquetil they nicknamed *Maître* (more usually the title of a lawyer). An example of his audacity on 29 May 1965. At 5.12 p.m. in Avignon he received the winner's bouquet after the Critérium du Dauphiné Libéré. At 6.52 p.m. he boarded a Mystère jet in Nîmes and flew to Bordeaux for the start of the Bordeaux–Paris race (358 miles) at 2.30 a.m. next morning. At 5.33 p.m, in the Parc des Princes, he rode in first. Sponsored by Ford; also by himself. In that race he fought a titanic duel with the great English rider Tom Simpson, who came in third.

In 1979, his second Tour, Hinault won the yellow and the green jersey plus seven stage victories. (Aside from Merckx, three other riders won both jerseys in one Tour: Coppi, 1949, 1952; Gino Bartali 1938, 1948; Sylvère Maes 1939). In 1980, tendonitis had forced him to abandon the Tour – a very public humiliation – leaving the field clear to the Dutchman Joop Zoetemelk, a specialist climber who had not, till then, made a strong run for overall victory.

Zoetemelk, admittedly a rather uninspiring rider, was much disparaged for 'wheel-sucking' – notably by Merckx – that is sitting on the wheel of more energetic, more ambitious men and getting a free ride to his own advantage. (A rider in the slipstream of another bike has to do up to a third less work for the same speed because of reduced wind resistance.) This is a little unkind, maybe, because Zoetemelk certainly did not lack class. Moreover, a horrific head-on collision with a car whilst out training in 1974, left him in a coma with a fractured skull, close to death. Lesser men would have thrown in the towel but Zoetemelk recovered and in his first stage race after the accident, the 1975 Paris–Nice, he beat Merckx into second place by a thumping one and a half minutes. Like many Tour winners, the one field of combat Zoetemelk never joined was the massed sprint finishes of the flat stages – far too dangerous: why risk broken limbs for a few seconds' bonus? That madness is for the men built like wrestlers with more nerve than sense, many would say; chancy, twitch-nerve men like Abdoujaparov, the Tashkent Express who, head down in the mad drive for the line, collided with the crash barriers on the Champs-Elysées and had to walk the last metres with a broken collarbone to claim final ownership of the green jersey. The last few years have seen a rash of desperate pile-ups on the flat stages and wiser men stay clear. Merckx and Hinault never avoided the sprint if it was on offer. That willingness to mix it with all and sundry shows in the impressively long lists of their stage victories: Merckx 35 (a record), Hinault 28. Hinault returned to win in 1981 and 1982.

In 1983, he was forced to withdraw from the Tour before it even started; this led to a souring of relations with his manager and mentor at Renault, the exceptional Cyrille Guimard. (Guimard rode five Tours, 1970–74; in '72 he gave Merckx a pasting, only to be forced into the broom wagon with a knee injury, and from there watch the great Belgian take his fourth victory. He met the Tour finish in Paris where Merckx, in sympathy at his enforced retirement from the race, made him a present of his green points prize jersey.)

The argument began in a restaurant: Hinault wanted another glass of wine, Guimard refused to permit him one; the row thickened and widened. Hinault, a pugnacious Breton, like Astérix, and not famously diplomatic, told the Renault bosses they'd have to choose between him and Guimard. The bosses stonewalled and Hinault stormed off to join La Vie Claire. In his absence, the 1983 Tour was won by his former team-mate Laurent Fignon – the ex-dental student whose fiery temperament and Parisian cynicism disinclined him to think well of his former *patron*, or journalists, or press photographers or, it seemed on occasion, anyone in the immediate vicinity. He was always a contender, often winner, of the unofficial Prix Citron awarded by the French press to the sourest, least helpful rider in the *peloton*. Fignon was, by the way, just short of 23, a good age for winning a first Tour – Anquetil, Merckx, Hinault, Ullrich . . .

Hinault returned for the 1984 Tour and the former champion took on the usurper; had Fignon's victory been a fluke? Hinault didn't shirk the duel; he went for Fignon hard, but Fignon was out to prove he was no lucky profiteer of Hinault's absence. Hinault, a long-distance time-trial specialist, most unusually, won the short Prologue time-trial, riding at 49kph, but he lost time to both Sean Kelly and Fignon in the first major race against the clock. In the Pyrenees, Fignon began to flex his muscles and to ride with mature confidence and assurance, demonstrating class and bravura. In the Alps, wearing the yellow jersey, he caught the Swiss rider Jean-Mary Grezet 12km from the top of the day's final climb, went past and rode on alone to the mountain-top finish at La Plagne. That day Fignon showed himself to be a true champion.

Admittedly, Hinault's team was weak; he was having to do most of the work more or less unaided; Fignon's Renault team was supreme. Yet, Hinault showed enormous courage in taking on the rampant Fignon when none of the other grand men of the *peloton* would challenge the ex-dental student. His efforts were exhausting, however: dropped on the climbs – the Galibier seemed to take personal revenge by deriding his former superiority – he would ride manically along the flat to catch the leaders and, without pause for breath, attack instantly. This sapped his energy drastically and left him suffering, once more, on the climb. Merckx concluded that his attacks were more 'panicked than calculating'. But at least he was going for it.

Fignon countered his erstwhile leader's attack in the valley of the Oisans with obvious ease and taunted his rival scornfully at the finish on l'Alpe d'Huez: 'I don't know what the effort cost him; personally, I thought it was comical.' Fignon went on to win in Paris. Hinault, smarting from the reverse, shook himself down and, later that summer, took victory in the Grand Prix des Nations (an annual time-trial which saw Anquetil's début pro win, aged 19, the first of nine victories in the event); the Tour of Lombardy, 'the race of the falling leaves'; the Barrachi Trophy, a two-up against the clock, (what's called 'the race of truth') paired with the Italian ace, Francesco Moser. Some pride was salvaged.

In the 1985 Tour, Hinault crashed heavily head first in the dying metres of the bunch sprint stage into St Etienne, broke his nose and crossed the line, blood pouring. He'd been controlling the chase to allow his young team-mate, Greg Lemond, to lead home a break some distance ahead. The wound was patched up and, despite severe breathing difficulties from a bent septum, Hinault refused to quit the Tour and, in Paris, led Lemond, the American pretender, by a minute and 42 seconds. It was his fifth victory. He had already said he would retire on his 32nd birthday, a year hence, and declared that in the 1986 Tour he would work for Lemond. The king would sacrifice his efforts for the dauphin.

Within months he seemed to have changed his mind, though with typically Gallic enigma. He repeated his intention to retire in mid-November 1986, but added: 'Why give up the chance of another Tour victory or a World Championship title?' He added:

'I said I'd help Lemond win the Tour but he's got to earn it; he's got to be worthy of the yellow jersey.'

As soon as the Tour reached the mountains, it became plain that Hinault had no intention of simply handing victory to Lemond. Over the first 11 stages he attacked relentlessly and with characteristic passion, forcing Lemond to keep up or shut up. This tactic, though confusing to the American, was old hat to the wily Frenchman. He had been wearing the climbers down. 'By the time they reached the Pyrenees the climbers had nothing left, no reserves of strength. You've got to attack them until they can't recover. That's not hard to do.' The querulous Lemond wasn't impressed. He complained to reporters that Hinault was stiffing him.

Between Bayonne and Pau, over the col de Marie Blanque (a killer in disguise) and the first Pyrenean giants, Hinault once more attacked, in company with the Spaniard Delgado, to come in four minutes and 37 seconds ahead of the American. Lemond, for sure, never understood the arcane workings of the continental *peloton*, the intricate alliances and almost feudal sense of hierarchy and pecking order, the imperious requirement of wholesale, un-questioning loyalty. He was impervious to irony; neither, it seemed, could he distinguish between patronage and patronising. An intelligent, articulate and garrulous man, Lemond was a gift to journalists: he gave them reams of clean copy off the cuff which they could transfer direct down a phone line. But his amiability was a thin carapace for an aloof personality: he notoriously preferred to eat alone – ice cream and Mexican – with his family, lawyer–negotiator father included, rather than with the team in the hotel. He would even play truant from eve-of-Tour team receptions.

Nonetheless, Hinault's blatant flinging down of the gauntlet on the excuse of team ethics might seem a bit rich from the former boss who had promised him a lieutenant's support. 'I gave Lemond the chance to sit on my wheel today and relax.' Hinault explained. 'He knows we have to attack to make the opposition work, to tire them out.' Besides, who told Lemond not to keep up with Hinault? The fact is, Hinault made Lemond realise the brutal truth that victory would cost him, *must* cost him, dear; and what would victory be worth if Hinault merely stepped aside handed it over? To win the Tour is something; to beat Hinault in doing so, that's another thing.

Stung, Lemond, as fine a rider as he is strident a whinger, did rise to the challenge. He took a stage victory – one of very few over his career – in the Pyrenees, and erased Hinault's lead. Moreover, time was catching up on the Badger. So too were the High Alps. On the approach to l'Alpe d'Huez, Herrera and the Swiss rider Guido Winterberg, a Vie Claire team-mate of Hinault and Lemond, were first over the Galibier; while Hinault was leading the chase in company with Bauer, a team-mate, Zimmerman, Pello and Ruiz-Cabestany, all rivals. Lemond had been dropped. On the descent, taken at a furious speed, the group reformed and Lemond, in yellow, caught up. Along the valley, on to the Télégraphe, Hinault drove the pace like a fury. Herrera was the first to go off the back, then Winterberg. On the descent, Hinault and Lemond went clear and stayed clear for the final 70km, Hinault punishing them both without respite towards the foot of the col de la Croix de Fer. From the valley they climbed 32km and some 1,500m in altitude to the pass; thence another 30km sweep down the col du Glandon and so to the foot of the last climb of the day: l'Alpe d'Huez. They rode it together, Hinault in front, as he had been all day.

At the finish, Lemond came up alongside him and they rode into the mountain station side by side, hands clasped. It was the moment of transition, all smiles, the old wolf yielding leadership of the pack to the young challenger . . . as if Hinault would have surrendered. It wasn't in him.

'I've really thrown everything at Greg in the last 48 hours. I've pushed him as hard as I can, sparing him nothing to put him under maximum pressure. If he doesn't buckle, that means he's a champion and deserves to win the race. Next year maybe he'll have to fight off another opponent who'll make life difficult for him and he'll know how to fight back.'

Lemond, inevitably somehow, cast a very different interpretation on the psychological games and harsh treatment meted out by this devious Frenchman; in fact, he more or less discounted Hinault's share in his victory, a singular lack of generosity given the essentially corporate nature of *any* victory in the Tour. Hinault remarked: 'It wasn't my fault he didn't understand how to lead a race . . . I spent all my time wearing out his opponents. Throughout my career I worked hard for other riders without having the kind of problems I had with him.'

In the 1985 Coors Classic in USA, for instance, Lemond did what was unthinkable in a continental pro racer, he attacked his team-mate Hinault in tandem with members of rival teams. Loyalty wins loyalty. On the climb of the Stelvio in the 1980 Giro d'Italia, Hinault and René Bernaudeau were alone in the lead, Hinault waved his ally through for stage victory, to thank him for his help; the 1968 Blois to Chaville, Merckx pulled aside to give Guido Reybrouck victory as a reward for selfless help earlier in the season. Merckx never won the race; Reybrouck counted three wins in his *palmarès* – honours list – 1964, 1966, 1968.

A racing team of cyclists must function somewhat like a racing eight of oarsmen, the obvious difference being that the crew of a boat is always in the same place at the same time. However, merely because they are all in the same boat does not mean that they all work in perfect accord and synchronised effort; that harmony has to be worked for and achieved by total commitment to the united aim: to make the boat go faster than any other. With racing cyclists the united aim is to produce an overall winner, if there is a man capable of complete victory; if there is not, then daily stage victories. To those ends every member of an effective team must be devoted, sometimes – mostly – at cost of his own ambitions. A good team is a coherent unit, smoothly organised, each individual performing a task he is best suited for; those tasks differ with each individual. But even the most lowly, the most obscure contributions can often be the most efficacious for the team's greatest potential. Some riders are even rebuked for lack of personal ambition, in that they subordinate all their own effort to that of a markedly superior team-mate. Zoetemelk was one, till the absence of Hinault provided the spur to overcome self-doubt. Some men do not, apparently, suffer from such inner frailty: they ride at bust-a-gut limit for themselves or for others if they're having a bad day. But, *par excellence*, the Tour de France, much as the Bourbon kings of France, imposes a demand of total fealty from rider; in reward, the accolade of victory – be it the race or a stage – and recognition of the unstinting combined effort to win it. No more, no less.

This renders some of the tactics witnessed on the television coverage perplexing to the uninitiated: two riders well clear of the *peloton* (the same word in French as platoon, incidentally) will generally work together to get to the finish where they can duel for the stage win. Sometimes, however, they jealously refuse to work with each other and the pack, like a speeding whale, swallows up the pair of minnows and their chance for individual glory is blown. Or else that day, their team managers decide that the sprinters need a showing; a bigger splash in place of a small flourish. So, orders go down via the team car. (The cat-and-mouse tactics do draw scorn from many riders and race organisers: the patent lack of real desire to go for a win even at the risk of defeat on the line.)

The basis of team tactics is to protect the leader, or a member of the team who attacks. When one of their men goes off the front, the best riders, those of the *grand métier*, know how to worm their way to the front of the *peloton* and disrupt any other team trying to wind up the chase. They will sit in, let one of the chasing team get a metre or so clear and block any attempt to link with him from the riders behind; what they call a *cassure* or fracture. This slows the whole *peloton* by damaging jolts to the even rhythm of the pursuit.

Or, a break of several riders goes comfortably clear, none of them a great threat to the general classification. However, one of the race leaders sends one of his team men to sit in on the escape and do no work. This tactical 'wheel-sucker' is there to get an easy tow to the finish where, fresher than the rest, he may save his strength and thus have a better chance to slip through for a win; or, should the escape prove half-hearted, his failure to help it along will see it founder sooner, rather than later, and thus allow his own team men to race back into contention for the final sprint. Often, two escapees jockey endlessly with each other as the finish line heaves into view, one, a better sprinter than the other and anxious to choose the exact right moment for his jump – not too far out, not too close – only to miss out because his rival, no speed-man, suddenly determines it's all or nothing, do or die, and lets rip, hangs on by his nerve ends and imaginary strength to take the stage. This isn't tactics: it's opportunism winning over stupidity.

Most significant, though, is the surrender, the literal surrender, of time by a lesser man to his leader. The examples of it are legion and they belong to the peculiar masonry of this unique sport, a tradition positively seigneurial, where princes really do have to win their spurs on the battlefield to earn the right of their noble calling and the plaudits of their older peers, by perceived courage, by show of nerve under extreme duress.

Hence Hinault's passionate, unequivocal rebuke of what he called the gutless slipstreamers who formed the procession behind Big Mig – a supreme athlete without a spark of panache or wit in him; a man marginally less interesting than his bike, tallying an unprecedented five consecutive victories of bromide regularity and hypnotic boredom built on classic time-trialling superiority, the slavish efforts of a devoted and characterless team, limiting losses in the mountains by picky calculations of seconds rather than from any discernible *rage* to win. This metronomic accumulation of wins had been obediently abetted by the docility of the men who might have whipped up some opposition, or at least have exposed what the thoroughly likeable Basque had in his head when push came to shove and he had to get out of the saddle to fight a bit. Not much, it turned out. Rijs' taming of the rider that nobody thought could possibly fail to record a legendary sixth victory proved Hinault right: if you want to win you have to attack, to the point of exhaustion and a long way beyond it, on strength, nerve and mad confidence, the full monte. Until Rijs took the Spanish robot on, the Spanish robot was, apparently, ready to grind the rest into mincemeat as per usual. *Coup de maître*. There were excuses: Indurain didn't like the rain and cold, he forgot to eat enough, and so on. But no pro at that level and with that experience, forgets, like a rookie, to stuff in the daily quota of 8,000 calories. And cold and wet? *Please.* The fact was, he'd been hit hard, gone down and couldn't get up. The will simply evaporated. Desgrange always said it: to win the Tour you need your head as well as your legs.

Rijs' tactics that day on the climb to Hautacam, July 1996, when Indurain bowed to mortality, caused a few raised eyebrows, not least because of the prodigal expenditure of energy it took. This, ironically, was the ground Indurain had picked for his Tour-winning attack – he very rarely attacked – in 1995. He had recon-noitred two stages: the individual time-trial and this stage up to the mountain near Lourdes. Clearly he was nervous: he needed some security early in the race, a step-up to his fifth victory. When he jumped on the climb the rest of the pack were so completely mesmerised – Indurain going out alone? Must have sunstroke – that they lamely watched him go until it was too late; he gained a couple of minutes, ample cushion for a time-trial specialist and another win was shuffled into his hand almost without murmur.

In 1996, Rijs launched his assault on this very slope – unjustly, perhaps, one wouldn't naturally impute such wit to Danes. He flew away from a small group of leading riders, including Indurain and his own lieutenant Ullrich, Virenque and other danger men. Hammering at them, like Merckx, he sped off a hundred metres; then, inexplicably even to our own Channel 4 commentators, he sat up and waited for the others to haul themselves level, glancing over his shoulder at them as they approached. Then he soared off again. It was, I must say, obvious to me at the time what he was doing. Whereas the admirable Phil Liggett deplored this tactic as the act of a madman, what he ought to be doing was keep pace with the others waiting to see who would crack – a very English timidity, that seems – it was quite apparent that Rijs was testing them, flaunting his own strength and challenging them, old-style, to the duel. None answered. Rijs went away a couple of times more and then for good and he was uncatchable. What must Indurain have thought when he saw him disappear around the far hairpin? Only what he must have been thinking for several days already: that his meeting with the sad destiny had arrived.

Of course, questions were asked about Rijs' startling form, his unsappable energy and, later that year, he and Ullrich, both members of the Deutsche Telekom team tested positive in a pre-Olympics dope sample and were refused entry in their national teams. The communist bloc Eastern Germans didn't invent drug-enhanced sports performance but they certainly developed it into expert science and some habits have persisted. There is the alchemy of head and legs and the pharmacopoeia of who knows what else?

Indurain recently criticised Pantani and Virenque, both explosive climbers who have stood on the podium in Paris, for not riding more intelligently. 'They attack absolutely anywhere, even when they have no chance of succeeding, and these attacks cost them a lot of energy. To win a Tour you must concentrate on one consolidated strike and make sure it's a knock-out blow.' That *may* win a Tour; it wins no place in my roster of real champions. Jalabert, censured for wasteful solo efforts, retorted that he might as well attack as get dropped.

If I have been harsh on Indurain it is not through lack of consideration for his talent – no one wins a single Tour, let alone five in a row, unless he is a remarkable sportsman – but rather from disappointment in his disposal of it. For example, by stage seven of the 1995 Tour, Indurain's fifth victory in store, Rijs had already emerged as a, or perhaps the, danger man. The route, from Charleroi, led the race into Liège and the Belgians would certainly be on the alert for a possible win in front of their home crowd. Towards the end of the stage, a group went clear and Indurain, acting on orders from his *directeur sportif,* joined. Here was a chance to put some time into the impatient Viking from Telekom. When they were 15km from the finish, the group confronted the fourth category Les Forges climb, one of the sudden sharp inclines for which Wallonia is noted; Indurain surged up it, offered only perfunctory support by the Walloon Bruyneel and the Canadian Boyer. They went clear of the other chasers, including Armstrong, usually a man for exactly this kind of break, but not lively enough this day. Boyer fell away, too – doomed, like the rest, to be swept up by the following *peloton* which was still moving quite sluggishly – neither Berzin nor Rominger, named threats to the big Spaniard, seeming much bothered that he was robbing them of precious seconds a long way before the mountains.

Over the top of the climb, Indurain and Bruyneel were in tandem now, Indurain beckoned the Belgian through to help in the pacing. Bruyneel, presumably acting on orders, refused. Either the break would succeed, in which case he'd be fresh for the final dash to the line, or it would fail and Indurain would have used up energy for nothing and a Belgian sprinter could crash out of the pack for the day's honours. Indurain shrugged his shoulders and got stuck in. On the 50kph descent of Les Forges, into the outskirts of Liège, he took every risk imaginable, on tricky corners and a chancy surface – one of the riders in the pursuing pack misjudged and flew into a shop window – and built a 50-second lead, Bruyneel clinging to his wheel. Behind them Rijs and the Belgian ace Museeuw were, at last, cranking up the chase.

Into Liège, Indurain was plainly in some distress, elbow wobbling, head tilted to one side, mouth sagging, but he was generating phenomenal speed. Flat out for the line, inevitably he had no change of gear left in him and Bruyneel came past, a smug grin on his face, to acknowledge the cheers of the locals as he swiped the stage win and with it the yellow jersey from the man who had towed him to the line. 'It was like riding behind a Derny motorbike pacer,' he said afterwards.

And Indurain? 'My legs were hurting.' But he'd gained 50 seconds on Rijs and next day in the 54km time-trial he added a further 50. Rominger lost 58 seconds and Berzin a massive minute and 38 seconds. With that power in his frame, what adventure Indurain might have put into his riding, instead of sheltering in the bunch. Lovely man; no brain.

Hinault, most assuredly, had a head on his shoulders. An interesting insight into his psychological toughening was that when he started work as a 16-year-old, he cycled daily from his home village, Yffiniac, by bike. Outside the village is a 2 to 3km long, steepish hill, where he would wait for an approaching lorry. He'd start riding towards the slope and, dicing with the possibility of misjudgement, latch on to its slipstream to ride close behind it at 50kph. To stay with the fast-moving vehicle became a matter of pride. On the way home at night, he'd try to match cars for speed going *down* the same hill. This, he said, developed both his muscles *and* his will to win, as well as the challenge of keeping a good rhythm.

These competitive rides entailed pedalling as fast as he could, but this isn't where he found his strength as a rider; that strength was innate and the fast pedalling on low gears would eventually lead to rapid turning of the cranks on the big gears, eating ground at ten metres a revolution. No, I'd say the principal benefit of those daily lorry-chasing rides was psychological; Hinault got used to racing flat out beyond what he might imagine to be his normal limit. There is, in many of us, a fear of succeeding far more crippling than any fear of failure, which is, by comparison, fairly routine. In his boyish refusal to give in to those lorries, Hinault was doing himself the precious service of eradicating from his spirit any dread of one day riding everybody else off his wheel. He is, too, a Breton, heir to the legacy of two of the finest Tour riders, rivals in their day: Bobet and Robic.

This goes through my head as I grind up the col du Glandon. It is a pig. I have no stomach for it and, bad sign, I am complaining. Complaining about the gradient, the scenery, the wet, the fact that there is a bloody mountain in the way of my basking in the earlier triumph of the day. How dare this ugly, endless, unforgiving col du Glandon muscle in on the glory of my l'Alpe d'Huez climb?

Hinault himself wasn't shy of bitching about excessive physical demands: for instance, he denounced the Paris–Roubaix – the Queen of Classics, part of which traverses the 'Hell of the north' the wicked *pavé* (cobbles) of the old wagon roads – and called it 'this stupid race' after winning it in 1981, 25 years to the day after Louison Bobet's victory, the last by a Frenchman. 'It's a circus' he said. 'Why risk a fall that would mean missing the Tour?' A resolutely professional attitude. Riding a bike was a job; the old 'giants of the road' stuff was romantic myth, though he did describe his victory in the 1977 Liège–Bastogne–Liège as a 'beautiful thing'. (A few days earlier he had won another Belgian one-day classic, the Ghent–Wevelgem; a double achieved only by one other man – Merckx.) Yet, when Hinault deplored a time-trial stage of 140km as 'inhuman', Marcel Bidot scoffed. In the 1927 and 1928 Tours they rode 200km *contre la montre,* against the clock, every day, except in the mountains. And the 1973 Tour, the stage from Bourg-Madame to Luchon, in the Pyrenees, was to include the col de Péguère, three and a half kilometres of horrible gradient, the early part one in five and scarcely more forgiving after that. I've ridden it twice: it's a brute. The day before, a rest day, when France was commemorating the fall of the Bastille, the national radio news reported that: 'The Tour organisers have just announced that two of their technical experts have been inspecting part of the itinerary for tomorrow's stage and, as a result, the col de Péguère has been eliminated from the route. The descent is considered too dangerous.' Local reaction was contemptuous: the riders had complained the climb was too steep and chickened out. The big names did not want to be caught getting off their bikes and walking. Modern Tour riders don't know how to suffer.

In 1978 Hinault was asked to lead a protest by the *peloton* against late arrival times, early-morning starts, enforced transfers by train or air – no fewer than five that year – which was all the fault of a system which allowed commercial interests to supersede those of the riders and the sport. The result: an inhuman race. When they were 50m from the finish in Valence d'Agen, the *peloton* dismounted and walked in; the stage was declared null. Jacques Goddet responded: an inhuman element was integral to the very nature of the Tour; excessive demands lay at the heart of its mystique, its ageless success. He claimed that the proper course of preparatory training for any rider should be two years, 80,000km of road-riding and a hundred post-Tour criteriums – one-day races – in towns dotted round the hexagon of France.

And yet, however pampered a rider is in the form of material and psychological support, there remains the equation on which all calculus of *who has it toughest* is based, and that is: man/woman + bike + mountain = hard work. There is a corollary to that unforgiving solution which is that proving yourself against mountains and achieving the top is extremely satisfying, even if it doesn't feel much like pleasure.

This rotten col du Glandon certainly doesn't feel like pleasure. At the risk of hearing the ghost of Marcel Bidot scoff me off the road, I was complaining.

Trouble is, I'm not sure how I feel about complaining. The fact is, I'm up against it, face to face with heroic sentimentality, picking a heavy plastering of romantic fiction off Pandora's sealed box containing truth. I want to ride the mountains and I am, so far. But can it really be as hard as this? I have no option but to confront my own weakness and sort out romance from reality. (Getting off and walking isn't an option. I'm a cyclist.) At least this climb is forcing me to a new discovery, a peep into the darker places of my psyche; because I do want the whole story, complaints and all. I want to observe my reactions closely and here I am, head down into the handlebars, observing my reactions.

The impression is that I am riding naked, on nothing more substantial than willpower; when the willpower runs out, that's it, *finito*. I have a sudden recollection of Boardman's face in the Alps, 1996, 'the worst day I've ever spent on a bike,' he said. He had nothing left but the tenacity to hold on till the end of that awful day and a wild hope there'd be enough left to get him through tomorrow. The image of his pain and distress was as eloquent as any anguish panted into a microphone. Fatigue may be only skin deep, as a nutcase sculling champion once remarked, but fatigue does exist and it can't always be held off: even heroes crack. But that's when the tougher heads get belligerent; the struggle to get back into the action when you've been dropped takes even more juice than the effort to hang on, and pugnacity is no more than hardboiled complaint. What you don't want is raw complaint: like liquid egg it goes all over the place.

Cursing a headwind or a broken engine, ranting at lost keys to come out of hiding, pleading with a bus stop to send a bus may kill time but, as Thoreau said, 'You can't kill time without injuring eternity.' We occupy the time we are in, its now, its past and future. I'm dicing with a kind of cosmic suicide here.

Of course I am not racing. The Tour, amongst a whole battery of inflexible rules, imposes a strict time limit based on a ratio of the daily winner's time – a rider who comes in too late to duck under the barrier is eliminated. In the mountains, the anti-gravity men – sprinters, *domestiques* – form what's called 'the bus' for mutual help, aiming to scrape in inside the limit. They also bargain on the race officials waiving the rules if too many riders miss out. Not to deplete the field drastically, the Tour finds some arcane clause – usually money – which permits *ad hoc* bending of the inflexible rules and reinstatement.

A few hundred metres outside the village of le Rivier d'Allemond, the road ahead begins to dip and blow kisses at the high ground; not a slight downhill, a headlong black run; bad news, very bad news. I go on, but I begin skidding down a glacier of suspicion.

The road twines like a rubbish chute to the bottom of a gorge dredged by the Eau d'Olle in spate. Beyond stretches a dismal valley, the Défile de Maupas, a sombre cleft between the towering Grandes Rousses to the east, le Massif d'Allevard to the west. Défile . . . Grandes . . . Massif . . . they make me feel very puny all of a sudden. The uphill looks villainous too, even as I freewheel into the trough of the descent, and villainous it proves. I pedal at it furiously. Momentum shoots me no further than 20m up the slope and peters out. I am numb, reduced to a gasping crawl, nearly forced into the zigzag routine back and forth across the hill to soften the gradient. A brief spell of utter dejection: I am simply *not* going to make it; I'd teeter to a halt and have to get off and *walk*.

I recollect a weekend training run before a school continental cycle tour: we tackled a steepish hill near Ivinghoe. One boy got off to walk. When one of the others ribbed him, he patted his bike and said, laconically: 'Metal fatigue.' (Not so fatuous, actually: the severe torque of wrenching at a bike can twist the frame out of track. From what I remember of him, though, wrenching anything, apart from himself away from work, wasn't his style.)

Getting off to walk is utterly against my instincts and I've rarely been compelled to; but even pros walk. The Koppenberg, 1km-long cobbled acclivity – one in four at its worst – like the outside wall of a pyramid on the Tour des Flandres (one of the Belgian one-day classic races at Easter) has them dismounting their over-geared machines in droves. The whole race is peppered with similar obstacles, why bother to slog up slower than you can walk?

Well, I didn't come to the Alps not to bother. Pride is the spur and pride dug its big-rowelled spurs in.

Hinault fell on the descent of the col de Porte and tumbled into a ravine, Critérium Dauphiné Liberé, 4 June 1977. The motorbike television camera zooms in and France watches as Guimard pulls him up on to the road. A momentary grimace of sheer dismay on Hinault's face as he clocks what might have happened. Then he is taking his bike from the mechanic and riding on. He wins the race over Thévenet (a few weeks away from his second Tour victory) and a true champion is born. Victories alone don't make champions so much as victories fashioned out of defeat.

Knowing when to get your arse out of the saddle is how Marcel Bidot put the difference between a champion and an also-ran: a mixture of not being too proud to work like a commoner and being too proud to allow a commoner to beat you.

The Tour passed this way in July 1995 heading for the Madeleine and beyond. My tyres cross names daubed in white on the road; the usual smattering – local heroes, national heroes, foreign heroes – but a lot here for the Italian trio of Chiapucci, Bugno and one Bourgni, except that he's no rider I know of. I conclude that Bourgni is *tifosi* slang for 'dig in', an alternative to the more common *Forza!*

Italian cycling fans – *tifosi* – are notoriously partisan, deeming it a time-honoured part of their national duty to spit at, abuse and jostle foreign riders invading the home turf. (*Tifoso* properly means 'typhus patient'. Typhus, also known as pestilential, putrid or gaol fever, produces severe nervous symptoms.)

Nicholas Freeling recounts how he saw Anquetil, the hated Frenchman, riding up a *passo* in the 1960 Giro d'Italia, jeered and spat at by the *tifosi*. He took it all, impassive, aloof, and made the best riposte by winning the Giro, the first Frenchman ever to do so.

In 1987, Stephen Roche famously took back the leader's pink jersey in the Giro from his co-leader of the Carrera team, Roberto Visentini: the Italian had reneged on their mutual agreement that whoever proved stronger should go for victory. 'Let the road decide,' they say; so Roche attacked. His team did not want to chase, Visentini was screaming blue murder at them, other teams refused to co-operate – they weren't offered enough money. The Carrera manager, Davide Boifara, bowed to partisan claims and drove up alongside Roche to tell him the team were in pursuit.

Roche said: 'Well, Davide, you tell them to keep something under their saddle because they'll need it later.'

He was caught but had enough left to stay with the lead; Visentini, meantime, had cracked and was blown off the back. Roche actually punctured 10km from the finish, but no one told Visentini, a selfish rider and extremely unpopular. Next day, though, the *tifosi* were baying for Roche's blood, lining the roads, some of them, waving chunks of raw meat: very Mafia. Roche rode flanked by Eddy Schepers, his team-mate, and his fellow Celt Robert Millar, on a rival team, for protection.

Forza Bugno! Forza il Diablo! (the nickname they give the unpredictable Chiapucci, hot as devilled sauce who attacks when he feels like attacking, even when it makes no tactical sense, just for the sheer hell of it, because he's got a worm in his head telling him to give it a try and because even out of form he's a menace – Mountains Prize in 1991 and 1992, hero of a prodigious, all-day solo ride across the Alps into Italy that year – always ready to ginger up the action to see if anyone will respond).

I stare at the *Forza!* It's like a V-sign.

I so badly want to come and ride these Alps with flair but that's pure fantasy. Chris Boardman, speaking of a race early in his pro career, recalls how he was riding in the bunch – some 100 riders – at full stretch, when they hit a hill and the front riders simply changed a gear and flew off at such a pace he watched them go and thought: 'No way. If this is pro racing, I'm not going to make it.' Holder, since 1996, of the World hour record and the world pursuit record, he is one of the great speed-merchants of all time, but this road-race business was an entirely new reality. Such revelations of how we match or do not match up to demand are a shock, and few riders who enter the Tour for the first time can have any conception of the extreme demands it makes; even if, on the flat stages, the real action tends not to pick up until the final hour or so.

More of my own fictions are being deflated by the shock of a new reality. On this tiresome alp, imagining myself up with the rest, steaming up l'Alpe d'Huez at 32kph, tyres drawing a long cancel line through the tarmac autograph book – Yates, Kelly, Breukink, Roche, de las Cuevas, Indurain el Grande, even Merckx, still lionised, I'm pleased to see. But even as my efforts sag, I gain insight into 'attacking spirit'.

In 1997 Pantani, *Il Pirata*, from the gold earring he wears, raced up l'Alpe d'Huez – that implacable arbiter of uphill speed – in 39 minutes, beating his own record. He arrived at the foot of the climb with Ullrich, Rijs, Virenque and Casagrande. One hairpin was enough for him to settle in and he was gone, a spurt of pace which left Rijs and Casagrande for dead. The others tried to match him but 3km from the top he was 25 seconds ahead of Ullrich and at the *Arrivée* the deficits ranged from Ullrich at 47 seconds to Rijs at two minutes and 28 seconds. Customarily, it is the Dutch fans who monopolise the slopes of this climb; this day the *tifosi* crowded them off the verges to cheer their man who was making his comeback after a bad crash a year before.

Pantani celebrated stage victory; Ullrich moved forcibly into the limelight; Rijs, who had been repeating his view that Ullrich was too young to carry the day-to-day pressure and burden of leading the race, had to accede to the old adage 'If you're good enough, you're old enough' and found himself nine minutes 42 seconds in arrears on his erstwhile lieutenant. However, the emerging dominance of the most consistent *grimpeur*, climber, around – Virenque – in the Alps and Pyrenees was, I believe, the crucial factor in the 1997 Tour. He set out to win if not the Tour then decidedly the mountains prize, and did so for the fourth time in a row, but his attacking spirit animated the field in a way which made this race one of the most exciting in recent history. In the mountains, his Festina team were at the front constantly, forcing a relentless pace. Rijs announced that Ullrich had him to thank for his second place in 1996 and that he was coming to the 1997 Tour as the man to beat. For a while, team tactics dictated that Ullrich accept his incumbent role as second. So, the big challenge to Rijs in 1997 came initially from the uncompromising aggressive effort of Virenque at the head of the pack, launching into the mountains with ferocious intent. Pantani fuelled the drive to win summit finishes, but even he nearly caved in, victim of the unpredictable Italian temperament (typified by the arch drama queen Cipollini, a rider with legs and vanity in roaring health and the moral power of a spoilt brat. Showman, show-off, he is, of course, a publicist's dream and a sporting director's headache). After the Alpe d'Huez ride Pantani complained of a sore throat and wanted to abandon. His team manager talked to him (gave him a bollocking) and two days later he took a second mountain stage and, eventually, third place in Paris. So much for waking up with a bit of a cold and wanting to skive off work.

Virenque's impetus never flagged, however. His capacity to chase a break on the punishing climbs has never been in doubt, but his combativity at the front of every mountain stage in 1997 undeniably broke Rijs and allowed Ullrich – quite clearly an exceptional talent on whose backing Rijs took victory in 1996 – to emerge as an indisputable champion, a leader in his own right. Whatever Virenque and Pantani did, he followed with the sort of implacable inner resolve that is intimidating to lesser men. Rijs, who had claimed to be even stronger than in the year of his victory, had no answer; he was dynamited out of the race for final honours, though, to his lasting credit as a sportsman, he worked tirelessly for the man who had replaced him as leader. The plaudits – 'Yes, Jan is stronger, he deserves his win' – are expected, which doesn't make them insincere; the actions, though, cannot be anything but genuine support, the leader being the leader in fact, not theory. Emerging from the Alps, Rijs succumbed to a bad stomach bug and, with the Tour lost, might have quit; he didn't. The year before, on the stage into Pamplona, patently marked out as a victory parade for the local man Indurain who was on his way, or so everybody had predicted, to a sixth successive win, Rijs lost the stage win by a whisker and Indurain trailed in already minutes down, his Tour lost. Rijs, however, beckoned him on to the podium and gave him the leader's bouquet. It was a magnanimous gesture.

Stage 14 of the 1997 Tour began with the col du Glandon. Several heroes of the previous day's charge to l'Alpe d'Huez were blown out before the finish at Courchevel, 2,004m, via the 2,000m of the mighty col de la Madeleine. Rijs lost a minute and 24 seconds on the day, Pantani three minutes 26 seconds, Casagrande three minutes 38 seconds. The winner, Virenque, pushed the race ahead from the start and arrived in imperious fashion, with Ullrich two bike lengths behind.

Approaching the Barrage de Grande Maison, I see ahead what had every chance of being another excruciatingly steep bit of misery. My heart sinks. I ride up to it and, in some remove of delirium, up it. Can't be so far now. Some way on I find out how far: a whole lot.

Once again, the road gets altitude sickness and dives for low cover. It is almost too much to bear. I charge at it manically and console myself with pondering the treat I have promised myself when I eventually reach this col du Glandon, wherever it is located in the stratosphere beyond silver linings and rainbow crocks of gold. At the summit of the col du Glandon, the road forks: left to La Chambre, right to another pass, the col de la Croix de Fer, an extra 2.5 km and 159m to 2,067m. I tell myself, kid myself, that this could be no longer or tougher than Highgate West Hill and worth the detour. Down in the valley, far from queasy air and solitude, the plan had seemed reasonable. From the moment this same road went AWOL down the slide, I reserve judgement on the idea. And the way things are going, reserves, whether of judgement, energy or any humour better than fractious, might very soon run out. Nor am I going to bother about the col de la Croix de Fer. Nor am I going to bother that I am not going to bother.

In the 1956 Tour, ten years after I was born, the col de la Croix de Fer was the scene of a famous break by Roger Walkowiak, an unlikely-sounding Frenchman, who, like Cornet in 1904 and Lambot in 1922, did not win a single stage *en route* to victory. (Firmin Lambot, first man to win in the yellow jersey in 1919, was down by 48 minutes quite early in the 1922 Tour; the Belgians seemed to have the race sewn up but Heusghem was docked an hour penalty and Lambot took the final yellow jersey.) 'Walko', who must have had *some* Polish impetuosity in his make-up, was noted for his willingness to tag on to what the bosses of the *peloton*, the *patrons*, team leaders, called *échapées bidon*, attacks doomed to failure incurring a waste, perhaps irreclaimable waste, of effort. To their cost, on this occasion. Walko went off with some small fry, and the big fry – including Bidot's French national team – left it too late to reel him in; the gains he made held until Paris and he took the overall victory without winning a single stage. It didn't endear him to the French public or the press, who called him 'wet' for his lack of enterprise, strolling into yellow with neither merit nor panache. After ten years of pro bike riding he went back to working in a factory.

An attack off the front is always a test of nerves: whether to follow or at least send a team member, if there's one strong enough, to join and hamper it by sitting on the tail doing no work. If the attack succeeds, it means you're fresher than the rest and better poised for a stage victory; if it fails then your own team leader is in at the finish. Nobody ever knows it's too late till it's too late.

In the 1955 Tour, the leading riders reached Bédoin at the foot of Mont Ventoux. Among them, in the rainbow jersey of World Champion, was Louison Bobet. Five days before, Charly Gaul had beaten him by 14 minutes over the Galibier in foul weather; but Gaul hated heat and that day the Provence skies hung over them like hot lead. At the start of the climb – 22km to 1,583m on slopes between four and 14 degrees – Bobet allowed the Swiss Ferdi Kubler, 'The Big 'un', and his own French team-mate Géminiani, to go ahead. Keeping his nerve, riding his own race, his own rhythm, his own speed, he watched as they surged away and went out of sight. Bobet came on, steady as a metronome. Halfway up the climb he'd cut the gap to a minute and a half. Then, 10km from the top, Kubler, as was his custom, launched a crazy attack. He'd never ridden the mountain before and Gém called after him:

'Careful Ferdi, Ventoux is no ordinary col.'

'Nor is Ferdi an ordinary rider' cried Kubler, accelerating away. Higher up the climb he cracked; Bobet came on, passed both men and reached the summit alone, in the lead by 50 seconds, and then began the descent. By the time he reached the town at the foot – Malaucène – 60km from the finish in Avignon, the advance was one minute. His attack was looking shaky; it had stemmed more from the default of the others than from his own aggression. Nonetheless, he was ahead and over the next 23km he increased the margin to two minutes and 20 seconds but then punctured and lost a minute changing the wheel. The chase was bearing down fast. Rattled by the enforced stop, jarred out of his rhythm, Bobet had grave misgivings about the wisdom of this *échapée bidon*. His team director, Marcel Bidot, drove up alongside to urge him on. Bobet asked how much lead he had. Bidot prevaricated: there was sufficient advance to see him home. Bobet wouldn't be put off. 'I want to know exactly; if it's less than a minute, I'm sitting up [giving up].'

Bidot checked: the lead was 55 seconds and they were 16km from home into a headwind. Bobet grew impatient.

'Come on. How much?

'A minute and 10 seconds.'

For 20 minutes Bobet put his nose in the handlebars, as they say, and took the stage by 50 seconds. Bidot, who records the story in his excellent *L'Epopée du Tour de France* (The Epic of the Tour de France), said it was an appallingly long 20 minutes, sweating on whether he had obeyed a good instinct or blown the gamble. Bobet was a brilliant rider but very suggestible; his morale could be brittle as an eggshell.

Kubler reached Avignon but he was finished; eyes rolling, raving to other riders: 'Go on. Ferdi's gone crazy.' Behind him on the mountain, Jean Malléjac fell to the ground in a delirium, the bike on top of him, his free leg pedalling like an automaton. Unconscious for 15 minutes, he was revived with an injection of the decongestant solucamphre and oxygen. That evening, Kubler lay on his bed muttering: 'The Tour is finished for me. Ferdi's too old, too sick. Ferdi committed suicide on Ventoux.' Words that would resound with appalling truth 12 years later.

There will be no one waiting on the col de la Croix de Fer for me to shout *Ça vous en bouche un coin* at and by now, frankly, I couldn't care less. The *croix de fer* must be one of those ornate, wrought-iron filigree items set by the side of the road to mark the old pilgrim routes; my own pilgrimage was well beyond such pieties.

Another clutch of tight hairpins and a steep gradient bring me back to the level I'd had to wave goodbye to a mile back. I cycle on towards Le Rocher Blanc, a giant bluff projecting from the side of the Massif. Cloud pours over its rim, as it were from a hidden chimney serving the troll furnaces in the mountain's heart. Billows of smoke as white as steam, enough to herald a whole consistory full of new Popes. A diabolic machine stoking up ready for the engorging of the lone, the *intrepid,* Knight of the Campagnolo Gears advancing to meet the Dragon of the Mount Vicious in its swirls of inspissated mist.

With the mist comes a thin drizzle, a damp lining to the veil of fog. The sky moans like a turbine starting up and is soon whining a gale and discharging its ballast of rain, the full-weight article from pewter-grey clouds in a lead-grey sky on to my battle-grey spirits; everything is sinking, sinking, sinking. The road is one long dipsy-doodle. I'll be cycling off on to the grassland soon, convinced I'm a sheep, baaing at clouds which bark back at me like collies.

Suddenly, out of this unremitting slog, there looms up through the opacities a signpost which indicates the col at 0.5km. I grit my teeth. You do grit your teeth, it's a way of showing off about the effort you're putting in. Sleet mixes in with the rain. More cold mixes in with the existing cold.

One switchback turn past a hostelry. It's closed, deserted, dark. 'There is nothing,' said Dr Johnson, 'which has yet been invented by man by which so much happiness is produced as by a good tavern or inn.' Nor anything, perhaps, more depressing than a shut pub when you need an open one. A short drag upwards, another turn and there it is, unmarked, a hump in the road and flat ground: the col du Glandon in all its all-its.

As I draw near, I sense a brackish jubilation rising in my chest, something akin to that stupendous relief (it's wonderful) and discomfort (it hurts) when you get to the WC at last and pee out from a bursting bladder. I round the final bend, hit the last slope and am at the top, where, to a bemused audience of sodden, bedraggled sheep rambling about as aimlessly as BR commuters waiting for a cancelled train, I yell: 'FUCK! FUCK! FUCK!' at the top of my voice. My treat.

I roll down once more, over a road that has recently done duty as a river bed, but down, and in the direction of the evening's comforts.

Gloves soaked through, my hands stiffen with the cold and from pulling the brakes near full on. The worst drawback of descending is that the heart engine slips into neutral, burns no fuel and stokes no heat.

A signboard for a hotel at 10km. My knuckles and wrists are aching horribly with the strain of braking. I can't see far enough ahead to risk any speed and the road is slick and skiddable. I am lucky. On such a night in 1919, Léon Scieur (winner, 1921) rode the Le Havre–Cherbourg stage carrying four spare tyres wrapped round his shoulders; in short succession he got punctures in all four. He spent what money he had left from food and drink on two new spares and, for security, decided to mend the others. This required unpicking the outer easing of the 'balloon' tyre, sealing the hole of the puncture, then resewing the case. There was a bitter wind blowing. Scieur took shelter in a house doorway and, by dim lamplight, set about his repair work under the watchful eye of two witnesses: the old lady who lived in the house and one Lucien Cazalis, Desgrange's right-hand man, a race commissaire, on duty to check that the rider didn't cheat by asking the old woman to thread the needle for him because his hands were too numb to do it. If she did . . . penalty.

At 10.5km there is a sign for St Colomban des Villards. A second sign: *Centre*. Ahead there looms a deserted village street, flanked by houses, one street lamp valiantly aglow like a good deed of 'welcome' in this naughty world of 'piss off'; one side of the road beside it is a covered market place, and, opposite, a bar with a lit doorway, and therein food, drink and a bed for the night and no commissaires to penalise me for begging help or stealing comfort.

CHAPTER THREE

COL DU TÉLÉGRAPHE

Tours of the 1920s

Front-runner for the title 'Most Unlucky' of Tour riders must surely be Eugène Christophe; motto: 'He does his duty who does what he can.' In 1921, Cri-Cri lost the Tour yet again when his front forks broke for the *third* time and he had to descend the Galibier on foot in search of a blacksmith's forge. Three times . . . you begin to suspect that it might even have been a protracted publicity stunt, *grâce á* Desgrange, sponsored by a rival tube manufacturer.

The first, and most celebrated, fracturing of the forks occurred in 1913 on the descent of the Tourmalet, the highest modern main-road pass in the Pyrenees, at that time a goat track. It was a calamity, but this was no time for tears and tantrums. Christophe held the overall lead by 20 minutes. He simply shouldered the broken bike, trotted 8km – two hours – to the nearest village, Ste Marie de Campan, and rooted out a blacksmith's shop. He begged a length of metal, softened it in the fire, shaped it into an 18mm pipe to match the broken fork, punched a hole in the end to receive the axle and set to to weld it in place. This took another two hours. Tour officials stood by in relays to ensure fair play – HD himself, then two others – and observed as Christophe made the crass mistake of asking the smithy's boy to pump the forge bellows for him. Restricted to just the two hands, he couldn't manage the job without a third. Now, he clearly wasn't a man to cadge assistance on a whim, but such mortal frailties as not being possessed of three hands or prehensile toes cut little ice with a tartar such as Desgrange. The man was another Draco, a Bligh. (When he was told of Lapize's choked cry '*Assassins*' he took it as proof that the race was as tough as he intended it to be.)

The commissaire hovering in the doorway of the forge docked Cri-Cri ten minutes for accepting help. That the breakdown had already cost him four hours was of no account. The rule was the rule. After two hours, one of the commissaires felt peckish and asked Desgrange permission to go to the restaurant next door for a sandwich. 'If you're hungry,' growled Cri-Cri, 'eat some coal. You're holding me prisoner: you stay on guard.' Christophe reassembled his bike, remounted and rode on, any chance of final victory gone but determined to finish. He came seventh, 14 hours and 41 minutes behind Philippe Thys, who sacrificed his celebrated walrus moustaches that year to cut down wind resistance. The French Cycling Federation put a plaque on the wall of the old forge where Christophe mended his bike to commemorate the Homeric gallop down the mountain. It concludes:

'Eugène Christophe did not abandon the race which he might have won. An example of wonderful determination.' Hear hear.

(The plaque records that he covered 'many kilometres on foot'. The figures I give are those of Christophe himself, aged 74, in an interview with the late Jock Wadley, cyclist extraordinaire – Paris–Brest–Paris – and for many years correspondent at the *Daily Telegraph*. His ashes are scattered on the road through the Défile de Maupas.)

At Valenciennes, on the Metz–Dunkerque stage in 1919 (468km), having caught an escape by Firmin Lambot over the infamous monster cart-track cobbles of the 'Hell of the north', Christophe's forks started to shudder and then snapped. He avoided a fall but, as he climbed off, a voice from the *peloton* shouted: 'The old man's dropped: let's go.' Firmin Lambot, 28 minutes down reached the finish and pulled on yellow; Christophe had lost 70 minutes finding replacement forks in a small bike factory. When the race reached the Alps, Christophe was clawing some time back, but Thys got away over the Vars and Izoard cols – the first crossing by the Tour – pursued by Lambot, and the attack effectively gave Lambot the final victory. However, the readers of Desgrange's *L'Auto* were so impressed with Christophe's fortitude that, although he arrived in Paris in third place, he was awarded the same prize money as the winner.

Incidentally, he wasn't the only man to shoulder a broken bike and continue the race. One year, Alavoine's bike broke under him 10km from the finish in the Parc des Princes, Paris. He picked up the bits and ran in. A nice irony for the man who never got off and walked in the mountains. These precautionary tales had a deep impact on Firmin Lambot. He never set out without 500 or 600 francs in his pocket, in order to buy a replacement bike if his broke. The 'touch wood' precaution paid off: in 1922 he won the race aged 36, a record.

Christophe was a meticulous man, analysing gear sizes, careful what food he ate to provide high energy – rice cakes, bananas, ham sandwiches, chocolate – but such ill fortune he suffered; they said he was a victim of the 'witch with green teeth', the rustic bugaboo who scatters bad luck on the mountain winds. He never did win the Tour, *le vieux Gaulois*, though he surely deserved to. He was second in 1912, in spite of having a faster overall time than the winner, the Belgian Odile Defraye, but victory was awarded on points for positions on stages at the time. This was clearly unjust; even Desgrange could see that and the system reverted to classification on time the following year and forever after.

Christophe holds a unique record appropriate to the galvanised-iron breed of man he was. He rode his first Tour in 1906, his eighth and last in 1925, aged 40. *Chapeau!* Well done! (He sold millions of toe clips with his own brand name on them; my own toe straps put money into the Christophe estate.)

On the subject of accumulated masochism, Zoetemelk rode 16 Tours, Van Impe 15, Kelly 12 (15 starts) Darrigade 13 (14 starts) and Poulidor 12 (14 starts) – three times second and five times third. Several men, including the British rider Sean Yates, have ridden 12 Tours.

The second night I can't sleep a wink: too tired to rest, too tired to read, tossing and turning as if round an endless gyration of hairpins. Half-dreams come and go on the small screen of my feverishly active mind: riderless bikes cast in goblin silver . . . a scraggy Bo-Peep in hobnailed boots slumps drunkenly on a boulder, torn skirt, lips stained with blackberry juice and hair like seaweed . . . a gauntlet of dwarf shepherds in soiled wool capes brandish blackthorn cudgels at me as I hobble past in cycling shoes with pedal plates stuck to the soles like squashed tar-pats, scribbling frantically in a tiny notebook with the stump of a blunt pencil – the writing smears like mascara in the driving rain . . . a donkey tramples my bike and brays derision at me . . .

What makes tiredness unmanageable is having to be around while it's happening to you, to have to prowl around in its locked waiting-room till it decides to let you out. In the old days we'd already be on our way.

The 1920s were the epoch of the original *touristes-routiers*, freelance professionals independent of the trade teams. They provided everything for themselves, even to booking their hotel rooms each night. No *soigneur*, no *directeur sportif* dictating tactics. They fended for themselves completely – like the Parisian Robert Jacquinot, six Tours (1919–24) photographed with spare tyres looped round his shoulders, his legs caked with mud, at a table in a small *estaminet* gulping down a bowl of soup, glass of wine and hunk of bread to hand, precious bike propped against the table. And the Belgian Brackeveld sprawling in thick grass in a field at the side of the road eating sandwiches, two tin bottles of drink in the rack on his handlebars to wash them down. They all had to do their own repairs – a buckled wheel tied on to your back to carry to the next blacksmith's shop, maybe – but at least with a team the loss of time from running repairs, or accidents, could be limited.

Departure time: midnight. Setting off to work like miners down the long, unlit tunnels of the night. Hubert Opperman, the great endurance cyclist – who won the Paris–Brest–Paris in 1931, some 50 hours non-stop – says he rode up alongside another cyclist in the dark on one Tour stage and addressed him in French. '*Comment ça va?*' The other man didn't respond. Oppy repeated the question. No reply. He got angry and swore at him, in native Australian, whereat the other guy swore back, in native Australian.

Emerging from the night into day, it's cold, unfriendly and still two thirds of the stage to ride. No ready-made energising drinks in bottles passed up by race cars. Food bought from villages *en route*, eating as they climbed the mountains – chickens, bananas, fruit tarts, biscuits, toast, bolting the food like Pantagruel. No spare wheels, tyres, parts or clothing on tap; what they needed they had to carry, weighed down like a First World War *poilu*. No doctor in the caravan, no masseur waiting in the hotel room. Moreover, the draconian rules Desgrange imposed seem eccentric if not insane. For instance: no item of equipment was to be discarded; what you were carrying at the start of a stage you had to carry in at the end. No help was to be offered or received from fellow riders; any rider *not* pursuing victory *or* sacrificing his own chance of victory in favour of a team-mate would be eliminated; any rider sticking to another rider's wheel would be instantly disqualified. Not only were there fixed controls, but secret checkpoints where the commissaire would spring out and stamp an inky time and date on the riders' wrists.

In 1920, having won the stages into Brest and Sables d'Olonne, Henri Pélissier quit the race when a commissaire penalised him for throwing one of his spare tyres away. Desgrange, who had a Luddite aversion to new-fangled technical advances and a slave-driver's distaste for anything contrived to make life easier for the men who rode his Tour, remarked of Pélissier's defection: 'This Pélissier knows nothing about suffering; he'll never win the Tour.'

He was wrong. Henri, perhaps the most able of three Pélissier brothers, had his victory in 1923, when two-minute bonuses for stage winners were introduced to liven up the racing. Speaking for the three brothers, Henri told journalists: 'We're out to win, to prove to Desgrange we're not clowns.' He made big gains crossing the Allos and Izoard cols, followed by the Galibier and the Arravis, enough to put him out of reach. In the first half of the Tour, Henri had been badly adrift. Robert Jacquinot trounced him one day in the Pyrenees, crossing first the Aubisque (1,709m) then the mighty Tourmalet (2,115m) riding over it as did the great Merckx in his first Tour, 1969, *comme un bolide* 'like a meteor', wrote one journalist. Except that poor Jacquinot had shot his bolt. A kilometre from the summit of the third climb, the Peyresourde (1,569m) a relatively undemanding ascent these days, he cracked with fatigue and fell off his bike into the ditch to recover. Watching Jean Alavoine surge past at a brisk pace, he croaked: '*Je te salue, gars Jean.*' I salute you, young Jean.' Chivalrous gesture.

Jacquinot's early flourish seemed to have cut him to size; on the other hand, Henri Pélissier was nowhere. Desgrange must have shrugged: Pélissier *was* feeble, a loser. And, a couple of stages later, he trailed into Nice a full hour down on the leaders. That seemed to have written him out. What happened overnight? Did he say, like the Civil War General Ulysses Grant assessing the day's defeat: 'Give 'em a hell of a licking tomorrow,' and go to sleep? Or did he lie awake and turn his miserable insomnia into creative rage like Dickens stomping 15 and 20 miles around the London streets during the nights when he was working on *A Tale of Two Cities*? Whatever, he made up his mind all right, and tore off next morning as if his life depended on it.

Pélissier gained a quarter of an hour on his pursuers, but they got the wind up and clawed back. He had it all to do again if he was going to do it at all, and surely they wouldn't let him give them the slip a second time? But he did go again, took one minute, two minutes, ten and, by the time the Tour left the Alps he was in yellow. Desgrange recounted the story himself in glowing terms, eight years later in the journal, *Match*. Time hadn't mellowed him, it never would, but he'd changed his mind about Pélissier's exceptional talent; although I suspect he always liked to believe that he had invented his winners. Needless to say, victory was Pélissier's way of sticking it to the old bastard, and the old bastard loved his winners, especially if they were French, just as he reviled his losers, especially if they were French. He knew how hard victory came; he made extra sure it came as hard as it could be made.

Vapouring about that 1923 Tour, Desgrange compared Henri to Debussy and Monet: sheer artistry on a bike. 'His victory has the beautiful order, the classicism of Racine's works . . . the mountains seemed to sink lower, shrunk by the victorious thrust of his muscle. More than a score of times on the most vicious gradients, hands on the top of the bars, he looked down at the valley bottoms, hairpins twisting endlessly out of sight, like an eagle staring at its prey.' HD was a journalist first and foremost, after all, lavish with vitriol and saccharine in promiscuous quantity, inspired by his own publicity, convinced that his opinion moulded the champions who came into their own in his great bike race.

Riding for Pélissier's trade team, Automoto, was a young Italian, Ottavio Bottechia. The French fans were sceptical about the recruitment of this ex-bricklayer and horse-coper from the wrong side of the Alps, ignoring the fact that he was a fervent racer and a brilliant climber. Perhaps his own attitude to cycle racing – 'You don't need to be any good at this job' – got up their noses; the fact is, he'd won his first races by such huge margins that he hadn't yet grown conscious of his class. He won the second stage of the Tour, Le Havre–Cherbourg, autographed his yellow jersey and made a present of it to his team leader Henri Pélissier whom he eventually followed into Paris. Little 'Toto' Grassin broke his forks on the Le Havre stage, did a Cri-Cri and rode the rest of the 300km on his own.

Pélissier was generous about the country bumpkin with the style and grace of a fluent athlete, his legs in perpetual motion. Desgrange, too, was full of praise: the Italian had stormed over the Galibier and consolidated his second place; he was in the hunt every day; he may have fouled up on the Izoard – forever stopping for drinks – but when courage was needed, Bottechia was always at the forefront of the action. He didn't even speak French – can you *imagine?* – but here he was teaching some of France's homegrown champions how to ride in the Tour de France.

Bottechia was the revelation of the '23 Tour, and in 1924 he became the first Italian ever to win, and remarkably he wore the yellow jersey from start to finish. He crossed the Aubisque in a record time – 37 minutes and 40 seconds – into the bargain.

But the big news was made by the Pélissier brothers, Francis and Henri, who quit the race at Coutances. They had been penalised for '*abandon de matériel*', namely ditching one of the jerseys they had started out with. Desgrange counted the articles of clothing out and he counted them back in. Outraged that instead of a bike race they found themselves participating in a sort of militaristic fashion show, the Pélissiers packed, pulled up outside a bar and ordered coffee. The journalists flocked in. One of them quizzed Henri: had they abandoned on impulse?

> No impulse; only we're not dogs. This morning in Cherbourg, the race commissaire came up to me, pulled up my jersey, didn't say a word. It was bitterly cold so I was wearing two jerseys. Later he stopped me and did the same thing; the sun was burning hot by then and I'd ditched one jersey. What would you say? I won't take behaviour like that.
>
> 'Two jerseys, three, it might have been 15: we have to arrive carrying the same number we set out with. We not only have to ride like animals, they want us either to freeze to death or suffocate. Seems it's all part of the 'sport'. I went off to find Desgrange and asked him why I couldn't discard my jersey by the roadside. He said: 'You're not allowed to throw away anything belonging to the organisation.' I told him it didn't belong to the organisation, it was mine. He said he wasn't going to discuss it in the road and I told him if he wasn't prepared to discuss it in the road I was back off to bed, and got on the bike. 'We'll sort it out in Brest' he said and I told him that *everything* would be sorted out in Brest because we're packing it in, and we have.

One of the scribes listening, Albert Londres following the Tour for the *Petit Parisien*, wrote up the débâcle and entitled his article: *Les Forçats de la Route*. The phrase had probably been coined in 1913 in *L'Auto*, Desgrange's own paper, and he was characteristically exasperated at the plagiarism: he had meant it as a compliment; Londres had used the term pejoratively. *Forçat* means galley slave or chain-gang convict. Worse, Londres wasn't even a cycling journo. In 1923 he had published an exposé of the penal colonies, the *bagne* in French Guyana in *Le Petit Parisien*. The brutal Napoleonic penitentiary code was still despatching men to prison colonies and Devil's Island, where Dreyfus found himself. The Pélissier story caught Londres's prison-fever attention and, working the parallels for all he was worth, he painted a grim picture, as he saw it, of Desgrange's martinet mentality. Desgrange riposted: these Pélissiers, so-called stonebreakers, were in fact millionaires, fractious, dimwitted, myopic; they hadn't prepared themselves physically and had just given up, beaten, without a fight. One wonders how badly podgy little HD was bullied when *he* was in short trousers.

An unsolved mystery surrounds the death of Bottechia, who took a second victory the following year; and Henri Pélissier made a curiously ominous remark after the 1924 win. Bottechia – a strikingly featured man, darling of the Italian papers, a sporting hero – had been pursued by an obsessive woman fan plainly suffering from amorous fixation. Bottechia had been flattered, tempted to put ego before domestic peace. Pélissier voiced the fear that Bottechia's wife, a volatile woman herself and volubly jealous, might easily flip and blow Bottechia away with the family shotgun – a traditional Italian vendetta. The circumstances of his death were quite as strange.

On 14 June 1927, he was found unconscious at the side of a country road in Italy, his head and body broken and drenched in blood, his bike, undamaged, leaning against a tree. He was murmuring *Malore, malore . . .* it hurts. He can't have fallen: the bike proved that. Had he been attacked by peasants, enraged that he was stealing grapes? Yet in June grapes are sour. Rumours, even, of a Fascist killing – Bottechia made no secret of his socialist leanings – yet his status as sporting hero leant weight to a pro-Fascist national subscription to raise money for Mussolini. An anti-Fascist plot, then? Or, wait a minute, a Fascist conspiracy, after all, to eradicate a man whose popularity threatened to eclipse that of their Duce?

In the mid-'30s, an Italian immigrant, dying from stab wounds on the New York waterfront, confessed that he had murdered Bottechia. He had lain in wait for him when he was out on a training ride; a contract killing, ordered by a man called Berto

Olinas. He died before he could enlarge on the story and no Berto Olinas was ever traced.

In 1973, the Italian priest who had administered the last rites to Bottechia in a back room at his church, to which a group of men carried his body after his 'fall', corroborated the version that it had been Fascists livid about his massive popular acclaim who had zotzed him. Perhaps it's not so unlikely. On the '24 Tour he came down on several mornings to find his tyres flat; one night in Toulon, he received an anonymous note in his hotel: 'Anti-Fascist: you'll get what's coming to you.' Whether the reasons for his death were political, vengeful or accidental, his loss was a tragedy for cycling. Maybe Desgrange took umbrage when Bottechia swapped his own purple jersey for the leader's yellow because he wanted to go unrecognised by crazy Italian fans. We shall never know.

The *maillot jaune* was introduced in 1919, halfway round the Tour at Grenoble, a publicity gimmick, advertising Desgrange's paper which was printed on yellow paper. The first wearer was Eugène Christophe; it was a slight but worthy recompense to a fine rider. For years, it bore no markings at all; then, after Desgranges died, his initials, HD, were embroidered on the right breast; subsequently, a strip showing the team name of the rider was fixed across the chest. These days, like all the rest of the jerseys, it serves as yet another portable advertising placard.

Only three men apart from Bottechia have worn it from the first day to the last: in 1928, the Luxembourger Nicolas Frantz, wearing yellow as the '27 winner, won the first stage into Caen and is the only man to have worn it literally 'end to end'.

In 1935, on the first stage from Paris to Lille, the 22-year-old Belgian, Romain Maes, not reckoned to be a contender for victory, but clinging to a slender lead with the *peloton* breathing down his neck, rode through a level crossing at Haubourdin, a few miles from the finish just before the barriers came down on the rest of the bunch. While the train roared past and the bunch cursed, Maes went crazy for home, took the yellow jersey by two minutes and never relinquished it. Also on that same Tour, on 11 July, the diminutive Spanish climber, Francesco Cepeda, fell during the descent of the Galibier, fractured his skull and, three days later, Bastille Day, he died: the Tour's first fatality.

In 1961, André Darrigade won the opening half-day stage, Rouen–Versailles; Anquetil took the afternoon time-trial and wore yellow from then on.

There is, though, some doubt about the first appearance of the yellow jersey. In the July 1953 edition of the Belgian magazine *Champions et Vedettes*, Phillipe Thys – then 67 and in lively good health – said: 'In 1913, I was leader on general classification and one night HD came to me with the idea of a coloured jersey: would I wear it? I refused – it would make me a target for everyone else. He pressed me but I was adamant. HD wouldn't give up and persuaded my boss, the unforgettable Baugé, to advise me to give in as the jersey would be great publicity for our Peugeot team. We went to the shops and bought a yellow jersey, more or less my size, but the neck was so narrow I had to enlarge it, and rode several stages, *décolleté*, like a society woman.'

The yellow jersey probably only made sporadic appearances, a passing gimmick, in the 1913 and 1914 Tours. By 1915, the armies were entrenched along the Marne, Luxembourg's first winner François Faber (1909) had died at the Front and not till after the War did the jersey establish itself.

They called the 1926 edition 'The Tour of Suffering', the longest of the 20 so far: 5,795km (the modern race rarely exceeds 4,000km), 17 stages averaging 340km, the last three stages alone totalling 1,000km. From Metz to Dunkirk, 435km, over the wicked cobbled cart-tracks of old France; a marathon from Cherbourg at the tip of the Cotentin peninsula to Brest in Brittany, thence all the way down the Atlantic coast to Sables-d'Olonne.

Between Mulhouse and Metz, the shank of Marcel Bidot's pedal snapped and he was left pedalling one-footed. A hasty repair, improvising with a strap from the toe-clip, jammed the pedal in position for a while but it soon failed again. The chief commissaire allowed Bidot, riding his first Tour, to borrow a bike from a local man who was following the race, on condition that he swap its wheels for his own. This done he remounted; the bike was entirely the wrong size for him and he finished the day in a state of collapse and ready for the next instalment of misery.

The race moved south. Midnight. Bayonne in the torrential

rain, 76 riders set off into the Pyrenees. The road up the Tourmalet was awash with mud; a cyclocross course; wheels slithering about till there was no ploughing through it and the only option was to get off and plod up. Even Lucien Buysse, a dromedary of a man, more nervous, they said, about his gears than anything human, like thirst. Bystanders were kept busy heaving the following cars out of the sticky mud drifts.

The descent off the Tourmalet plunged into a dense icy fog which so frequently tumbles out of leaden Pyrenean skies. At this point, Bidot's 24-tooth freewheel broke. In those days, the back wheel carried a freewheel sprocket either side of the hub; a larger size for the mountains, smaller for the flat and downhill. Later they carried two either side; a gear change was effected by turning the wheel round. The breakage of Bidot's larger sprocket meant he had to ride up the Aspin on the downhill sprockets, 43x22, a strenuous development of 4.10m. The deluge got worse: cold rain obscured vision, eating into flesh and bone, its carrying wind lunging at the frail machines. Snug inns nestled temptingly by the way; oh to stop for a bowl of hot soup . . . no, no, *retro me Satane* . . . once you stop you'll never get back on.

Buysse took this hellish mountains stage 330km, crossing five massive cols: Osquich, Aubisque, Tourmalet, Aspin, Peyresourde and the yellow jersey by 25 minutes. At midnight, only 47 riders had clocked in; a dozen of them called quits on their torment and scrambled into the commissariat cars, pardoned for this licence 'in view of the sky's anger'. Others never made it home: lost on the dark mountain slopes, they had to be sought out and rescued in charabancs. Bidot trailed in an hour and a half down on Buysse. Desgrange scolded: 'Bidot doesn't know how to suffer. He won't finish the Tour.' Buysse later became proprietor of a hotel and named it 'L'Aubisque', one of the Pyrenean giants, in memory of his epic ride.

A rest day followed and the next midnight they set off for Perpignan over another beastly mogul of mountains: col des Ares, Portet d'Aspet, Puymorens, col de Rigat and la Perche; three spare tyres looped around the shoulders, pockets crammed with food, spoke key, spare toe-clip, extra spokes strapped to the bike frame to restore the almost inevitable buckled wheels, they had 18 hours in the saddle ahead of them. Lucien Buysse won again, and led home his brother Jules by seven minutes.

Between Perpignan and the Alps, Bidot incurred further wrath from Desgrange who blasted him in a newspaper article, accusing him of controlling all the escapes, sitting at the front of the *peloton*, managing the pace. In other words, doing his job, a determined, professional job, for the Alcyon team and its leader Nicolas Frantz, a potential winner. 'As for me,' wrote HD, 'Bidot can ride any race he chooses next year between 19 June and 19 July *except* the Tour de France.'

Frantz agreed to reward Bidot's service with the stage win into Nice, then outsprinted him along the Promenade des Anglais; the instinct to win couldn't be kept down and loyalty to underlings came cheap. The team manager tore strips off Frantz at dinner that night.

Into the Alps and Bidot punctured twice *en route* to the col d'Izoard but caught the Buysse brothers on the lower slopes; Lucien attacked and went clear; Jules followed. At the foot of the climb proper, Bidot rejoined and passed them when they stopped to change their wheels around on to the climbing gear. Bidot went by as Lucien shouted 'Change your bracket.' He demurred, feeling good, surged ahead and then, disaster: a third puncture. Hands so cold he couldn't peel the tyre off the rim, he tried to pick it off with his teeth. Impossible. Minutes passed; the Alcyon car drew up and the driver tossed out a knife. The commissaire – they seemed to have been, like vultures, ever-present at calamity – strode up: 'I forbid you to pick up that knife.' Bidot unscrewed a butterfly wing nut from one wheel and used that to prise off the holed tyre, just as the Buysse brothers rode past; but he repaired the tyre, caught them and was third into Briançon.

Desgrange wrote: 'I fancy Bidot has a somewhat sluggish temperament, he lacks drive, a bit lazy, not much of a head on him; he could have won that stage, I believe. However, he's strong, in good shape, solid; he climbs well, descends adroitly and he doesn't stop at water fountains. Such a début in the Tour de France suggests he is a man of courage.'

Never pulled his punches, HD.

For 1927, all the flat stages were team time-trials: this guaranteed fierce racing, since the whole team of 12 had to stick together as long as it could. The tendency to conserve energy in a muted approach to what they all knew was the real proving ground in the mountains had become ingrained. The drama of the Tour went limp and journalists could not be inspired, or inspire their readers, with a saga of monotony. On the first stage, the Alcyon team sustained a total of 20 punctures but the least known of the Pélissier brothers, Francis, had his moment of family glory and put on the yellow jersey. On the second stage, Bidot was left behind when near Cherbourg both wheels punctured simultaneously.

He slogged on through Brittany, thoroughly demoralised, and eventually abandoned. His team-mate Frantz fulfilled promise and won. Amongst the riders that year were two who would join the all-time greats: André Leducq and Antonin Magne.

Another innovation in 1928 was that Desgrange ruled that the nine regional teams, including the Australians, which had replaced the trade teams, would be allowed to call on substitute riders during the race. Bizarre. On one stage in the Pyrenees, Francis Bouillet and Arsène Alancourt were dropped and cadged a lift in a small lorry. The lorry slid off the road into a ravine – those mountains have witnessed many such incidents in this race – but luckily they all climbed out uninjured. More luck: a taxi drove up; Alancourt and Bouillet piled in and rode the rest of the stage in some ease. The *directeur sportif* coughed up for the fare and, three days later, in Marseille, draughted Bouillet back into the team after one of his riders, Gallotini, abandoned. Frantz took a second overall victory in a Tour which, perversely tame, eschewed the Aspin, Peyresourde, Vars and Izoard.

That year, the flat-stage team time-trials were axed as the teams could too easily conspire to control the pace; better, after all, to let individual ambitions have play. Bidot had a shot at the yellow jersey: he was on the same time as three Belgians, behind them only because he had not won a stage. A unique event in Tour history, this: the three leaders, Fontan, Frantz and Dewaele, each wore yellow at the end of the stage into Bordeaux. A few days later, the trio still in yellow, the race was heading out of Bayonne for the Pyrenees and a good ride would put Bidot himself in yellow. Setting out, a woman stepped into the road in front of him, he went over the handlebars. Badly bruised, one wheel rim in pieces, he eventually reached the finish in disarray. But, he took the stage into Nice on Bastille Day and continued to help his team-mate, the Belgian Maurice Dewaele, to final victory. Dewaele had fallen ill and was on the verge of packing in the Alps but courage, sheer talent and the transcendant magic of the yellow jersey got him through his Calvary. Also the efforts of his team helped. They nursed him steadfastly after a sleepless night of malady and a fainting fit and rode shoulder to shoulder across the road out of Grenoble and prevented any other riders getting through.

At Luchon, in the Pyrenees, Fontan was clear; an exceptional climber, 37 years old but still in hot contention. Some 10km from the start, in pitch-black night, his bike collapsed under him, the front wheel ruinously buckled in a pothole. He lost 45 minutes and, despite valiant efforts to regain the time on the climb of Portet d'Aspet, abandoned after the descent.

A journalist, Louis Delblat, wrote angrily in *L'Echo des Sports*: 'How can a man lose the Tour de France because of an accident to his bike? I simply do not understand. The rules should allow a rider with no hope of winning to surrender his machine to his leader or provide for a back-up vehicle with spare bikes on board. You lose the Tour to a better rider; you should not lose it because of a stupid accident to your bike.'

It took a long, long time for those eminently sane suggestions to be adopted. Desgrange remained implacable. He was not impressed by Dewaele's win, either: 'How can such a soft touch retain the yellow jersey? Why didn't his rivals attack him more resolutely? What can one make of their tactics and the real worth of the winner?' Meantime, other complaints were being levelled.

Delblat moaned: 'What's wrong with the Tour? No French winner for six years and the public at large aren't interested in it.'

Henri Poulain lamented: 'What can be done to haul cycle-racing out of its rut of tedium? New ideas. Bold initiative.'

It was on the way: what amounted to a veritable palace revolution.

Professional cyclists were earning a good living, even if much of their work might justly be compared – as it was at the time – to life in a penal colony. In addition to a monthly contract of 1,500 francs, Bidot's purse for the 1928 Tour was around 10,000 francs. To give some idea of relative values, at the time a suit would set you back 300 francs, you could dine handsomely on 20 francs and a newspaper cost 25 cents (a quarter of a franc). That money was generated by commercial interest: the race itself had been inaugurated to sell more papers and it sold more papers; bicycle manufacturers sponsored teams because success in the Tour de France sold more of their machines. But, commercial interest then, as today (like the Grand Prix organisation *vis-à-vis* tobacco advertising) has, like the great champions, a ruthless *rage à vaincre*. Desgrange fumed about it, and he was not one to fume in vain. 'The constructors,' he fulminated, 'want to see their rider win, even if he isn't the strongest in the field. The organiser wants to see the best man win.'

No winner unless worthy – hence his disparagement of Dewaele, in his view unworthy – and the noble cause to be served above grubby, meretricious bargaining or worse. He set out to reform radically the Tour's creaking state.

All machines would be of the same make, supplied by the Tour and painted yellow; national teams of eight riders apiece; only five jerseys from the countries of the competing riders: France, Italy, Germany, Spain, Belgium; 60 *touriste-routiers* to be selected by HD and his organisation; an International Challenge prize, for the best showing of participating nationals; a publicity caravan of trade vehicles selling to roadside crowds, separate from the riders, but stimulating the very necessary commercial interest attached – but now controlled – to the Tour, and a source of new funding; prizes to be given in kind. Finally, for the first time, national radio and local stations in Paris, Lyon, Bordeaux, Toulouse would broadcast reports of the Tour's progress.

Of these changes a journalist wrote: 'The Father of the Tour has underlined his hardihood; he has erased the past. Commercial interests were, he was convinced, fatally prejudicial to the health of his cherished child. He has made bicycle manufacturers, sporting directors and managers subject to one licence: that of the Tour.'

L'Action Française, capitalising on the new multinational flavour of the Tour, published special profiles of the French and Italian team captains, Fontan and the *campionissimo*, Binda. (*Campionissimo*, 'champion of champions' was coined for Constante Girardengo, Italian road-race champion, 1913–25.)

The French team might have been riding a superior freewheel which gave them a higher development, useful in the mountain descents; nevertheless, Alfredo Binda arrived as favourite. Winner of the first World Championship Road Race at the Nurnburgring motor-racing circuit in 1927, his *palmarès* also included the Milan–San Remo, Tour of Lombardy and 10km, 20km and 50km world records. A fine climber and a peerless sprinter, he had taken the 1929 Giro d'Italia by such a devastating show of superiority – nine stage victories in all, eight of them (second to ninth) consecutive – that the organisers paid him a rumoured 22,000 lire not to enter in 1930. With Binda around there would be no race. He did return to win the 1933 Giro and still holds the record of 41 Giro stage victories. However, in 1930 he lined up for the traditional opening stage of the Tour de France: Paris–Caen.

Charles 'Charlot' Pélissier – probably the strongest finisher in the *peloton* – made a break 20km from the line; Binda chased, caught and outsprinted him on the Venoix track and pulled on his first golden fleece. In the next three stages Binda took second place, and if Pélissier was out of yellow, he was compensating with stage victories.

The French were up against it when another Italian leapt out of the pack: Learco Guerra. Outside Dinan, the Frenchman Mauclair jumped and took 300m before anyone reacted. Guerra flew off, caught Mauclair and sped past without a sideways glance. The French team rejoined Mauclair and gave him a mouthful: 'Listen, egotist, you make a break you make it work or else you *don't* make a break; you're with us, we're not with you . . .' And the whole team set out – time-trial fashion – to reel in Guerra, but he held them off took the stage by a minute and a half and with it the yellow jersey. He merited his sobriquet '*la Locomotiva*'.

A few days later, he threw down the gauntlet again and the Italians shot off. The French team, habituated to rough-riding over cobbles, launched a ferocious chase across the *pavé* in Labouheyre, an old market town in the flatlands some 70km south of Bordeaux. Then disaster – a touch of wheels and the bunch went down in a heap. They rallied, caught the Italians and the sprint was on with 60 riders haring for the line. Leducq led out Pélissier, who chose his moment and flew past Binda and the Belgian speed-merchant Aerts – a classic victory. Binda recorded his version for the Italian press: '120m from the line, I attacked, Pélissier grabbed my jersey and then catapulted himself off my shoulder. If this is French bike racing, I'm quitting.' Desgrange relegated Pélissier, gave Aerts the win and persuaded Binda to reconsider.

Next day, Guerra came back at the French on his own, but into Hendaye they placed six in the first eight home. The day after that, Binda had fallen and was in trouble; Guerra stayed with the Frenchmen; they attacked again, out of Bayonne, 90km on. He roared back; they gave it up as a bad job and let him go.

Alas for his captain Binda, *he* finally trailed in an hour and ten minutes down. The journalists swarmed like sharks to a pall of blood: Binda wouldn't start next day; he was finished . . . abandon imminent.

Binda refused. He had proved his quality but he had lost the Tour because of an accident; he owed himself a lap of honour. He took the next two Pyrenean mountain stages into Pau and Luchon. Then, on the road from Luchon to Perpignan, descending the col du Portet, the pillar of his saddle snapped and the repair took 15 minutes but he caught a small group containing the yellow jersey Leducq on the climb of the Portet d'Aspet. Yet, some 130km on, 1,436m up the 1,915m-high col de Puymorens near Andorra, he packed.

On to the Alps. In yellow still, Leducq flanked by Pierre Magne (Tonin's brother), reached the top of the Galibier, two minutes behind a leading group comprising the Italian, Guerra – whom Leducq led overall by 17 minutes; the French *touriste-routier* Benoît Faure – a tiny man, prodigious climber, nickname The Mighty Mouse; another lightweight, the Spanish Flea, Vicente Trueba; and the Belgian Jeff Demuysère (second in 1929). The two Frenchmen hurtled off on the descent at 80kph; Leducq lost control of his bike – probably hit a stone – overshot a bend, somersaulted off the bike and was knocked unconscious. He came to, badly bruised, his knee cut and pouring blood, shorts ripped open to his right hip to reveal a deep graze, the fingers on both hands lacerated. In addition, one pedal on the bike was bent out of true. His Tour seemed to be over; he slumped at the side of the road in terrible distress. Marcel Bidot, a short way behind, rode up, saw Pierre Magne standing at the side of the road, assumed he'd punctured then learnt the truth. He and Magne talked Leducq back onto his feet, Magne bent the pedal back into shape and they remounted. A hundred metres on, Leducq's brake failed; another repair stop. Leducq was in poor straits.

'They had to work very hard simply to get me back into the saddle again.' The trio set off downhill, but painfully slowly; 19kph reckoned Leducq, his hands hurting so cruelly he could hardly pull on the brake. They staggered into Valloire on the valley floor and on to the first slopes of the col du Télégraphe. Leducq, too shattered for any vocal complaint, was struggling to find any speed or rhythm and, no more than half a mile up, out of the saddle, desperate to keep going, his right foot shot off – the damaged pedal had snapped. It looked like curtains; Guerra must be building an unassailable lead. But Magne and Bidot refused to give up. Bidot even offered Leducq his own bike – strictly forbidden in those days.

However, the bad luck was running out and a spectator cyclist offered them a pedal; a car belonging to the newspaper L'Ami du Peuple provided an adjustable spanner and, like the US Cavalry, up rode three more members of the French team: Charles Pélissier, Merviel and Magne's brother, Antonin. The timing was perfect: the rules forbade any more than two riders attending any rider who had fallen or needed repairs. Another man arrived, the touriste-routier Guiramand, who undoubtedly pocketed some money for his assistance in the chase. They calculated that they must be some 20 minutes behind the Italian and his breakaway, which made Guerra leader on the road by three minutes.

'I was totally dispirited,' said Leducq. 'The winding descent of the Télégraphe passed safely but we took it very easy. At the bottom we joined the fast valley road of the Arc and heard that Guerra's lead was now only 14 minutes. I felt my courage restored, gradually my muscles warmed up and soon the whole team was riding at 40kph, working flat out, all of us, in pursuit of the group ahead. My pals swapped turns at the front and rode with their noses in the handlebars.'

(The modern slang is 'eyeballs out' or 'on the rivet' – on the brass rivet at the front of the old-style leather saddle.)

They rode the 40 miles along the valley in two hours. Merviel stopped to switch his back wheel round – to change the freewheel – and was dropped; they didn't dare wait for him; he came in alone. By Albertville, the lead had been cut to one minute, and shortly afterwards, they caught Guerra and the others. There were still over 140km to ride to Evian but, within sight of the finish, the entire French team launched Leducq out in the sprint and he won the stage; Pélissier came second. That day, starting from Grenoble, they had covered 331km through the mountains. Leducq tottered off to the hotel to be patched up by a nurse.

André Leducq won to be sure (Guerra was second at 14 minutes and 19 seconds), the first French winner since 1923, and confirmed the promise he had shown on his début three years earlier. Desgrange penned an encomium. 'André Leducq is a pure child of France. He will tell you that life is good not only in the flush of victory but equally good through the most strenuous efforts and moments of anguish.' We don't have Leducq's version, but that victory in the 1930 Tour was, emphatically, built on the celebrated pursuit of Guerra, an epic of individual grit and team co-operation. The French team won the International Challenge prize.

As to Binda, he explained the faint mystery of his abandon 50 years later. He'd had no thought of riding the Tour because he wanted to concentrate on the World's Road Race – he'd won the 1927 inaugural race but been dispossed twice by the Belgian Ronsse. HD had bribed him to ride: the same fee for every stage as he'd earn for a race on the track.

And Faure? In his version, he admits his mistake in not helping the breakaway. He'd towed Guerra and the others to the top of the Galibier and sat on their wheel on the flat. He thought he'd be able to jump them, tired out by their efforts, and win the stage and the prize money. The freelance instinct; it didn't pay off. Had he worked with them, whoever took the stage, Guerra, not Leducq would have won the Tour and Faure would have come fifth not eighth. But, as for Bidot and Magne, they helped Leducq because he was their man, their potential winner; self-interest and selfless hard work need not cancel each other out.

The following year, 1931, having become a team man, Benoît Faure was still getting it wrong: he found it hard to know when to help or block an attack because, he said, he couldn't remember what jersey he had on and therefore where his affiliation lay. With his team leader, Tonin Magne, up on the Italian, Pesenti, by ten minutes, it was Faure's job to shadow Pesenti and keep tabs on any attack. However, as they approached the lead-in to a 2,000 franc *prime*, the old instinct surfaced. These prizes were offered as bait to ginger up the action, to guard against the whole race being stifled by team tactics. Extra cash on offer, Faure jumped; the Italians, Pesenti included, leapt on to his wheel and they all flew off ahead of the main pack. Pesenti eventually took the stage and gained five and a half minutes on Magne, who subsequently had to work like a horse to keep the yellow jersey. Magne was furious with Faure, the whole team was furious with him but angriest of all was Desgrange. Faure just blundered along on his legs; where was his *brain*? What offended him most was the vulgarity. Desgrange was a notorious stickler for rules and regulations but he was an unapologetic romantic, too. Riders must ride hard but, above all, they must respect the concept, the high idealism of his, Desgrange's, Tour. The team co-operation – augmented by some ready cash for extra help – was, by and large denied to the *touriste-routier* whose only obligation was to their earnings from various prizes and one-off pay to help other riders; they were mercenaries, pure and simple. The origin of the word 'freelance' was just that: a knight with no fealties other than to his pocket.

The man Jacquinot saluted on the Peyresourde, Alavoine, never won, but he was a great stayer, always difficult to shake off. Second twice, third twice, he was one of those men who scorned walking, too. When others got off, which they frequently did to tramp the mountain passes on foot, he ground on. He probably weighed up the economies on blisters and shoe leather. They said he could look at a map and point to the exact spot where he would have to change his rear wheel round. Incidentally, the *dérailleur* gear had been long since invented, but the tyrant Desgrange derided it as an unnatural gadget and forbade its use; he didn't lift his embargo until 1937. (His resistance lay partly in his belief – correctly – that they weren't reliable and would cause endless mechanical problems to impede the race; also that a larger number of gears would make the mountains too easy to climb and diminish the incentive to ride hard.)

Professional cyclists were never averse to the darker skills and the changing of the back wheel offered the opportunity for 'professional' skulduggery. A man who knew the road ahead might leap off his machine at the top of a climb, pretend to change his wheel to engage the higher gear and remount. The other riders who didn't know the road would follow suit, only to find that after a short descent there came another big climb and have to change *again* while the local man flew off, turning the large gear he never actually shifted.

Tuesday. St Columban-des-Villards.

A slow start. The clothes all just about dry, except for the gloves which we put back into the oven to bake. We slouch down for breakfast at 9 a.m. and don't wheel out the bikes until past 11 a.m. in warm sunshine. Roads, houses, roofs, trees freshly rinsed. We oil the chains and gears, turned orange and squeaky with rust from yesterday's rain. The *femme de maison* waves us off. Halfway down the long, steep descent into La Chambre, not the best way to put heat into stiff legs, we pass a lone cyclist toiling up the climb on a mountain bike loaded, back and front, like a pack mule: panniers, top bags, bar bags, tent roll, bag roll, pockets bulging and a crammed rucksack hitched to his back. Poor creature probably thought that by schlepping it himself he was saving his bike the weight. He keeps pace with the grass growing in the verges. Forgetting my misery of the day before, I wonder what could be the pleasure in it; total independence for 5kph and 48km a day. Not for me to say. It was his choice to sleep in a tent and rejoice in nature at ground level. He doesn't even glance up as we pass:

locked in his thoughts and the long struggle; we know how far he has to go and he knows we know.

I check on the local saintly *patron*, Columban. He pitched up in this village in AD612, an Irish monk, a whole-hog killjoy with uncompromising sentiments on moral fibre and penitential toil, ancestor of the notorious Maynooth hellfire and damnation wallahs. He'd been sent to put some bogside backbone into the continental brothers – lacing their soup with gravel, ensuring that bare knees were on cold granite during prayers . . . that kind of thing. Plainly the sort of hairy ascetic Desgrange might have pledged to dig some true grit out of the *Frères* Pélissier. He quarrelled with almost everybody, including the neighbouring royalty – accused them of slacking – and the encumbent Pope, a ne'er-do-well. The similarities between him and HD fall smartly into place the more you ponder them. His emblem is a bear – with a sore head presumably.

The Glandon valley is ripe green, lush and chilly from the previous day's downpour. Ahead lies the col du Télégraphe; beyond it, depending on the time, the Galibier – two climbs traditionally linked on the Tour. It doesn't seem likely we *will* make them both today; we have set out too late. After some discussion last night, we have shelved our original plan to move north from la Chambre to cross the col de la Madeleine (2,000m) and ride the big loop round to the col de l'Iseran, (2,720m). The Iseran will have to wait for another trip.

On his last Tour in 1959, the triple winner (1953–55), Louison Bobet, abandoned on the descent of the Iseran. He'd been suffering and clearly was not going to make it to Paris; for two days he had been riding on reputation, glued to his bike by willpower. When he finally packed, he was asked why he'd persisted so long in a lost cause. He made the astonishing reply, the simple answer of a true lover of the bike: 'I'd never climbed the col de l'Iseran. It's the highest road in Europe. I wanted to ride up there.' It's probably the loneliest moment a rider ever encounters, the moment of abandon. Bobet is done with the 1959 Tour, with the Tour for good; someone from the team car brings a fawn gaberdine raincoat to put over his shoulders against the cold; Bobet's face is drained, his eyes shut, the humiliation of the defeat on that high road palpable; to one side stands the former Italian ace, Bartali, Coppi's great rival – sad, contemplative – holding Bobet's bike.

There is, perhaps, sometimes more than a dash of sentiment in this love of the bike and it was probably sentiment alone that kept Poulidor, a decent man, if unimaginative, from the winner's podium. He won plenty of other races but never the Tour, though he came close several times. He never even wore the yellow jersey. But his sunny disposition fended off the demons which drove Anquetil and they speak of Poulidor's love of the bike, of Anquetil's pride. Anquetil, who spared no feelings, least of all his own, in his incessant ambition to win, informed by Bidot, then French team manager, that Poulidor had promised to ride for him in the World Road Race instead of for himself, said bluntly: '*Il est plus con que je croyais.*' He's more stupid than I thought. Bidot walked out and slammed the door. Anquetil didn't win, never did win a world title but that reply was lack of sentiment in spades. How did he sum up his glittering career: five Tours, two Giro, one Vuelta, two hour records, five Paris–Nice, nine Grands Prix des Nations, a hatful of one-day Classics? Prosaically, almost dismissive: 'I earned a living by countless millions of turns of the pedals.'

After he retired, Anquetil never rode a bike, though he did command great respect as an intelligent, shrewd commentator on the sport in general, the Tour above all. Poulidor, however, evinces, still, something of the poor farm boy from Limousin given his first bicycle, a blue racer, by a local bike-shop owner when he was 14; till then he had been riding, and winning, races on his mother's old sit-up-and-beg rattletrap. He never really escaped that upbringing; you might say that he couldn't really believe how big his talent was. He assessed his life as a pro with the ingenuous: 'Even a hard day's racing never lasts as long as a working day in harvest.' (It is appropriate then that the first bikes were advertised as 'The horse which does not need hay.')

Yet, it's difficult not to see in that first vault to liberty on to the blue racer – all cyclists make it, one way or another – the laying of hands on the bike, a near-consecrated taking up of a long destiny. Anyone who remembers the exact thrill, the magic of that moment when you ride a bicycle free for the first time must recognise that. In my case, I was six when Christopher Thompson, whose bike it was, a powder-blue-framed item with solid rubber wheels, took his hand away from the saddle and left me to my own flight in balance on a machine which, since its invention and popular acceptance has symbolised, embodied, independence. Anquetil, son of a Norman strawberry grower and never as poor as Raymond, Poupou, borrowed a friend's bike and discovered a mysterious affinity. Or, could one detect in that act of borrowing, the inherent disdain which was central to Anquetil's character, the need not to be owned by anything, anyone, any outside claim. Exceptional, focused rider he was, but he never allowed his *bon viveur* tastes to be hampered by the strict calls of pro racing. He drank champagne late into the night; ate amply and with gusto. During a rest day in Andorra on the 1964 Tour he was invited to a social bash, he wolfed down a hearty meal of barbecued lamb with sangria. The other riders were out for a rest-day ride and Anglade remarked of Anquetil's gourmandising: 'Does he take us for idiots?' Antonin Magne, now a team director, turned to Poulidor and said: 'Okay Raymond, this is where you make your play.'

Next day, on the big Envalira climb Anquetil felt sick and heavy, his sunken face showing all the signs that he was in a bad way. Poulidor, in company with Esteban, Bahamontes, Jimenez, Man-zanèque, all class riders, attacked. Anquetil showed no sign of being prepared to counter. One Vuelta he'd actually vomited, still on his bike, trying to make sure that no one saw him. This was different: his will seemed to have evaporated. The escape was well established when Géminiani, a veteran rider now director of Anquetil's team, drove up and, passing his man a *bidon* full of champagne, rounded on him. 'Jacques,' he said, 'you're five minutes and 40 seconds down on Poulidor so if you feel like dying please do it at the front.' It was insult enough to Anquetil's pride. He bestirred himself, his team rallied and they made hot pursuit with Anquetil belching a nauseous aftertaste of roast lamb. At the foot of the climb he caught a small chasing group, among them Anglade, who asked: 'Are you riding with us, Jacques?'

'I'll tell you in 10km' he replied. His legs were still leaden; but 10km on he was flying.

The accompanying team car speedo read 50kph and the Poulidor–Bahamontes break was doomed. In Paris he sealed his last victory; the luckless Poulidor once more second.

In truth, after l'Alpe d'Huez, the Télégraphe – in clear warm sunshine – is not hard; after the Glandon it's a positive treat, and I am beginning to find the new steadier rhythm – physical and mental – you need for the long hauls. Any activity that stretches you to the limit physically trims unwelcome flab off the morale. My heart sings.

> I count life just a stuff
> To try the soul's strength on.
> Robert Browning, *In a Balcony*

It is a pleasurable climb; hard in places – as is inevitable when the hairpins are kinked like nipped wire – but a steady ascent into the heady aerial company of the Dôme de l'Arpont, Chasseforêt and the Aigle de Péclet, crowned with glaciers, dwarfing the Télégraphe (1,566m) from the ethereal vaults above 3,600m. Amply rewarded, too, with the sight of St Michel de Maurienne in the valley, where Leducq and the others got their time check; there it is dwindling through the trees, snapshots of Lilliput as the hairpins wind us up, up, up. And I am there.

CHAPTER FOUR

COL DU GALIBIER

The 1930s

The sun on the Télégraphe is warm. I park the bike, unpack a sweater to insulate me as the sweat cools and go into the café on the mound. I calculate that the others will be about half an hour behind me and by the time they come it will certainly be too late to press on towards the Galibier. That, and the next leg into Briançon, will take at least four hours, maybe five. I order a beer and scan the racks for postcards.

My bicycle postcard collection numbers 1,600 to date – modern, reproduction and original – some of which date from the 1860s. Here's a gem: family of four picnicking by a roadside, salute the Tour de France *peloton*. Father waves a plastic sauce bottle, mother makes conductor's left-hand *fortissimo* gesture, the elder child, about eight years old, sitting on the grass behind the table, scans a map, while at the table the toddler turns to watch in wonder. This is St Veraud, 1954. You can tell it *is* the Tour from the numbers on the bikes; spare tyres looped round the shoulders. They set out from Amsterdam that year; Bobet gained his second victory and either the 'witch with green teeth' or her demon sidekick *Hammerman* pushed the great Swiss champion Koblet over the edge on a climb in the Pyrenees. The man on his wheel, Robic, swerved and rode straight into a photographer. Koblet, 'the pedaller of charm', survived. An exceptional rider, he won on his first attempt in 1951. He sealed his superiority – as all great champions do, some time or other – with a stunning solo break of 135km between Brive and Agen. He told his team director Alex

Burtin he'd had enough, he couldn't go on just 12km from the *Arrivée*. Burtin dissuaded him. As he rode up to the line, he nonchalantly sat up in the saddle, took a comb from his pocket and combed his hair. He never went anywhere without a flea-rake; best-groomed rider on the Tour. The Frenchman Mahé, halfway up a very steep climb on the 1951 Tour of Switzerland, gasping on, empty with the effort, was flabbergasted to see another rider come up alongside him, take his hands off the bars and proceed to comb his hair. Koblet psyching the rest of them out. It was effective: Mahé climbed off. (The story got out that he'd been suffering badly from piles and kept it quiet in case the others attacked him.) Next day, the sun so hot the tar was melting, he went again, 140km, the rest of them – Bartali, Bobet, Robic, Ockers, Géminiani, Coppi (still in mourning for his brother and way below his best) – toiling in his wake. He just sat rock steady and rode them off his wheel.

After Koblet's victory in that Tour, Jacques Goddet described him as the 'perfect specimen for demonstrating the miraculous power of the human race'. Goddet's purple prose notwithstanding, Koblet was never the same rider again and his life ended tragically when his sports car hit a tree in 1964.

Robic 'Biquet', The Kid, five-foot nothing was so light in weight, he ballasted his water bottles with lead to increase his momentum on the downhills. Tiny guy, blond curls crimped under a string-of-sausages racing helmet – another nickname 'Leatherhead' – gnarled face and Mr Punch hooked chin and nose, he could sprint, climb and roll flat with the best. He won the first post-war Tour in 1947 and was still giving his fellow Breton, Bobet, a ride in 1954. He wore a ring inscribed *kenbeo kenmaro*, 'to life, to death' in Breton.

Jacques Goddet, who took over from Desgrange after his death in 1940, called the first edition of the Tour after the Second World War 'an act of faith'. The occupying Germans had pressed him to run the Tour during the War to demonstrate that life in France was good, that the country was *en fête*. 'Out of the question,' he said. In 1947 he wrote in *L'Equipe*:

'This Tour de France sends a message of joy and of confidence . . . because it spreads a frieze across all the radiant landscape of our country, a moving, inspiring, astounding frieze of a heroic adventure from which hatred is absent.'

(There might be no room for sentiment in cycle racing itself; in the journalism, particularly the French journalism, the scope and appetite for it was always bottomless.)

The departure was uncertain, right to the last minute. Post-war stringencies bit deep. The Government intervened. The President of the Council called for widespread economies *except on the Tour*. Potential entrants were asked to confirm their ride by telegram (the French Post Office was on strike) and to validate their passports for Belgium and Luxembourg. Rationing was severe; the organisers rustled up a ton of meat, 800kg of sugar and the same of bananas to provision the Tour.

On 25 June the field of 100 riders – 90 newcomers, 10 *brisquards* ('old soldiers, veterans') – rode out. The hot favourite was René Vietto. In 1934 young René had made all France ache with compassion at the picture of him sitting forlornly by the side of the road on the col de Puymorens, in tears, alongside his bike, minus its front wheel. 'The living image of despair.' Having ridden back down the mountain to give up his wheel to his team leader, Antonin Magne, who had punctured, he sat and waited, and waited, and waited for the service lorry. By the time it came his race was over. Nonetheless an amazing talent, a thoroughbred cyclist, had burst on to the scene. Only 20 years old, the man from Cannes took the King of the Mountains title and was, surely, due his own victory eventually. In 1939 he wore the yellow jersey for 11 days. When Sylvère Maes failed to shake him off on the Izoard, Vietto offered him half a peach. He paid for the generosity: Maes raced over the mighty Iseran at an average of over 16kph.

On the opening stages of the 1947 Tour, Vietto was riding well. He took the yellow jersey with a solo escape of 130km into Brussels; lost it at Grenoble, in the Alps. Over the Galibier, Robic began to show his hand and would have taken the lead had he not punctured and lost a lot of time. He clawed it back little by little and positively flew over a four-col stage in the Pyrenees, where Vietto reclaimed his yellow jersey, at Digne. One reason given for Robic's growing threat was his access to plentiful food. Wearing the white jersey of the Western France team, he and his fellow

Bretons had bypassed post-war stringencies and were tucking into 2kg of butter, three baskets of fresh eggs and ten dozen oysters daily, all supplied by regionals keen to see their men prosper. Nevertheless, three stages from Paris, Vietto appeared to have his first Tour victory within grasp. But in the time-trial in Brittanny, 139km from Vannes to St Brieuc, he cracked and lost nearly 15 minutes to a recently married Robic, cheered by a parcel of 72 letters from his family, friends and acquaintances. Robic had told his bride: 'I have no dowry, but I'll give you the Tour.'

She wrote to him: 'Show them you're the strongest.'

Had Vietto succumbed to the ill-effects of a bottle of iced cider? Had the obsession with a Tour win broken his nerve? Whether the collapse was moral or physiological, he slumped to third place by five minutes on the Italian, Brambilla, in yellow; Robic was second, nearly three minutes behind. On the final stage, Caen to Paris, the race crossed the côte de Bonsecours; 140km from the finish seven riders were in the lead but none of them of any threat to the leaders. The heat was intense. Robic records:

'Ahead of me I could see everybody out of the saddle, a mass of heads bobbing about. I spotted Brambilla, surrounded by his guys. Instinct kicked in. The *pavé* was smooth as mosaic. I took 50m out of Brambilla. He closed on me; I went again, he came again. He thought I'd shot my bolt but he was as exhausted as I was; spent. I got going again and took 50m. He came back at me. It was agony; we were both near asphyxiated, cooked. And at that point my generous-hearted friend, Brambilla, a man of superhuman energy, cracked, he was completely shattered.'

That didn't finish it, however. One of the French team men, Fachleitner, six minutes and 56 seconds down on the overall in fourth place, saw that Robic hadn't much left and offered him a deal: 50,000 francs and he'd ride for Robic. (That was the equivalent of two post-Tour one-day contracts – from which most of the Tour men used to make the bulk of their money.) In Robic's words, he needed to drop some ballast; he agreed and they rode on. Shortly after, Fachleitner upped the ante to 100,000. Robic coughed. The point was that if they co-operated, Robic stood a chance of winning the Tour and Fachleitner of coming second; if they didn't there was a chance that Brambilla would recover and the bigger prize money would have been lost. In the event, Robic did win by three minutes and 58 seconds – Brambilla at ten minutes and seven seconds – having never worn the coveted yellow jersey once the entire Tour. Brambilla took the mountains prize.

Besides Robic, another man won the Tour without ever wearing the yellow jersey; that is, he never led the race until he crossed the line in Paris. In 1968, the Belgian, Van Springel, led the race by 16 seconds to the last stage, a 55km time-trial from Melun to Vincennes, to the east of Paris. But he lost the Tour by 38 seconds – to date the narrowest winning margin – to the Dutch rider Jan Janssen, already three times winner of the green points jersey, a prize for consistently finishing towards the front on each stage. The first Dutchman to win the Tour, Janssen, like Robic in 1947, hadn't worn the yellow jersey once. Janssen was actually more of an all-rounder, boasting a lively mix of one-day and stage races in his *palmarès*, or list of victories.

Another sad end for Poulidor that year: forced out when he crashed near Albi.

A curious symmetry was at work here. Robic's last-minute victory in 1947; 21 years later Janssen scraped home; 21 years after him, in 1989, Lemond won by the smallest margin ever, eight seconds, having started the final time-trial on to the Champs-Elysées 50 seconds down on Fignon. Hitherto, the narrowest margin had been the 38 seconds that Jan Janssen held over Herman Van Springel.

In pleasant warmth and the satisfaction of a day well cycled, I ponder the Galibier.

One card in my collection is of a view north of the Galibier taken from Le Roc Noir, above the Briançon road, showing the approaches to the switchback climb up the southern slopes from the col du Lautaret as well as the peak of the Grand Galibier itself; at 2,704m it is nearly 60m higher than the col. The card is dated 6 April 1908 and the enigmatic message reads: *162 demain matin! Franck.*

No bike to be seen, but one of the most famous climbs in the

Tour. You can visualise the phantom machines picked out like microdots in the grainy sepia, the road traced like a thin trickle of quicksilver down a jumpy circuit board.

The audacious changes Desgrange instituted in 1930 had worked. Influential journalists had inveighed against the risk but the risk had paid off. Desgrange reaped a handsome profit: daily circulation of *L'Auto* rose from 500,000 to 750,000. Commercialism might be deemed bad for the riders but it was good for newspaper business . . . which helped to sell the Tour, and so on and so on. But, instead of a Tour providing a field of combat for industrial tycoons promoting their bike-manufacturing business, the race had been restored to the men who rode them. The Tour de France was proving itself adaptable; it could change, and with change grow even more popular, and become even more taxing proof of heroism. Unquestionably it helped having a French winner, and a personable, likeable one at that. More, the French team scooped 51,900 francs in prize money and counted four riders behind Leducq in the first nine. Of him, a journalist rhapsodised: '*Dédé, geule d'amour, muscle d'acier*' (Dédé, matinée idol looks, muscles of steel.) His time had come. He became *de facto* leader of the French team. Fontan ceded place. Pélissier, the strong man, won eight of the 21 stages, the last four consecutively, and came in the first three no fewer than 18 times; though in the course of three mountain stages he lost over an hour in time. However, a cyclist of great style and poise, he was, too, immensely popular. He landed a richer posse of post-Tour contracts than anyone else, Leducq included. Among the other French successes were the Magne brothers, Pierre and Antonin, 'Tonin' a man whose destiny had arrived.

Born in 1904, 12 days before Leducq, Antonin 'Tonin' Magne, third in 1930, was a quiet, even introspective man. Each morning he went to the bottom of his garden, hefted a massive chunk of stone into his arms, staggered a few feet and put it in a new position. This exercise he dedicated to the steeling of his will.

Every May he went into pre-Tour retreat in the Pyrenees, there to reconnoitre the cols, acquaint himself with the climatic vicissitudes, nerve himself for the battle, harden his physique on the big climbs. No detail of preparation was too small to overlook. Years later, as Poulidor's *directeur sportif,* he told Poupou that the work of the Tour de France is as complex and intricate as a spider's web and reproached him for his lack of method.

They talk of training for the great race as a bit like entering the monastery. Desgrange yielded to the call of natural impulses but said that once the racing season was on, women were in the same category as a pair of socks. Merckx described entering the Tour and penetrating its strange world as a quasi-religious experience: 'The paradox of the test condemns the champion, by definition a public figure, to the life of a recluse for 20 days.' (This reclusion is complicated by the daily obligation of press conferences – an added 45 minutes or more to the already gruelling demands of the ride.) On and off the road, he might have said. Yet, why else is sport inspirational, if not in the magnified example it sets for life, a life in or out of the limelight? Achievement and the manner of achievement in any pursuit of goals beyond easy reach is governed by similar tolls. The Tour de France as *Odyssey?* Certainly. Odysseus the lone wanderer overcoming vicissitudes and disaster. And that side of sport, the reclusive nature of being number one, your entire existence embattled in continuous rivalry is little appreciated by the public who thrill to the exploits. Anquetil put his view of it bluntly: 'Follow a career in sport and it must be like passing through a jungle: you beat your own path, you fight on your own.'

In contrast to the ascetic Tonin Magne, Leducq seemed to need no extravagance of effort: he enjoyed robust health, had natural class, unshakeable morale and sweet temper but was passionate to boot. Like Anquetil, a *bon vivant,* he would declare that he owed his victories to good humour. Magne said he imputed his to sleep. It was he who said: 'Wearing the yellow jersey doubles your strength.' And, in proof of the old adage that if you believe in yourself you can make your own luck, Magne's second victory came partly thanks to an ex-hotel pageboy who gave him a bike to replace his own broken machine. Leducq won the 1930 and 1932 Tours, Magne the 1931 and 1934. (Georges Speicher kept the tricolour flying in 1933 when Guerra came second for a second time.)

In 1932, Desgrange endeavoured to swing an advantage behind Charles Pélissier, a rider whom he favoured and, perhaps, felt had been unlucky not to win at least one Tour. Poor climbing had reduced his chances, so Desgrange inaugurated time bonuses. Pélissier, a consistent stage victor would profit. First home: bonus of four minutes; second, three minutes; third, one minute. In the 1930 Tour this would have shortened Pélissier's time by 56 minutes, nearly enough to give him victory. However, Pélissier withdrew from the field, Leducq took yellow on day three in Bordeaux and kept it. He also won six stages, one of them over the Galibier in a snowstorm.

The intense Leducq *v.* Magne rivalry was gentlemanly, however; there was never the bitterness which marred the Poulidor–Anquetil duel, for instance. On their last Tour in 1938 the two of them rode into the Parc des Princes five minutes ahead of the *peloton* and acknowledged the plaudits of the French crowd by linking arms across their shoulders. It was a mutual gesture of respect, affection, shared privilege in the talent they had so generously deployed. Hinault and Lemond may have done the same on l'Alpe d'Huez, but the motives were very different.

We book into a hotel in Valloire – the town where Merckx had his neutral zone fall in 1975 – bath, wash clothes, hang them in Widow Twanky garlands on the balcony to dry in warm evening sunshine. I go off to explore the town and recce options for dinner; trawl in a few cards, several pictures of the Galibier, the Desgrange monument on the south side and La Louison Bobet, a *touriste-routier* event.

It is a pleasure, dawdling along that tangle of quiet streets in the late-afternoon sun, sniffing at the aromas issuing from fruit shops, bars, restaurants with dinner and wine in store. I stroll back to the hotel and instal myself with Virgil and a bock in the bar. The others join me after their perambulations and we agree on the restaurant, local cuisine just round the corner: *tartiflette*, a Hell-of-the-north-sized cobble of melted cheese, potato and onion, speciality of Savoie; Savoy sausage, creamed potatoes and sauce, in a dining-room plainly decorated for the après ski, pitch-pine panelling festooned with old wooden tools and implements, cooking utensils, copper pots and pans.

I sleep ill, wake far too early and hear the rain start. By 6.30 a.m. it is teeming, the sort of rain which, if it had a sense of humour, would be pleased with itself; except that it has the monotonous insistence of a Scottish presbyterian minister. Dawn rises with all the enthusiasm of a late-night drinker evilly hung over. We're in for a soaking. I pray there isn't wind.

Galibier. Giant of the Alps. Desgrange's favourite (introduced in 1911). Next to the Galibier, he declared, the Tourmalet, the Bayard, the Laffrey cols are like 'colourless, common-or-garden gnat's piss'. The Galibier is *grand cru*. On its south side they built a memorial to him, *father of the Tour*. Born 1865, died 1940. International tensions had kept the Germans, Spanish and Italians out of the 1939 Tour, but on 14 April 1940, Desgrange contumaciously announced the 33rd Tour, albeit over a reduced itinerary. Paris fell undefended to the invading Germans on 14 June. Admitting that little hope for the Tour remained but clinging to it anyway, Desgrange, HD, Le Patron, died aged 75 on 16 August. 'A will of pure steel, tempered without finesse, a blade levelled at *action* . . . Born for sport, it is as a sportsman that HD dies.' (R. Coolus, *L'Auto* 18 August 1940). On the rest day of the last Tour he directed, in Perpignan, he'd gone for his traditional 12km run. He returned to Paris before the finish to be there at the Parc des Princes, in his suit, to welcome his family, the giants of the road. An amiable Spartan, someone called him and let this – his own words – be an epitaph:

Le Tour idéal serait un tour où un seul coureur réussirait à terminer l'épreuve. (The ideal Tour would be one in which only one rider would complete the ordeal.)

There was something decidedly Knights of the Round Table

about Desgrange; he knew what evil demons inhabited the high passes and what terrors they awoke in the cyclists he sent up there. And a touch nostalgic of this latterday French *petit général* to refer to the Laffrey, a col of no great height or difficulty nowadays, but cited because it was one of the first included in the Tour. At Laffrey, *en route* from exile on Elba to Paris, Napoleon and his ever-growing army were intercepted by a battalion sent out by the military Governor of Grenoble. Napoleon marched up, alone, confronted them, opened his coat to reveal the Légion d'Honneur on his chest and invited the troops, many of them veterans of his European campaigns, to shoot. To a man they broke ranks and swore fresh allegiance to him on 7 March 1815. He marched directly to and into Grenoble, boasting that he had only to 'knock at the gates with his snuff box to gain admittance'. Curiously, there is a French slang expression *faire à quelqu'un une conduite de Grenoble* which means 'to run someone out of town' but that must refer to the 'day of tiles', 7 June 1788, in the run-up to full-scale Revolution, when the independent-minded Grenoblois bombarded the royalist forces from the city rooftops and forced them to capitulate.

From Valloire (1,430m) to the col (2,646m) is 17km, via Plan Lachat, (1,961m) at about halfway, at which point, as we can see from the map, the climb begins to get up on its hind legs: double chevron denoting severe gradient. We load the bikes and wheel out into the downpour. Rain slanting into us, we fill water bottles at the town fountain and set out. John and Angela in full waterproof togs, as suits their more laden pace, me in shorts. Legs take a while to warm up and I've left my gloves off – better to keep them dry in reserve for the downhill. Somewhere up beyond those cloud-swathed ramparts at the head of the long valley rears the Galibier.

The King of the Mountains competition was instituted in 1933: The first winner, the diminutive Vicente Trueba, known as the Torrelavega Flea, a featherweight with no claim on the overall classification or stage wins. Points are awarded to the first men across cols which are classified in categories: fourth (100–300m), third (300–600m), second (600–1,100m), first (1,100–1,500m) and *hors catégorie* – super category – (1,500m-plus). Classification is based on a fairly arcane system which takes into account quality of road surface and steepness. The paving of some of the remoter Pyrenean climbs is very poor and they are rated higher in consequence; and because the Pyrenees were less frequented by cars in the early days, the gradients tend to be sharper than those of the Alpine cols, an exception being the Alpe d'Huez ascent, super category because of its steepness and the fact that it always comes at the conclusion of a stage. Ratings are not consistent, moreover: the col de Bordères in the Pyrenees mounts only 300m but, depending on its location in the stage route, has been variously marked third or first category. And the col de la Madeleine, which has a mile downhill section on the northern ascent – enough for a short breather – is either first or super, even though it tends to be in mid-stage, depending on whether it's approached from north or south. The ability to climb – like perfect pitch – is innate; it's a misconception that you have to be born in the mountains to be a climber: many of the best climbers come from the flat lowlands. In 1997 Paul Sherwen, commentating on television, expressed surprise that Laurent Brochard, a team-mate of Virenque's should have held the lead in the Mountains competition 'because he was from the north of France, which is very flat'. Northern France isn't very flat, actually, and plenty of the finest climbers have come from Holland. Strength is what counts; a light body frame is a bonus. All the other attributes – stamina, fitness, morale – are essential to any Tour rider, whatever his speciality. Boardman, a natural speed-merchant, has I believe, made the costly error of purposely reducing his body weight in the past three years to adapt himself to the demands of riding the mountains. The assumption is that a reduction in body weight and the resulting loss of a few metres of speed over time-trials – his speciality – will be more than recompensed by greater efficiency on the climbs. This has, on the evidence, drastically cut into his natural strength. In 1997, shattered by a heavy fall and four days of riding in intense pain through the Pyrenees and a long mountain time-trial – 'I've never been forced to ride so far below my full power,' he said – he looked horribly gaunt when, finally, he had to retire on the Alpe d'Huez stage. The confidence he expressed in 1994, that in three years he would be physically capable of winning the Tour was, I fear, too much based on laboratory calculations. A computer can tell you many things: it can't tell you to forget about monitoring effort. After his magnificent attacking victory in the 1998 Giro, Pantani – 56kg of heart, say the *tifosi* – disparaged the gadgetry of modern bike racing. Riding out of his skin in the final time-trial to defend his narrow lead he actually beat Tonkov, a time-trial specialist. The pink jersey lifted him into another level of effort and he's no stranger to that. But he had his head buried in the handlebars not a cardiometer. 'That instrument,' he said, 'has detracted from the nobility of cycle-racing.' A view confirmed by Roche when he observed that young riders, festooned with computers and gauges, would do well to remember that riders rode hard long before the invention of the heart-rate pulsometer.

The Tour is a race like no other; the devastating changes of rhythm and physical stress it unleashes are vicious, abnormal; simply finishing it cannot be subjected to analysis in the same way that track racing – Boardman's great arena before he turned pro – can be. Refining technique and patterns of lung litrage, heart rate and watt output may work to brilliant success in a pursuit race; the Tour imposes its own reality and, like humour, it can't be explained logically. The Tour's learning curve is as steep as the mountains themselves; the psychological strain is enormous, the physical toll crushing. Merely seeing those bloody great cols from the valley floor can reduce the finest athlete's ability to perform at his best.

Boardman has, though, worn the yellow jersey longer than any other Briton – Tommy Simpson and Sean Yates both held it for a day – by winning two Prologues. The first in 1994 saw him in yellow for three days; the second in 1997 and in yellow for one day. I believe he does, or did have the capacity – mental, physical, moral – to win the Tour; there is a fine element of steel in his moral power, something so candid and nerveless in the courage of his ambitions; but he probably needs to follow something like the Tonin régime to achieve them. As Tonin said: 'To shine in the Tour, you have to learn staying power, to be as effective at the end as at the beginning.' *And* you must train on the battlefield itself.

Only four Frenchmen have won the Mountains prize – Vietto, Bobet, Géminiani, Virenque. Spaniards and Belgians share the most honours with the Italians third: Van Impe won six, though Virenque is currently on four consecutive wins. Merckx and Jimenez collared three, but the record holder is Federico Bahamontes, the Eagle of Toledo, overall Tour winner in 1959 and six Mountains prizes in all. ('54, '58, '59, '62–64) a man inclined to fly up the cols and sit at the top eating ice cream waiting for the rest to catch up. 1959 marked the last year of national teams and the French were top heavy: Anquetil, Bobet and Rivière. Their internal rivalries, compounded by the moral blow of losing Bobet in the Alps, allowed Bahamontes to keep going down once he'd gone up and become the first Spaniard ever to win the Tour.

I ride on and muse about punctures: none so far but it would be a drag in this weather on the exposed lower approaches to the Galibier, on this rainswept, down-in-the-mouth day. Lower down the valley, clumps of farm buildings, which high summer could hardly make handsome, crouch dishevelled, sodden and morose in muddy yards. Shuttered chalets. Bleak moorland. The waters of the Valloirette river course unseen. Water everywhere. To the west, a massive wall of mountain, the Aigles d'Arve; to the east La Sétaz Vieille. It's an impressive show of mountain force. Ahead looms the col overshadowed by two mighty steeples of rock at the end of these opposing ridges – the Grand Galibier and the Pic des Trois Evêchés.

In 1967 a puncture committed Poulidor to defeat once more. He came to the race as the odds-on favourite: his team was strong, he was at the height of his powers, Anquetil had retired. Misfortune struck again, almost inevitably. Had he but been blessed with luck . . . it was the quality Napoleon most prized in his generals – luck, above all luck at two in the morning (or in the high mountains) when moral power is at its lowest ebb. Poulidor punctured and fell on the Ballon d'Alsace; there was no help to hand and he lost 12 minutes. His own chance of victory gone, he decided to work for the Frenchman Roger 'Pinpin' Pingeon against their main threat, Gimondi, winner in 1965. Gimondi was a better climber than Pingeon and Poulidor's sumptuous riding over the Galibier in tandem with Pinpin effectively snuffed out the Italian's challenge and launched the Frenchman to final victory which he ensured with a solo escape between Roubaix and Jambes. Poulidor was, as ever, gracious in defeat, one of nature's gentlemen, though that is not to detract from his class – no stranger to heady success he was no willing loser, either. Or his wise good humour. He once said: 'My big luck was to meet plenty of bad luck.'

Say what you like, some of these Tour riders have a queer way with aphorism.

Plan Lachat heaves into view, a huddle of ugly, wooden ski chalets in a crook of the ranges. The meandering road swings a sharp corner to the right and steeply up; the first of the ramps. I have been in my lowest gear since we started; the only shot left in the locker is out of the saddle.

Asked for his opinion on the best rider of all, Bidot replied: '*Merckx. Faut voir son palmarès. Il savait lever le cul de la selle, pas comme certains champions très médiatiques mais peu entreprenants.*' (Merckx. You have only to look at the list of his victories. He knew how to lift his backside out of the saddle, not like some champions who are very conscious of their media image but not very daring.)

An indication: taking one point for a win in the Tour, Giro, Vuelta, Paris–Nice, Tour of Switzerland, World Road Race, nine major classic one-day races, Merckx scores 46, ahead of Anquetil 24, Hinault 23, Kelly 21, Coppi 20, Indurain ten, Bobet nine, Lemond five.

Hardly a controversial claim, therefore, choosing Merckx, who dominated pro cycling during the '70s, although the reasoning might seem eccentric. Anquetil, who dominated the '60s, was famous for rarely getting out of the saddle, but *in extremis* he would be dancing a fast treadmill jig on his pedals squeezing more speed out of the machine, like a jockey urging the last gasp out of his mount.

Bidot's summation of Merckx does not neglect to say that if he had spared himself more, he would have won even more victories; but caution was alien to the man and he saw it as part of his talent, part of his calling, an essential part of his professional requirement, too, to ride and ride and ride, wherever the calendar offered races. In December 1994, to mark the retirement of Sean Kelly, the great Irish rider – a record four green jerseys, bronze in the 1982 Worlds Road Race, Vuelta a España and a long list of Classics – his home town in Ireland, Carrick on Suir, organised an open invitation race: pros, current and retired, amateurs. They all came, including Fignon, Roche, de Vlaeminck and Merckx. 'I am very busy,' he said, 'but I had to come. Sean is such a great champion.'

Kelly said: 'The people have done me a great honour turning up in such numbers [1,200] and that riders such as Merckx have spared the time makes me even prouder.'

That's cyclists for you.

During his first Tour in 1969, the veteran English sprinter Barry Hoban put this joke round the *peloton*.

'Did you hear? Poulidor and Gimondi have been fined 50 francs. They took a tow from a lorry all the way up the Tourmalet, didn't turn a pedal.'

'What about Merckx?'

'Oh, he got done 50 francs too: he was towing the lorry.'

Merckx has said, and repeated, that that first victory meant more to him than the other four put together. The accident on the track later that same year not only meant that from then on he was never completely free of pain when riding; it jangled his nerves, too, made him extremely pernickety about the setting of his bike. He'd get up in the middle of the night to make minor changes of adjustment. And, during races, the team car would come up alongside to lower his saddle a fraction to reduce the centre of gravity going into the mountain, then raise it for greater leverage on the flat. His resistance to the incessant physical discomfort was remarkable; he owed his unequalled success as much to durability and stubbornness as to sheer class.

A revealing story about Kelly and the physical demands on class riders appears in Paul Kimmage's book *A Rough Ride*. Not so much a book as a protracted sermon of self-pity. Kimmage, a first-class amateur, never settled in the pro ranks and moans incessantly about how hard his chosen career turned out to be. He also, as they say, 'spits in the soup', breaking the fraternal code of the pro racers by sneaking on the practice of dope taking. At the end of the book, he recalls how he and Kelly went for a sauna one time and Kimmage tottered out, drained by the heat. 'I've never felt so knackered.' he said. Kelly, the consummate pro replied: 'I feel like this all the time.'

In praise of Kelly, Merckx said: 'Kelly [then aged 30] has an exceptional professional awareness. That is his only secret. Like me, he loves competition and never thinks of taking part as an also-ran. For Kelly, only winning counts and you will see him fighting like a demon in the Basque Tour in April, a few days before the Paris–Roubaix (48 hours after the finish) as if the hell awaiting him further north didn't exist.'

Asked if he didn't look out of the window on some grim winter days and wonder how cold and wet it was and if he'd go training after all, Kelly said: 'You never know how cold and wet it is till you get out there; so you get out there.'

Hoban's joke reminds me of a story Merckx tells of a prank his team-mate, the Dutchman Wagtmans, pulled that same Tour. The *peloton* lined up for the start of the stage from Clermont-Ferrand but, before the gun heralding the off, Wagtmans jumped and disappeared from sight. Immediately the gun went, the *peloton* streaked after the cheeky fugitive. He, meanwhile, had nipped down a side alley and dismounted. Hidden, he watched the bunch roar by, slipped out and picked up a tow from one of the support vehicles and surreptitiously rejoined the bunch. They were going crazy, a mad speed, when Lucien Aimar launched a sudden attack off the front, in pursuit of the man who was actually bringing up the rear.

The Galibier is very exposed; the road up it breaks every vertebra in its back over bare rock. No trees obscure the way forward. I can see the next hairpin on the climb swinging past me overhead, as the hairpin I'm on bends open from the tight turn. Progress is slow. Suddenly it's very daunting: this is a massive alp with a deserved fearsome reputation. I feel as if I'm gatecrashing the giants' committee. Occasionally, I stand up on the pedals to relieve the ache in the small of my back, 50 yards or so, and then settle back again. I am reminded of Charly Gaul of Luxembourg sitting near motionless in the saddle, turning his low gears, lower than anyone else's, flying up this mountain on his way to a stage victory in the 1955 Tour and they dubbed him 'The Angel of the Mountain'. He sealed overall victory in 1958 with a heroic escape in the Alps – cols de Porte, Cucheron and Granier – through torrential rain and won by 15 minutes, over a field including Bobet, Géminiani and Anquetil who had dysentery and was spitting blood and vomiting by the finish. In the mountains – the Massif of the Chartreuse, near Grenoble, and Ventoux – he was untouchable that year. There was little love lost between him and Bobet – Bobet had attacked him one day in the Giro d'Italia while the Luxembourger was taking a pee – so the Tour victory was sweet. Gaul himself ended sadly at first: a virtual recluse, dishevelled and run to fat, after a failed comeback in 1964. He has since retrieved himself.

Something is bugging me: the matter of stage wins and the relation to overall victory. The record of stage wins recorded by winners is instructive. Head of the list is Merckx with 35, Hinault 28, Leducq 25, Frantz 20, Faber 19, Anquetil 16, Indurain ten, Coppi eight (five in the '52 Tour) and Lemond five. Out of interest, in the Giro after Binda's 41 stage wins, Girardengo won 30 (two overall wins), Merckx 25 (five overall) Coppi 23 (five overall). No victor in the Tour deserves less than frank admiration but there are wins and wins. And as to the manner of victory, nothing testifies to fighting spirit more conclusively than the strength and swagger it requires to challenge the rest of the field to take your slipstream. 'If that's all they're prepared – or able – to do,' Eddie told his son Axel, now a pro himself, 'then let them.'

This Galibier is packed with history. Where exactly did Leducq fall on this descent that I am ascending? Not far from the top, I catch sight of a huge gully to my right, a funnel between two massive pillars of rock, a chasm plunging over a precipice, swirling with spectral white flurries of snow in spirals of wind. The ventilating chimney of an erl-king's refrigerator. Winter doing the dance of its ice veils. Awesome portico of monsters. I am riding into the lost regions where frost makes rainbows and the witch with green teeth trails nets of crystal snow for unwary summer, and unwary summer is caught fast, like the fish in the frozen lake. This is the realm of Ice-Blink and I am riding a glacial brook not a road.

I get nearer and the realisation begins to break, although I don't tempt the moment by cheering it too soon. Then I see the snow-plough, beyond the cars, facing me, beside a large buttress of rock above the left-hand verge. I ride up and say to one of the spectators of not very much happening, all togged up in mufflers and warm coats:

'*C'est le col?*'

'*Oui.*'

No ceremony. This is it. What? I get off the bike and lean it against a low wall of this mountain's fundamental stone and attack the saddle-bag containing my fleecy-lined top and gloves. The gloves are a saviour. I hadn't packed them originally, and put them in only at the last minute. Suddenly I feel the cold intensely, my fingers unlocked from the handlebars. I can only fumble woodenly at the bag straps. It's painful and clumsy. I'm just peeling my waterproof *off* so I can get the jacket *on*, when the driver of the snowplough, cigarette drooping from pursed lips, catches my eye and shouts. '*Vous nous assistez avec cette voiture glissée au défaut du bord.*' (Come and help us with this car, it's slipped over the edge.) More of a statement than a request. I stare impassively back at him.

'*Je viens de grimper le Galibier au vélo et vous me demandez assistance avec une voiture, merde.*' (I've just cycled up the Galibier and you want me to help you with a *car*?) More of a statement than an answer.

He stares impassively back at me, unimpressed. '*Oui.*'

I suppose the fact is that these mountain johnnies can't properly relate to any silly bugger trooping up their locale at any time of the year, and as for mad foreigners doing it by bike, *unpaid*, well, *c'est faire le con, quoi*? . . . that's just plain stupid.

I pull on my warm clothes, hobble over on the tip-up sole plates to join the snowplough driver and his mate by the car which had slipped off the road a yard or two down the slope. Danish, from the number plate; the driver, also Danish, from the passing resemblance he bears to an iced pastry, stands by with his hands in his pockets. I know he is the driver: he gets straight in without a word of thanks or apology the minute his motor is back on the road.

The three of us artisans clap on; I'm braced at a wheel arch. Monsieur Chasse-Neige chants: *Un, deux, trois*: we heave. *Un, deux, trois*: we heave. Inch by inch we swing the rear end into a position where a tow rope from the snowplough's winch can be attached; they hook on and safely up comes the motor, only after one violent twang, a broken line and a rehitch.

Monsieur Chasse-Neige makes no comment, simply coils up the rope and looks vacant, all in a day's work. No one else says anything. I hobble back to my bike, remount and head off for the first sign of hot drinks. The descent looks treacherous. As I tip over the flat of the col into the fall of the south side, a woman standing under a chandelier of icicles says: '*Chapeau bas.*' ('Hats off'.)

A surge of elation and wonderment flows through me. The Galibier. Wow.

A short way from the summit stands the monument *A la Gloire de Henri Desgrange, Créateur du Tour de France Cycliste*, a stumpy obelisk thrusting up out of the snow like a petrified tarboosh.

In Briançon we settle the price at the hotel with the woman owner and, pointing to the open garage adjacent to the building, ask if we might leave the bikes there, under cover. She quivers in protest. She flaps her hands and arms, eyes glaring, head shaking – charading *Non, non, NON!* We've overstepped our welcome; but no. She explains that she wouldn't dream of letting us expose the precious machines to villainy, for villainy there was all around, a wicked lawless contagion and endemic thieving, everything down to humble rivets going missing. Apparently, a team of club cyclists had stayed in the hotel the night before a race, parked their racing machines in the garage, come down for breakfast at 5.30 a.m. and found the cupboard bare, every bike nicked.

She insisted that we bring our bikes into the hotel and park them at the far end of the restaurant. We drip through and park the bikes against tables. She looks relieved; we feel awkward. I express our gratitude. We go off for hot water and clothes-drying.

The yellow bike with which Desgrange furnished the riders in the Tours of the 1930s was an all-steel affair – frame, wheels, handlebars; total weight around 12kg. (The French army's target of 10.5kg had to wait till the '50s.) It carried two brakes, of the caliper variety, shoes clamping either side of the rim, which hasn't much changed since. The single 'bean' brake had been a rectangle of rubber fastened to a metal pad which a rod and lever simply pushed down onto the front tyre: inefficient and dangerous. The dropped handlebars were mostly of the ram's horn shape, though Nicolas Frantz favoured a distinctive curving top bar and a shallower drop, a sort of eyebrow in outline. Hooked over each tyre, affixed to the frame behind front stem and seat stays, was a flint-scraper, a simple half hoop of thick wire which rubbed the tyre and, with luck, dislodged inhering pointed stones before they got driven into the inner tube. Nicolas Frantz placed little trust in them, preferring to scan the road ahead of his tyres constantly and thus avoid the sharp stuff. It worked. He rarely punctured.

The back wheel sported up to three sizes of freewheel on either side. Gear changes were still effected by switching the wheel round, and butterfly nuts made that operation swifter. (A sensible rider carried spare wing nuts: easy to lose one in the fumbling to mend a puncture or change gearing in the darkness of night.)

Desgrange still held out against the *dérailleur*, but the influence of *dérailleur*-using cycle tourists on the refinement of the bicycle and its equipment was decisive. The Tour riders might have to conform to puritanical edicts against an easier ride; Joe Public did not and Joe Public was stimulating the quest for lighter metals with high resistance to stress, such as duralumin, an alloy developed at the instigation of a cycle club called the Parisian Mountaineers.

The single chainwheel usually varied in size – between 46 and 48 teeth; the freewheels round 16/18 for the flats and 22/25 for the climbs. (Benoît Faure, recalling the Leducq-Guerra pursuit, said that they rode 46 x 22 on the climbs then switched to 16. For a flat stage they'd ride on a 48 chainwheel. Riding such big gears almost always necessitated tackling the climbs *en danseuse*, the modern preference tends to be towards a fast-whirring smaller gear, such as Charly Gaul favoured, though specialist climbers like Virenque and Pantani get out of the saddle as soon as the gradient steepens and swing into a remorseless hip-rolling rhythm which calls the full body power into play.)

'A bicycle is a work of art which you take up to the bedroom every night. Anybody who doesn't is not a real cyclist.' René Vietto.

I attempted to follow Vietto's advice in a small hotel by Lago di Como, *en route* home from the Dolomites: the proprietor thought I was joking. In Barcelona, asking where I might park my bike, the reception clerk simply assured me that the room was plenty capacious enough to accommodate me and my bike comfortably.

René Vietto was not preaching bike-fetishism or sentimental attachment. Care and scrutiny of the bike was a wise precaution

against more than coincidental breakdown. During the Boule
d'Or, a 24-hour track race in Paris, Hubert Opperman's chain
broke and he lost several laps before he could get back into the
race – which he won. His rivals had sawn partway through the
chain to eliminate him. By the closing laps, and a long way in the
lead, he was also on schedule for the 1,000km record. He wouldn't
hear of it and climbed off. His pal Bruce Small shouted across:
'They'll never forget you in France if you do it. 'He rose to the
task, rode on for another hour and 19 minutes, the crowd yelling
'Oppy! Oppy! ' and took the record. He said he hardly felt that
extra hour and a bit. A seemingly tireless long-distance cyclist,
Opperman arrived with two fellow riders from Australia to ride in
the 1928 Paris–Brussels race, 361km; he came third. They raced
in the Tour that year, when every stage, except those in the
mountains, was contested as a team time-trial. Given that the
major teams put ten men into the race, Opperman's 18th position
is astonishing. One rider who rode the 1931 Paris–Brest–Paris,
1,200km, said he'd ride into the checkpoint towns and ask if
they'd seen Oppy. Yes. Where did he stop? He didn't. He was still
cycling aged 90.

Gustave Garrigou (first 1911, second 1909 and 1913, third
1910 and 1912) took his bike up to his bedroom every night. The
commercial rivalry of the bike manufacturers was ferocious and
unprincipled. Garrigou won his early fame as the first man ever to
cross the Tourmalet on a bike – 1910, the year of the great duel
between Faber and Octave Lapize, a head to head which increased
the daily sales of L'Auto massively. Halfway through the Tour he
went to bed, took his bike with him but forgot to bolt the door.
Shortly after the start of the next stage, 3 a.m., crossing the Lunel,
near Montpellier, his front wheel began to buckle. Ballbearings
spilled out over the road. The opposition had sawn through the
ball-race. The repair cost him an hour and a half – he probably
performed the celebrated trick of bashing the wheel rim into
somewhere near round, then standing on it to make it true
enough to go through the forks and rode on – he finished third.
Garrigou formed part of the Alcyon team which dominated the
Tour 1909–12. Alcyon sales rocketed: everyone wanted to own
the bike that had won the Tour. Another Alcyon man, Duboc, was

leading the 1911 race, sauntered up the Tourmalet with insolent ease but, at the control in Argelès grabbed a *bidon* from a spectator. Ascending the Aubisque he drank the contents and almost immediately pitched off the bike with violent stomach cramps. Since he was in the lead the intention seemed blatant: to impede if not actually to poison him. He lost an hour and Garrigou assumed the lead. A rider of few words, minimal gesture and a studiously economical style of riding, he unexpectedly beat the more flamboyant Luxembourger, Faber (winner in 1909). Duboc recovered to win two stages and finish second overall, but after the race he returned to his carpenter's shop in Rouen and never mounted a bike again.

To conclude with the story of another drama played out on the Galibier.

It is 1966 and the riders are 70km into the stage from Bourg d'Oisans to Briançon, Tom Simpson of Britain in the rainbow jersey of World Road Race Champion breaks clear; 10km on he's built a small lead and begins the climb of the Télégraphe with one and a half minutes' advance on the *peloton*. It's an ambitious move: 60km still to ride and the Giant of the Alps to cross. One minute and 20 seconds after him, the eventual Mountains' winner for the second year in succession, Julio Jimenez, riding for Anquetil's team, appears, clear of the bunch. By the time he was 5km up the 12km climb, the lead over Jimenez has fallen to 20 seconds; the chasing group of 20 men, including several Spanish riders as well as Anquetil and Poulidor, is at one minute and 30 seconds. Simpson's solo effort was all but over; the Spaniard catches him, sits on his wheel briefly and then sprints past. Now begins Simpson's long torment of trying to hang on, fighting against oxygen debt, sagging morale, sapped strength. He launched the break too early. He tries desperately to match Jimenez's pace; it's beyond him and Jimenez dumps him, rubbing the desolation in with every turn of the pedals. All Simpson can do is grit his teeth and wait to see who comes up in his slipstream next along the valley towards the monster at the head of it. The following group has split; Poulidor and Anquetil are on their own having dropped the other survivor, Huysmans. Anquetil has won five times; he's written off a sixth victory this year. He has one ambition only: to stall Poulidor's chances. Being a team-mate of Jimenez, he could legitimately sit on Poulidor's wheel and let Poupou do all the work. He had too much pride to do that and on to the first steep ramps of the Galibier they ride side by side, reeling in Simpson. There he is; Anquetil out of the saddle, Poulidor, that awkward swaying leaning gait of his on the climbs, but firmly seated, go past the ailing Briton. It's always a melancholy moment for most riders, to drop another fine rider who will have to slog on alone on an empty tank.

But here comes the Belgian, Huysmans; Simpson takes his wheel for a short distance, the Galibier one in seven gradient exacting a fearsome toll; he has paid a heavy price for going early and trying to outdistance a man of Jimenez' ability. Huysmans allowed Anquetil and Poulidor to go and has reserves of energy as a result. He'll reach the col in better shape and has the long easy descent to come. Simpson will be in a sorry state by then.

At the col, Jimenez has already taken the *prime* (£140) but Anquetil goes flat out for the second prize (£70) to show the Poulidor fans gathered at the summit that he is still the boss. Then the descent begins. Back down the road, Huysmans is two minutes and 30 seconds adrift, Simpson at four minutes and 30 seconds in company with a small group of chasers, including the reigning Tour champion Lucien Aimar.

Anquetil lets Poulidor go ahead – no fans here to boo him – and he can't risk helping Poulidor catch Jimenez. His own man, Aimar, is well placed to win a second time. Huysmans, a strong decender, is breathing down their necks and Aimar is taking all kinds of risks behind him, flinging himself and his bike into the hairpins at an outrageous speed. Simpson has taken a boost from the arrival of the others and is redressing his losses.

When they are 20km from the arrival in Briançon, Jimenez is in no danger; he leads Anquetil and Poulidor by two minutes and 30 seconds; Huysmans at three minutes; the group with Aimar three minutes 45 seconds. Suddenly, a motorcyclist carrying a TV cameraman skids on some loose gravel and brings Simpson down. Blood streaming on to his rainbow jersey, he remounts and rides into the finish in severe pain. Next day's stage begins with the second category climb of the Montgenèvre, 9km and 524m.

Simpson's right arm is virtually useless and, 15km on, he abandons. The customary ritual of removing the numbers from bike and jersey – so reminiscent of the breaking of Dreyfus: badges of rank torn from his uniform – and another Tour is over for Simpson; another lucrative post-Tour circuit of one-day events vanished.

Why did he attack? He explained that he expected Anquetil to control the race behind him, that the climbers wouldn't bother to go until the last kilometres of the Galibier and that he'd made the fateful error of trying to stay with Jimenez and blew up.

CHAPTER FIVE

COL D'IZOARD

Coppi and the Modern Era

Briançon, *petite ville et grand renom*, held out for three months against a besieging Austrian army with a garrison of 300 in 1815. Vauban's fortifications, built after the sacking of the city by Sardinians in 1692, perch on a high prominence way above the new suburbs, an untidy conglomeration of faded grand mansions – some Italianate – and ghastly concrete modernity. The usual civic architecture on ugly, self-satisfied authoritarian scale: massive school, barracks of an Alpine regiment, administrative offices, hospital . . . it's not easy or rewarding to distinguish which is which as you stroll by.

We walk up the steep hill towards the old city in the shadow of the church of Notre Dame, another of Vauban's bastions; this one, cordoned with cypresses and dedicated to God rather than gunpowder, though carefully sited to double as a defensive salient if need be.

In a small bar, cosy, coffee-warm, redolent of black tobacco and anis, we talked ourselves back up the Galibier and down; and panegyrics of the bicycle. Angela sums it up:

'I feel really sorry for people who have never discovered the fun of a bike.'

★

Perhaps one doesn't associate Tour riders with the fun of a bike. The melancholy tale of the 1906 Tour winner, René Pothier – first home of a mere 14 survivors from the field of 75 – who, on 25 January 1907, after a broken love affair, hanged himself from the garage hook from which he suspended his bike. Not so much fun, more an obsession.

'*Le problème avec Eddy c'est qu'il a été vacciné avec un rayon de bicyclette. Une semaine sans courir et rien ne va plus.*' – Madame Eddy Merckx. (The trouble with Eddy is that he's been vaccinated with a bicycle spoke. A week away from the bike and nothing works.)

We have been vaccinated with a bicycle spoke, too, though we share more with the old *touriste-routiers*, of course, than with the champions like Merckx – save in the deep fascination with and love of the bike. Bidot summed up why Desgrange – an unapologetic admirer of the 'Aces' or 'first violins' as opposed to the mere trombones, the drudges created the freelance *touriste-routier* category.

'He particularly liked them because they stirred things up, turned the race into total disorder. He sent them off at different times which was a nightmare for us. If they rode in a bunch, they could block the entire road all day long.'

There was, too, the innate antagonism between team men, riding to tactical order, and the freelances, ready to go for any prize on offer, not giving a pint of stale air for anyone else. There was big money to be won and the independents flew after it, mindful of no team responsibility, no larger tactical scheme which, so often, throttles genuine competition in every Tour.

The earning life of a racing cyclist is, generally, short. Anquetil, who put all his money into property and land, also pointed out that as freelances, the riders made their money 'under the constant surveillance of the tax inspector. Lucky amateurs, not to have that.'

Taxmen see sportsmen as fair game: bungs and backhanders are as old as sport itself, even – especially – among the ancient Greeks. Olympian–Corinthian amateur idealism is a modern invention. In 1951, Hugo Koblet, the pomaded *pédaleur de charme*, was arguing about tax returns with the Swiss revenue men. They demanded more tax; he ducked and dived. One day the inspector returned to

Koblet's house with photographs of two famous Swiss bike riders of an older vintage, now dead, and asked if he recognised them.

'Of course.'

'And you know very well they won a lot of races, as you have. And they wound up destitute, dependent on public funds to live. They owed the daily bread of their old age to public charity. So, since you're going to end up the same way, don't bitch about paying taxes – you're contributing to the fund you'll have to draw on one day.' Bleak prospect.

Poulidor, who perhaps epitomises the fairly uncommon combination of the race-hardened pro who still loves riding the bike (Kelly is another), retired a wealthy man. How much would he sacrifice to have won the Tour, to have worn the yellow jersey? He won almost everything else: burst on to the scene in the 1961 Milan–San Remo (the 'spring' race) and beat Anquetil's lieutenant, Stablinski, to become Champion of France later that year; but the self-doubt set in.

He was giving Anquetil enormous trouble in the 1964 Tour but, on the stage into Toulouse lost time after a stupid fall. Next day he mustered a near-decisive punch over the Pyrenean cols and won, on his own, at Luchon. Interest in the Tour revived but he lost, just as he missed out in that year's Worlds at Sallanches – the bronze when he was ideally placed for the gold. He often beat Anquetil and was far more popular – he still is. But, his destiny was, it seems, less for his own success than to force even sterner efforts out of his formidable rival. Anquetil admitted it: 'There were times when he crushed me, this Poulidor.' But this was the man who swore fealty to the old cliché that winning isn't the most important thing it's the *only* thing. Poulidor never could evince that merciless attitude to racing, what amounts to a bloodlust. Yet the love affair with the bike survived. Robert Millar now loves the motorbike the same way he loved the bike in the beginning, before it became a machine he earned his living on. In retirement, Poulidor still went for bike rides. The days of 250km races were over; now he could ride 60km without any thought of performance and declare that he'd keep going till he was 65, then he'd see.

And tomorrow the Izoard. I've seen pictures of it. The famous, the clichéd 'lunar' landscape of the Casse Déserte: huge rock stooks amid boulder rubble, like windworn columns of a collapsed arcade. The camera surveys the desolation of scree, the tiny road cleared by dwarvish pickaxes and a lone rider ascending, bike and man, wayfarer braving the ambush of sun, thirst, exhaustion, puncture, even the circling buzzard. The archetypal rock and hard place in one. Arid. Totally exposed. Fearsome heat in summer, reflecting off the bleached stone. A meteorite artillery range. A foundry for Titans' stone slingshot. This is the Tour mountain terrain *par excellence*, the traditional *High Noon* battleground of the alpine stages.

On the Izoard, Sylvère Maes delivered his *coup de grâce* to beat Vietto in 1939. He'd nearly lost the yellow jersey in the Pyrenees – a team-mate launched a withering attack and Maes chased with Vietto glued to his wheel. In the Casse Déserte, Thévenet sealed his victory over Merckx in 1975. Here, in 1972, Merckx had left the rest toiling behind him to take his fourth victory, the 60th edition of the Tour. He capped that by taking the hour record. Across this wilderness Coppi and Bobet in their time launched what the French call the solo exploit. It's the heroism at the core of this race.

Ill-named Fausto (Italian for 'Lucky') Coppi died aged only 40; cursed with fragile bones, he missed years through injury and the War. Born in 1919, he turned professional in 1937 and, aged 20, won his first Giro in 1940. Drafted into the Italian army, his unit was captured by the British 8th Army in Tunisia and he spent two years as a PoW.

Coppi ushered in the modern era: the first complete bike rider, inspiration of Bobet's early career, Anquetil's ambition, Merckx's childhood. Won the Tour de France twice, five Giro d'Italia, five Tour of Lombardy, Paris–Roubaix, Milan–San Remo, World Hour record, two World Pursuit champion. First man to use a double clanger (two chainwheels) . . . even Desgrange's actuarial supervision did not extend beyond the grave. But he had known, as Coppi knew: winning depended on the intelligence as well as the physique and an event as brutal and demanding as the Tour de France took more than exceptional talent and the strength of a packhorse. Coppi said: 'The mistake made by young cyclists is that they are over-eager, too impatient to be world champions. They must look after themselves physically, they must learn the fibres of muscles and body, they must learn tactics, they must live, eat and dream road-race.'

Put another way: it's no earthly good being capable of winning unless you know how to. Winning, succeeding as a professional in whatever sphere, it amounts to the same. To be the best, you compete not with the opposition but against yourself. They don't call the time-trial the 'race of truth' for nothing.

The journalist Pierre Chany dubbed Coppi 'the heron': 5'10", ten and a half stones, long spindly legs, hunched, scrawny shoulders, disproportionately small torso, handsome aquiline features with long beak of a nose and high cheekbones, he seemed an ungainly man off the bike, yet:

> *Dans un ensemble paradoxalement harmonieux, ce héron . . . haut perché sur une selle invisible . . . ne connaissait pas la hantise du poids morts et des muscles inutiles que certains hissent tels des mulets jusqu'à la cîme des montagnes.*

> (The paradox was that his physique was perfectly attuned; this heron perched up on his saddle carried no dead weight, every muscle was brought into play unlike other riders who drag themselves to the mountain summits like mules.)

Heron is an apt image: observe the ungainly bird stalking its prey at the edge of the water, stiff and awkward in its movements, then lumber into flight and once aloft float effortlessly on the breezes.

Gino 'the Pious' Bartali was already established – winner of the 1938 Tour – when Coppi arrived on the scene in 1939, but the ignition of the great rivalry came in 1946, Milan–San Remo, when Coppi went clear for 147km, led the second man Tessière by 15 minutes and Bartali and Ricci slugged it out for third place along the Via Roma ten minutes after him. When Bartali found out who'd won, he knew he had a fight on his hands.

The Coppi v Bartali duel animated cycling, particularly in their native Italy, during the late '40s and early '50s. Coppi, the radical thinker who revolutionised methods of training and racing, versus the Tuscan Bartali of peasant stock; atheist ranged against devout Catholic. Culzio Malaperte said of them: 'Bartali is for the orthodox, his talent is spiritual, the saints look after him; Coppi has no protection up there. Bartali has blood in his veins, Coppi has petrol.' Bartali had such a slow heart rate that his doctor insisted he smoke three cigarettes per day: one in the morning, one after a race, the third in the evening before bed. If he won a race he smoked a fourth to celebrate. Coppi's attention to diet was fastidious, and he fortified his strict régime with vitamins. It was no secret; though Bartali occasionally searched his hotel room for secret potions, the wonder dope that the lanky wonder from Piedmont must be taking. On one occasion, the story goes, he retraced the route of a race to hunt for a bottle he'd seen Coppi discard. He found it and had the traces examined: it was bicarbonate of soda in water.

In 1948, at 34 years of age, Bartali took his second Tour; a ten year gap which remains a record. He slumped early on – 21 minutes down on the newcomer Bobet – and was written off. But he surged back in the Pyrenees – a stupendous victory into Lourdes, which must have pleased his Catholic heart and proved divine blessing – by the time they reached the Alps he really had sprouted wings and took three stages in succession, one of them over the Izoard . . .. through hail and snow on the Croix de Fer and Glandon (touché) and pelting rain over the Chartreuse massif. An emphatic demonstration of his class. He took the Mountains Prize and won overall by a massive 26 minutes and 16 seconds.

In 1949, spindleshanks Coppi trounced Bartali in the Giro and came to the Tour – a year before he'd planned to ride it – and left his indelible mark on it: yellow jersey, mountains prize and Bartali beaten into second place by ten minutes 55 seconds. Coppi bided his time while the tiny Parisian rider Jacques 'the Parakeet'

Marinelli held the yellow jersey for the first 17 days – surviving a bad fall on stage five – and then struck.

He didn't so much climb the mountains, they wrote, as levitate: cols de Vars, Izoard, Galibier where he rode past the newly installed monument to Desgrange, wearing the first yellow jersey to be embroidered with the initials HD. One day, when the race crossed the massive Alpine cols, Coppi dropped Bartali at the foot of the Izoard and won the stage alone by over 20 minutes; an awesome show of power. Contributing an article on his reflections on the world and sundry matters he entitled the piece 'We all have two legs.' It was something of an understatement.

He missed the 1950 Tour having broken his pelvis in the Giro; in 1951, his morale badly shaken by the recent death of his brother, he lost 33 minutes on the stage into Montpellier under the furnace heat of the Languedoc. He must have felt as if he were cycling through a still photograph. But he came back and so dominated the 1952 Tour that no one could live with him – in the mountains he simply vanished into the distance. In Paris he led by 28 minutes 17 seconds. Every day he made detailed notes about the course of the stage and the gear developments of the Italian team:

> Bagnères–Pau km 148
> Coppi 45–50 14 16 20 23 24
> Bartali 46–50
> Abagni 46–50 etc
> col du Tourmalet 1st category
> col d'Aubisque etc
> Limoges–Clermont-Ferrand km 246
> Coppi 45–50 14 17 20 22 25
> Bartali 46–50 etc
> Puy de Dôme 1st etc

In 1960 the cycling world mourned his premature death. The power of his inspiration and his influence on professional racing methods were incalculable.

Louison Bobet, who idolised him, won three Tours in succession 1953–55, the first man to do so. He did ride against Coppi, in the 1951 Giro. Penalised five minutes for changing a wheel, the Frenchman wanted to abandon. His *directeur sportif* dissuaded him but, at dinner, Bobet was still brooding. Then, his inner turmoil wonderfully cleared, he said, in level tones: 'I'm not only going to start tomorrow but I shall wear my French champion's jersey and take them on. It may finish me but I'll show them I'm a Bobet.'

He rode over the mountains in imperious fashion, Coppi on his wheel, the rest of the bunch weaving up the slopes behind in disorder. Bobet finally rode Coppi off his wheel in the sprint, and eventually finished 7th overall.

1953. The Izoard stage.

From the small village of Arvieux on the southern approaches to the summit of the col via the Casse Déserte is 10km along a road which was still a rustic track, corrugated with ruts, scattered with flints and loose stones, swathed in plumes of dust. Since the crossing of the col de Vars, Bobet had found la bonne carburation (writes Bidot, then manager of the French team): his engine working well, fire in his spirit, legs going like pistons, perfect efficiency, balance and rhythm.

> Not far from the col itself, on the left side of the road, I saw, amongst the spectators, Fausto Coppi, in shorts, a camera slung across his chest. As Louison [Bobet] went past, in the lead, Coppi gave him a friendly wave and said to me: 'He looks good.'
>
> The Italian champion clicked his stopwatch. Eight minutes later, he clicked it again when Bartali rode by. Coppi, on the look out on the slopes of the Izoard . . . it was a bit like the artist contemplating his work.

(This was Bartali's last Tour, ending a career that spanned an exceptional 26 years.)

That same year, Jacques Anquetil, aged 19, rode his first season as a professional cyclist. After the Tour he won the prestigious Grand Prix des Nations – the only Classic-rated individual time-trial – and immediately added the Grand Prix de Lugano. On 30 October he arrived at Coppi's villa in Novi Ligure, unannounced, hoping 'to see face to face the only man still ahead of him, the one man he dreamed of dethroning'.

Coppi had been out training; his *soigneur*, Cavanna, was massaging him. The message came through – a young man wanted to see the maestro. Anquetil was called in; Coppi asked him why he'd come, quizzed him – ambitions? training methods? diet? And so on. But what was all this about? To Coppi, another young admirer, self-possessed and evidently showing huge promise; but . . . a long way to go. And for Anquetil? Entering the presence. Measuring himself against his hero. Even the most prodigiously talented do not spring fully-formed out of callow ambition; rivalry, emulation, is the stuff of our first striving, till we learn to improve ourself, not our own necessarily inadequate version of someone else.

> Coppi stayed silent a long time and for that moment, those minutes when I had only the sense of a strange complicity between us, I would have gone round the earth. (Jacques Anquetil, *Je suis comme ça.*)

In fact, Anquetil accompanied Coppi on his last ride – an appearance race in Ouagadougou in the French West African territory of Upper Volta, now Burkino Faso, on 13 December 1959 – along with other stars: Géminiani, Rivière. It was there that Coppi caught the malaria that killed him but 20 days later.

Anquetil was known for an ice-cool temperament. Nothing unnerved or unsettled him. His focus was as concentrated as a laser. Bobet was altogether different. He could be as jumpy as a cat, as temperamental as a racehorse. A grease mark on his front tyre which he couldn't take his eyes off . . . the wrapping of his spare tyre in a colour he found disagreeable . . . such irritations could ruffle his nerves and send him into a decline, drain him of fight for the day's racing . . . a badly written letter could stop him sleeping. (Ah, insomnia: I'm suffering from a touch of the Bobet's . . . if only.) On one occasion, he despatched a *domestique* into a café to get some mineral water. *Domestiques* (second-string support riders) are often called 'water-carriers' and in the days before the team cars supplied everything – taking no risk of spiked bottles – they would often hustle drinks wherever they could, without payment if possible. However, this *patron* insisted on cash. The *domestique* pleaded: it was for his boss. The *patron* wouldn't budge; certainly he was a sports fan but he was running a café not a cyclist's charity.

'But it's for Monsieur Louison!'

'So Monsieur Louison pays.'

(He may have been an anti-Bobetiste. France was split into rival camps: Bobetiste and anti-Bobetiste.)

The *gregario* argued but to no avail; he stumped up for the bottle, rushed out, leapt back on his bike. The *peloton* was by this time eight minutes ahead: a lot of chasing. Still, he was no mean *coureur* and in 13 minutes of hard riding he caught the bunch. Very proud of his solo chase, he rolled up alongside Bobet and handed him the bottle – thoughtfully unstoppered so the great man could drink it straight off. Bobet glanced at the bottle, grimaced in disgust and spat: 'You know very well I don't like that brand of water.'

A lot of riders try to make do with the bare minimum of water intake, imitating, presumably, the camel. Besides, cold water tipped into an overheated stomach can cause severe cramps. It is recorded of Pierre Brambilla (who tracked Robic over the Izoard in 1947 and came third to him in Paris) that he was powerfully resistant to thirst, although he fought some chronic battles with the demon *Soif* . . . verbal duels with his own faltering will. His dessicated body weakening, he'd cry out in a parched voice: *Tu vas avancer, vieille carcasse. Ah, tu ne veux pas. Eh bien, tu ne boiras pas.* Like St Antony in the desert, wrestling with temptation. 'Get going you bag of bones. You don't want to? All right, no drink for you.'

One day in the Canicule, the torrid Dog Days of July, dry as a water biscuit, Brambilla cracked. Spotting a roadside fountain, he drank his fill in great gulps, then topped up his water bottles and remounted. He abandoned 10km further on. He never raced again and, to avoid any temptation to revoke the decision, he buried his bike in his garden. He did come back, though. When Jock Wadley rode the bi-annual Brevet des Randonneurs des Alpes time-trial in 1973 (from Grenoble over the Glandon, Croix de Fer, Télégraphe, Galibier and back to Grenoble, 245km and 4,500m of climbing) Brambilla was also entered. They were old buddies from Wadley's Tour reporting and met in Grenoble the day before the start. The race began at 2 a.m.; Brambilla caught Wadley on the approach to the Galibier. Wadley thought the Italian veteran (now 53 years old) would have been miles ahead, but he'd overslept and set out an hour late. He offered to give Wadley a tow up the Galibier; Wadley declined and Brambilla flew off. Wadley remembered the buried bicycle story and called out, but too late . . . the chance to confirm or scotch missed.

Jacques Anquetil once said: 'Driest is fastest.' And, like T.E. Lawrence, trained himself to survive on small intakes of water. He was frequently beaten on open stages; in five Tour victories he won only 15 stages. His abiding principle was to conserve every scrap of energy until he needed to make an emphatic push. The pictures of him out of the saddle show eyes glinting, body arched with effort, as if all the hounds of hell are chasing him. But he was a supreme strategist. Had victory in the Tour been more dependant on climbing than his speciality, the individual time-trial, experts agree that Anquetil would have made himself a climber.

He wasn't above professional cunning, either. Two seconds down on a Bahamontes in roaring form in the mountains during the '63 Tour, Anquetil's team manager, Géminiani, told him to ride one stage on a lighter bike than usual with lower gears. The race crossed the col de la Forclaz that day, close to the finish in Chamonix – a perfect launch pad for the Eagle of Toledo's *coup de maître*. However, since the descent was narrow and steep, Anquetil would have to change back to the heavier, more rigid bike for safety.

'But changing bikes is forbidden.'

'Leave that to me,' said Gém.

They rode to the foot of the Forclaz into rain and a headwind. Poulidor, who didn't know the climb, launched another furious attack but he blew and was soon zigzagging over the road. Anquetil stuck to Bahamontes, who varied his rhythm constantly to disrupt the Frenchman: dancing on the pedals, a cruel surge of speed, back in the saddle for a steady drive . . . he was giving Anquetil a real pasting.

At the summit, Anquetil glanced at Gém in the team car. Prearranged: he stopped riding, got off the bike and called out: 'My *dérailleur's* gone.'

Out leapt the team mechanic with the replacement bike, Gém signalled to the commissaire to verify the mechanical failure. Meantime, Anquetil was off down the mountain in pursuit. The commissaire checked the bike: the cable was indeed broken . . . snipped through, actually, by the mechanic. The trick was obvious but there was no proof. The following year a new rule came in: bike changes were permissible.

Anquetil had weaknesses, all riders do, but he never gave in. A day lost was never the campaign lost. His constant rival Poulidor, the gadfly who never metamorphosed into the stinging *maillot jaune* bee, famously beat him in a *coude à coude* duel up the Puy de Dôme on 13 July 1964. (A blunt tooth of volcanic rock, 1,465m high, 5km of 1 in 14 gradient, a level stretch and the last 5km of one in eight; the road ends at the top.)

'Elbow to elbow' it was too. The pugnacity, the hostility starkly evident in the photograph. Locked in a bitter contest, shoulders bumping as if each was trying to knock the other sprawling, bikes flung sideways, front wheels all but touching at the base and tipped sideways in a vee, like two haunches of a log split by an axe. Both of them in the saddle, at the limit, Anquetil in yellow, his cheeks sucked in, gasping for air, Poulidor holding the brakehoods as if they were the traces of Pluto's chariot, a flotilla of motorbikes and cars in attendance.

'France holds its breath.'

Anquetil snapped first, and at that level a jingle of the chain on a less than smooth gear change can turn the affair – momentary lapse of concentration, your opponent pounces, a gap opens, precious advantage. Poulidor went clear and won by 42 seconds. Anquetil held his overall lead by a slim 14 seconds. He'd already won four Tours; no one had ever won five. Next day, Bastille Day, final stage into Paris: the time-trial. The *maillot jaune* always sets off last.

Anquetil, crouched over the bike, the best possible position for streamlining, total absorption in the task: the beating of Poulidor and finish the job . . . dispatch the victim. A bird of prey, they called him. Worth remembering that the raptors eat their prey alive, tear them to bits still breathing; there's no merciful stunning and oblivion before the talons go in. Anquetil, riding the race he excelled in and relished because it released his killer instinct, that capacity to drive himself way beyond ordinary limits, a combination of impregnable self-belief and indifference to physical distress heightened by the fact that it was Poupou just ahead of him. Anquetil tore 41 seconds out of Poulidor – at that level a cruel margin, especially given Poulidor's undeniable class except that his effort seemed hampered by that crucial inability to exceed his natural limits. A failure, if failure it was, in imagination.

He did beat Anquetil in the individual time-trial in 1966; but Anquetil turned a deaf ear, as they say, to defeat. He set up his young lieutenant, Lucien Aimar, for victory in Paris. Everything – anything – to beat Poulidor.

In one one-day classic, an English rider, Robinson, team-mate of Anquetil's, rode up alongside Jacques and told his boss: '[Tommy] Simpson is looking good today. I know him. All you need to do is follow him and you'll have nothing to worry about.'

Anquetil replied: 'Forget Simpson: keep your eyes on Poulidor.'

It is my belief that Anquetil, knowing full well that Poulidor possessed a killer punch, despised him, as a rider at least, for lacking the moral capacity to deliver it at will. Despising him as a rival, he revealed just how much he feared him; perhaps the only rider he truly feared because defeat cost him so dear, and at the hands of Poulidor it was insupportable.

We roll out at about 9.30 a.m. and do a mini sightseeing tour of the suburbs in quest of the route to the col. The air is damp and chilly, as in a coalhouse. I am, this dank morning, about as yeasty as a matzo, musing Izoard . . . Izoard . . . eez so ard . . . bloody hell, and feeling hopelessly of another race entirely from the various aerial wizards who've soared up this one.

The Breton Jean-Marie Goasmat, '*Farfadet*', 'Goblin', in his element here . . . Charly Gaul the Angel cruising up the slopes, whistling happily like a thrush . . . Federico Bahamontes the Eagle of Toledo dancing on his pedals as if they were springs . . . Coppi the heron . . . Van Impe the canary.

I saw Van Impe once, at the Worlds in Belgium, 1975. The race went to Hennie Kuiper who broke from the pack two or three laps from the end and profited from the hesitations of the big men who'd rather let a small rival win than risk towing one of the *peloton* grandees to the line for an easy sprint. As we straggled across the dusty road after the race, Van Impe and Merckx rode by, Van Impe impassive, Merckx a wry expression on his face – *not our day*. Their faces brown with filthy spindrift off the circuit, tired, off for a bath, work done. Next year Merckx missed the Tour, but Van Impe came determined to swap the polka dots he'd won three times ('71, '72, '75) for the yellow. It was a big leap of imagination for the diminutive Belgian climber but Guimard, his manager, was convinced he could do it. So was Mme Van Impe. According to Geoffrey Nicholson in his book *The Great Bike Race*, when Van Impe's team-mate Tierlinck beat him to become Belgian champion in 1976, Mme Van Impe said: 'Lucien, I'm not having that: you'll have to win the Tour.' He took the yellow jersey from Maertens on l'Alpe d'Huez, lost it to the 33-year-old Delisle in the Pyrenees three days later and set out from St Gaudens two minutes 41 seconds in arrears and leading the Mountains Prize by a whisker.

It was 139km to Saint Lary-Soulan over two second-category climbs and two first. Over the col de Menté, Van Impe took the *prime*, but in the valley towards Bosost across the Spanish border a break went clear, none of the riders in contention for anything beyond a stage win; Ocaña chases for the honour of Spain and takes four men with him, including Maertens the sprinter who has swapped the yellow for the green of the Points Leader. At Bosost, the escape of 16 men leads the *peloton* by two minutes and 40 seconds. Van Impe had been acting up, pretending he's going badly and wanting more support from his team. He's got the idea that it would be best to wait for the last climb of the day, up Pla d'Adet to the finish. Zoetemelk and Poulidor, riding for the Gan-Mercier team, spotted his indecision and decided they could hot things up. One of Van Impe's team-mates got wind of this and told Van Impe to be on the alert. Van Impe wanted his rivals to burn themselves up with some aggressive riding: all he would have to do was sit in and pick up a tally of seconds, even a minute, at the end when he was still fresh. Guimard had other plans. He wanted a grand gesture, minutes in the bag not paltry scrapings from what other riders left him. He sent a message to Van Impe, via one of the *domestiques,* to have a crack now. Van Impe wasn't impressed; if Guimard wanted him to attack he could deliver his own messages. Ocaña flew off ahead; Van Impe paid no heed. Guimard raced up the *peloton* in the team car, klaxon blaring, alongside Van Impe and told him to go. Go now, you win the Tour, and if not *not.*

Out of Bosost, on to the col du Portillon, a long wind up through pine woods to the French border along the ridge, Van Impe attacked. He might have been reluctant to accept the command but there is no questioning his will to make the effort succeed, and this is his terrain, after all. Up ahead, Ocaña topped the climb with Van Impe four minutes and 20 seconds down and the *peloton* – Poulidor and Zoetemelk for the GAN team, Delisle and his team leader Thévenet among them – at five minutes 50 seconds. The Portillon drops down the helter-skelter into Bagnères de Luchon, a beautiful old spa town, the thermal baths still in working order, a low-roofed, arcaded building in a leafy square of tree-lined walks. The col de Peyresourde leads straight out on the west side, climbing from 630m to 1,569m in 14km.

At the col, Van Impe had caught Ocaña and Riccomi and the trio led the race; the escape group had fragmented, riders scattered down the slopes behind them; the first, Talbourdet and Menendez at 55 seconds.

Zoetemelk, meanwhile, having been told by his manager to attack near Bosost, refused; a defining moment. On the Peyresourde he mastered his caution and, finally, got moving. He was a rider of undoubted talent but never a great shaker of events, what the French call a man who never catches the sun because he's riding in other men's shadows. He produced a bold ride up the col and crossed two minutes and 25 seconds down on Ocaña and Van Impe, but the day was lost. Van Impe made the attack he planned all along and streaked into Pla d'Adet on his own. The seconds, the minutes ticked by, Delisle's lead evaporated, Van Impe pulled on yellow and, three minutes and 12 seconds after he did, Zoetemelk appeared. He had lost this Tour. His victory came in 1980, at his tenth attempt, aged 33. French commentators were disparaging. *Le Blaireau* wasn't riding; Zoetemelk's win was no more than a bit of insulation between the solid walls of Hinault's supremacy.

Over the following 46 minutes and 23 seconds, the rest of the field limped in: Poulidor is in fifth overall now and by over 11 minutes, Thévenet at 13 minutes 15 seconds, but his strength was waning – a crippling year of social engagements as Tour winner which the naive country boy wouldn't refuse – and he will abandon five days later after a disastrous time-trial. He had been riding on his strength alone for some time and there was not much left.

Van Impe held his lead and took the yellow jersey home to Mme Van Impe in Belgium. It was Poulidor's last Tour. Aged 40 he came third, once more the best-placed Frenchman. He'd come back from 19th in the '75 edition, his worst-ever placing.

At the conclusion of this Tour, Poulidor had a road named after him in Sauviat-sur-Vige, near his birthplace, where M. Marquet who owned the local bike shop gave the poor farmboy his first racing bicycle to replace his mother's old sit-up-and-beg which he'd been making do with, and ferried him to his first races in his car. He always acknowledged the genius of Anquetil but the telling factor between them was perhaps that Anquetil could support any suffering on a bike to stay number one. Anquetil said: 'Together we could have produced some incredible results but it wasn't possible: our interests were opposed and the public wouldn't have understood.' A plan to unite them in the Gan-Mercier team for Anquetil's last season, 1969, fell through. Anquetil became a television commentator. One day, his five-year-old daughter asked to go to a race with him so that she could meet her favourite rider.

'Which?' said Jacques. 'Poulidor, of course. He's the best.'

The year following Anquetil's last Tour, 1967, the Norman said to Poulidor: 'You know, Raymond, it would give me pleasure to see you win the Tour. To make sure of it, you mustn't let them take more than four minutes in the Pyrenees.' Sadly, the early fall in Alsace meant that by the time the Tour arrived in the Pyrenees, Poulidor's race was devoted to Roger Pingeon. But Poulidor had lost his old verve; resigned to yet another defeat for himself and, worn down by his stupendous riding in the Alps, he seemed incapable of any more and hesitant to boot. Pingeon left him to it; on the descent from Portet d'Aspet, Poulidor crashed into a police motorbike and fell badly. He rode out the stage but he was too badly injured, his nose was broken, and he retired declaring that without him the Tour would go on.

Something of an eccentric, Pingeon. He rarely declined an interview but insisted on being in the bath when he gave it, so as not to waste time, and occluded every single source of daylight in his hotel room and slept in a blindfold to ensure that no daylight disturbed his sleep. He reckoned that an extra half an hour each night gave him three night's extra sleep over the duration of the Tour. In the 1974 Tour he was leading the pack together with Ronald de Witte. Nearing Dieppe, de Witte decided the break was doomed and sat up. Pingeon flipped, got off his bike, kicked it and walked out of the Tour. (That year saw the Tour come to Britain for the first time – a stage near Plymouth.)

Thévenet came back for the '77 Tour in much better shape, drove himself into the ground to ride Hennie Kuiper off his wheel up l'Alpe d'Huez and got a tremendous ovation at the finish. He went on to his second victory. He said that two moments stood out in his career: that welcome on l'Alpe d'Huez and finishing at the summit of the Izoard on his own, in the yellow jersey, especially the last 3km when he was riding through a dense crowd of spectators.

★

I am already pulling ahead up the first slopes of the long haul to the Izoard when John pulls up alongside. I am ready to say 'Listen, you know very well I simply can't hack that brand of mineral water,' when he says: 'Nearest place for a drink?'

I say 'Fine' and he drops back to rejoin Angela, her aching knee strapped up with a woollen scarf. I turn, wave, and push on, wheezing as if my lungs were stuffed full of Copydex glue.

It continues to be damp, threatening rain. This southern approach imposes some 22km climbing from 1,321m to 2,360m. Ostensibly, a steady climb, but we know better now. The Glandon factor. Northward along the ridges, along which the grey clouds roll like vapourised cannonballs, looms the Sommet des Anges, among them Charly Gaul, no doubt. There is a Musée de Vélo at the summit. Postcards.

About halfway, the hamlet of Cervières with its fifteenth-century church dedicated to St Michel all that survived the destruction of the old village in 1944. The Germans moved several divisions into the Dauphiné to stamp out resistance, a ruthless campaign prosecuted until just before the end of the war. Centuries before Hitler's Germans came, their ancestors, the Teutons, were slaughtered by the world's first professional army: the Roman legions led by Marius. *Plus ça change* . . . Napoleon . . .

At Cervières, the road doubles back on itself, a real French pleat. And the rain starts, borne on a flukey wind. Only one hard spat of gradient so far; the worst to come, doubtless. Into an open stretch of country, the forest barricades pushed back across empty grassland. Headwind; 200m bent over the front stem and I am into the tree cover again. Two more steep sections which I take in my stride. Le Laus, a handful of houses about 16km away; well over halfway on the map. From the road I'd hardly guess it. The kilometre stones pass in ultra-slow motion in my imaginary record of the long grind to the top; the film where nothing much happens. Me thinking: oh for an hour to ride like Merckx, even 20 minutes, just to feel what it's like. But, I know from my imagination: the same effort, the same grisly sick feeling; the only difference, I'd be moving a whole lot faster.

It's not only talent, either, but mileage. The year he won the Worlds, Freddy Maertens habitually cycled up to a hundred miles to a day race, then raced – 60 miles or so, and not infrequently rode part of the way back. At the time, an insular rump of the English professionals were grumbling that they stood no chance in the Worlds because they didn't get enough racing mileage.

I think of my younger self; that day we cycled through the Ardennes (I was 14) over what the masters told us was the highest climb in the chain. I had an old Coventry Eagle, passed on to me by a distant relation who hadn't ridden it for years. He told me it was the lightest bike you could buy. It was not, however, the lightest bike you could palm off on a gullible kid, short of a loaded butcher's bike. It took me some years to grow into it, and by the time I could ride it, the Coventry Eagle was an extinct species. Most of the others in the party owned flying machines from a new generation; one in particular, Perkins, two years older than the rest of us, was a pretty sharp Club cyclist, handbuilt frame, alloy everything; lugs.

I found myself in the lead on the big climb and reached the top, none of the others in sight. I sat down contentedly under a tree to wait. Twenty minutes later, the first of the following group hove into view – the two masters with them – on foot. The dribs and drabs straggled in. When Perkins found out I'd ridden the whole climb, he was furious. He unstrapped his saddle bag and, while the others flopped on the grass in a boiled pink state of sweat and despondency, cycled back halfway down the climb and rode up it without dismounting.

The closest I ever got, I think, to where the dream is stitched into reality.

The rain becomes snow. The climb gets harder. I've got to get this mountain out of my head. *Rien n'est extrême qui a son pareil*, as Montaigne put it, in the era AV, *Avant Vélo* . . . 'Nothing is extreme which has its equal.' It is finally a matter of perspective out of experience; and patience. If I push myself too far, I'll be the first to know.

A sign nailed to a post: Réfuge de Napoléon; one of the Alpine hostels set up by him and confirmed in state ownership by decree in the 1860s. I know it to be just below the col. Another bend, and another bend and there's the building set back from the road. Hard to say whether it's open or not. The road swings by it and up, nothing visible but banks of squalid salt-white mountain emitting dry ice. I set my teeth and forge on. I want this whole climb in one.

Another kilometre, another stone and still no col. The gradient nearly defeats me, steep as a ladder it feels. I stay in the saddle, saving the last resort till I have no choice. My eyes ache with the strain; but at last I make it to the midget plateau which is the summit of the Izoard.

Half a blizzard, sky merging with mountain in a spectrum of frost. The Museum, a square shack has windows boarded up, probably shut since the end of summer. Opposite stands a large stone obelisk, a monument to a Tour which hardly needs one, but here is as good a place as any.

We meet up in the Refuge and an hour after omelettes, apple pie, hot chocolate and coffee are on our way down to the Casse Déserte. If there are ghosts anywhere on the Tour de France's tangled ley lines, they certainly hold their sabbaths in the Casse Déserte, lit by red Jack o'Lanterns. (The red lamp, *lanterne rouge*, is fixed to the seat pillar of the last rider in the race.) It's an eerie sight, an apparition to set the nape hairs tingling, as the prospective opens out below the falling road. Across birdless chasms, a massive rampart of rock leaning like a seawall, its slopes thick with scree. Midway down it, the road is scored across like a white Schläger scar. Below the road tower the weird rock stacks, a petrified dental template – gaunt worn molars moored in crumbling gums. On these gigantic stalagmites you imagine eagles perch or vultures or the phantoms of Desgrange's commissaires, keeping watch for the dying things crawling away from the merciless sun's glare . . . the puncture victims making illicit use of the clasp knife . . . the standing stones of the Casse Déserte make an awesome sight. The panorama that suddenly opens out as you round the bend on the descent quite moved and bewitched me.

It is hostile; there is danger in it; the immanent menace of a mountain waiting to unleash its worst temper. A dragon asleep, they'd have said once. It exemplifies the unique challenge of the mountains to the riders who compete in this great race. (Women, too: the Tour de France Feminin was inaugurated in 1984.) No matter what physical preparation they undertake, the awesome scale of the high cols interposes a huge psychological barrier for which no preparation is of any use, other than the experience itself. Riding up these ascents cannot be contained by statistics. Boardman, under the direction of his technical advisor, tried it: training on the treadmill, an hour of one in eight on a calculated gear development and at so many revolutions per minute. Better than nothing, but the mountains have a way of dealing with that. They instil an elemental fear, in torrid heat or biting cold and the Izoard, weird and remote, embodies that fear totally.

Even as we cycle down through that bizarre rockscape in freezing vapours, I sense that the Alp was shifting into its murky winter cruelties of which the precocious snow and mist we had ridden through was no more than a flurry. I say precocious though in the 1995 Tour, the stage over the Galibier had to be shortened because the col was snowed in, impassable, in July.

At the side of the road, not far from where Coppi watched Bobet ride past, stands a tiny belvedere and a monument to both of them. We stop for a photograph more in homage than wannabe.

Comparisons are impossible. I'm sure the ghosts compare times and squabble about how hard it was in their day, but even Merckx smiles after the last competition number is peeled off. Of Rominger's shattering of the hour record, he said with fulsome generosity: 'Seeing Tony today, I suddenly felt that I was a very, very minor rider. To achieve such a mark at sea level . . . I take my hat off to him.' *Chapeau.* Merckx achieved his own hour record on a titanium frame, tyres inflated with helium, in Mexico City, 1972. Sixty minutes, as he described it, of 'continuous battle with pain' for 49.431km. He said afterwards: 'That's not the sort of thing anyone does twice.' In October 1994, in a warm-up ride on an ordinary bike, Rominger covered 53.832km; two weeks later on a special bike he rode 55.291km. In some ways it was a surprise. Rominger's *palmarès* include the Giro and the Vuelta and he is a noted time-trialler, but this World Record seemed to come more as an afterthought to his career than its ultimate goal; even as a counterbalance to the major disappointment, that of not winning the Tour de France. His threat to Indurain in the Tour was probably the most serious on at least one occasion; it never materialised; perhaps through an uncertainty of morale. Indurain who had beaten him in four Tours de France, pushed the hour distance to 55.040km. Rominger's reply was decisive, at last.

In 1996, Boardman, erstwhile holder of the record, set an astonishing new mark of 56.375km to regain it. The week before, he'd beaten the world record for the 5km Individual Pursuit. This egregious double was totally ignored by most English newspapers.

Occasionally I glance behind me; we are going down what the Tour most usually comes up. Impossible to gauge its difficulty against the way we have ridden. It's hard work, the road is slippery, I'm frozen and wet, the brakes are on non-stop.

Guillestre: one of the stations where English prisoners of the Napoleonic wars were interned. Hot baths, full laundry session, a walk round the town; the church with a sundial on its exterior wall (the local vogue) . . . *Tempus fugit – Horas non numero nisi serenas*; a back garden where vegetables are interspersed with flowers to ward off pestiferous insects reminds me of Monet's garden in Giverny where the flowers grow in strips like vegetables.

John and Angela have set their sights on Corsica: a week in the sun to restore. Over the col de la Bonnette, 2,802m, and a delicious long descent into Nice to catch the ferry.

'Bit hilly,' says Angela.

'You'll hardly notice after this lot. Piece of cake.'

'No cols.'

'Sadly, no.'

'You concerned about your reputation, John?'

'No, just looking for a bit of excitement.'

'You can always get lost up a goat track at night and wait for Corsican bandits.'

'Don't encourage him, he *will*.'

As it turned out, the Bonnette was closed and they didn't make it to Corsica. They were lucky. I heard from friends who happened to be on the island that week that the weather was unspeakable.

CHAPTER SIX

COL DE VARS

Drugs in the Sport

If you didn't actually see it you'd never believe the amazing courage of these young men who ride 1,500km in four stages through mud, completely drenched with rain from the sky and puddles in the road. Wind, storm, hail, snow, biting cold cannot stop them. They wear bits of sacking or canvas in a vain attempt to keep the wet off. Whenever they get off their bikes, in next to no time their feet turn into lumps of murky yellow mud, treacherous mud that seeps in everywhere, even through the most resistant shorts, and scrapes the skin like emery paper.

So wrote Marcel Violette in 1909.

We're having it easy in comparison. Nor are we experiencing the depth of oxygen debt that racing exacts on the high climbs, the speeding heart rate, 180 to 200 beats per minute – Stephen Roche at the limit on the climb to La Plagne in 1987, to keep in touch with Pedro Delgado; not only hung on, he very nearly caught him, but the strain of the chase meant they had to haul him straight off the bike to give him oxygen.

As I gaze out of the window, first thing, the sky shows a band of swimming-pool blue above the mountains to the south, which, in topologies of piety, is the side of the *spirits made just*. Northwards dwell the faithless, barbarian no-hopers, Teuton scallywags, Tungrian bugaboos. Above the blue streamers of hope in a bright day hangs a dismal pall of gunpowder-black cloud: smoke from the Devil's chimneys. Even as I watch, the satanic cloud sinks; the blue droops and is squeezed out. Rain it will be. Odin's dog pack gathering for the hunt through the stormfields and cloudbrakes. What comfort? Remember Elihu the Buzite endeavouring to cheer up Job. 'Look unto the heavens and see; and behold the clouds which are higher than thou.' (Job xxxv; 5)

And Job saying: 'So?'

Today we part company and do so, inauspiciously somehow, outside the bank. John's front brake cable shears on the way there from the hotel and I emerge to find him rooting out a replacement from his repair kit. Maybe this is the moment to go; no ceremony.

'You won't have to wait for us at the top of the cols any more,' says Angela.

'Ah, but I'll miss your company.'

I give her a hug. John switches the spare cable into his left hand and we shake hands.

'Enjoy Corsica,' I said.

At the bar in Valloire, Angela had suggested I write something for the wind quintet she plays in. I store the idea, uncertain about it one way or another; but of course I will have to come up with something. Such ideas, like mountains, do not go away.

Angela's slightly bandy-legged riding style reminds me of Greg Lemond, another knees-out cyclist. Fine rider, triple Tour winner, twice World Road Race champion, he made no secret of being intent only on victory in the Tour de France; lesser races didn't interest him, hardly even the classics which are the salients of the continental racing season. He started a trend which degrades the sport. There are now two divisions of cycle racing: the men who concentrate on the Tour and nothing else and the real pros who honour the tradition of the sport. Thus Jean-Marie Leblanc, one of the Tour organisers, expressed the opinion that on the eve of the 1998 Tour, Ullrich could hardly be considered the favourite to repeat his 1997 victory. Ullrich's total failure to respect the dictates of his professional duty – putting on some eight kilos over the winter to reappear for spring training bloated and utterly out of athletic shape – was a disgrace. His early-season record was miserable; the example he set tawdry. In the not-so-distant past, racing cyclists felt an obligation to take the whole calendar of races seriously. It is partly the fault of the sponsors who encourage their big stars to expend energy only on the main chance and to use many other races as training rides, pulling out after a few stages if that suits them.

Indeed, Merckx criticised Lemond on this very point: for lack of generosity with his exceptional talent. Lemond, answering back, slights Merckx for being envious of him because his brand of bikes sells better than Merckx's. Hoo ha. Of course the Continentals did not understand the totally self-absorbed American who appeared to find his team-mates a nuisance and retired to his camper van every night to be with his wife, whereas the orthodox rule is for a celibate Tour . . . *sexe coupe les jambes.* Kelly said he abstained for some six weeks before the Tour. (Semen is a valuable repository of vitamins.) Desgrange's credo was simple: total commitment to the bike during the season; and, since men needed sex, self-denial of sex was the truest test of supreme willpower.

Lemond was, moreover, on record as saying that the *peloton* these days is full of riders as good as Merckx and, as if that weren't preposterous enough, claimed that the only reason why Merckx had the success he enjoyed was because he spent the entire preseason period in preparation. Well, now. Lemond always did talk a good race, before and after the event.

That Merckx was prodigiously generous with his talent cannot be refuted. His record of seven wins in the spring classic, Milan–San Remo, is unique anyway, but the very fact that Merckx was winning at the start of the year with a gruelling calendar of races ahead is astounding. That and a punishing round of winter track meetings . . .

But Lemond suffered a lonely and ignominious end. The acknowledged leader of the GAN team at the beginning of the 1994 Tour, he was soon in trouble and was clearly not going to make Paris. A team leader has always been allowed the singular privilege of abandoning into the team car, rather than the broom wagon – it has a besom tied to the back – which sweeps up the lesser riders. When Lemond's Tour seized, he underwent the indignity of being placed in the wagon; the team had a new leader, it seemed

(Boardman), and not sufficient loyalty left over to accommodate the old one at his demise. He didn't deserve that.

Lemond had made an astonishing return to pro racing after a gunshot accident in 1987 which very nearly finished his life, let alone his career. It was a painful, slow, morally punishing, often debilitating return to fitness and the form and ability to contend with the best. By 1989, he was showing some sign of his original class, but in the Giro that year – always Merckx's preferred ride to prepare for the Tour – he was dropped on the relatively simple climb to Mount Etna and lost eight minutes. He was going badly; he seemed to be out of the hunt. However, in the time-trial – always his speciality – he came second and, he said, it marked the turning point.

A month or so later, he lay second in the Tour and set off on the final time-trial into Paris; flying down the ramp, he passed Fignon, in yellow by 50 seconds, warming up on the road, waiting his turn. The 24.5km from Versailles to the Champs-Elysées offered no better than an extreme outside chance of making up the deficit. A Frenchman would, it seemed, win the Tour in this year of years: bicentenary of the fall of the Bastille, prologue to the French Revolution. Fignon, riding with saddle boils, could hardly bear to sit down. (To ease that excruciating pain and discomfort, Zoetemelk put raw steak inside his shorts.) But, the man with the reputation for foul temper nobly advanced none of the excuses he might have made. One can barely surmise the anguish which afflicted him when he came to stand on the podium alongside Lemond, having conceded victory by the narrowest margin ever: eight measly seconds. As for Lemond, he added gold in Chambéry that autumn in the Worlds. It was, truly, a stupendous return. Had he matched his outstanding athletic prowess and hardness of ambition with anything approaching a grace of disposition, I'd think better of him.

'Strange people, bike riders,' said Anquetil. 'They imagine a racing bike is made for going quickly. They're wrong: a racing bike is made solely for winning races.'

At the very start of his career, and no more than a highly promising beginner, he was given this advice by the veteran journalist Alex Virot: 'Young man, listen: if you concentrate on making money you'll lose races; if you concentrate on winning races you'll make money.'

Good counsel for much else besides bike racing. Alas, Virot didn't live to witness the accuracy of his wisdom. On Anquetil's first Tour, 1957, Virot and his motorbike driver René Wagner plunged off the road on a Pyrenean descent and were killed.

The Dog Day sun blazed infernally that summer and the tar melted on the roads. Bobet wasn't there and the 23-year-old Anquetil had to overcome a bout of dysentery and the shattering challenge in the mountains of the powerhouse, Gastone Nencini, to win in Paris.

It was 1957 that saw the Tour riders wearing jerseys plastered in commercial advertising. Teams had hitherto been sponsored exclusively by cycle manufacturers but that support had dwindled and more or less petered out. A new injection of finance was needed and Raphaël Géminiani, who'd come second to Koblet by 22 seconds in 1951, convinced advertisers from a variety of other trading marques that the Tour offered a fantastic marketing opportunity; the *peloton* might be a travelling billboard covering 4,000km of French roads, observed, what is more, (since 1952) on daily televised reports of race action. They bought it. On their team jersey, Gém and Anquetil sported an affiche for the aperitif St-Raphaël, the aperitif of France (plus quinine), whose faded mural adverts still cling to many a French roadside building in faded flaking paint. The range of advertisers was wide: food stores (Potin), ice-cream makers (Miko), brewers (Kas, Pelforth, Stella), insurance brokers (GAN), coffee-machine manufacturers (Faema), *charcutiers* (Molteni), car factories (Peugeot, Ford), tyre manufacturers (Hutchinson), cigarette brands (Gitane), as well as a rump of bike firms who saw a new boost in the Tour commercial (Bianchi, Campagnolo, Flandria) . . . Many other sponsors followed.

In 1958, Anquetil abandoned with severe stomach cramps – intestinal infarction. The remaining French leaders were beyond their peak: neither Bobet nor Gém had the legs any longer and Charly Gaul left them gasping, his supple turning of the cranks like a *perpetuum mobile*. His majestic conquest of Mont Ventoux was televised live; the storms raged over the Chartreuse Massif but nothing could stop him.

In 1960, the Frenchman Roger Rivière, aged 24, came to the
Tour as double World Pursuit Champion and holder of the hour
record. In 1956, Anquetil had set 46.159km; three months later,
Ercole Baldini topped that by 234m. A year later, the 21-year-old
Rivière stepped on to the track, mounted his bike and set off,
turning the classic 52x15 gearing deployed by Coppi in 1942
when he extended the Frenchman Archambaud's 1937 mark of
45.840km by 31m.

At the side of the track stood Coppi himself, the maestro
encouraging the young pretender. Rivière scorched off at a
perilously fast pace: the first 5km in six minutes and 15 seconds,
nearly 50kph. He held the speed, flagging briefly – 40km at an
average of 47kph – to finish at 46.923km, a staggering improvement of 530m. A year on, he pushed that record to a mammoth
47.346km. Now, bagful of promise, he began his first, and last,
Tour.

Leader of the French team, he took the first time-trial stage in
Brussels, the flat stage into Lorient and opened his account in the
Pyrenees with a win at Pau. Healthily placed, a minute and 38
seconds behind Nencini, he was descending the col du Perjuret,
crashed, fell 20m into a ravine and broke his back. He was
crippled and died 16 years later. It was an apalling tragedy; what
dark sadness overhung Nencini's only victory.

The Pyrenees claimed another victim in the 1995 Tour: the
young Italian Olympic gold medallist of 1992, Fabio Casartelli.
Virenque, horribly unaware of what had happened, was already
way out ahead, riding to a courageous all-day solo win. Next day,
in muted tribute, the entire *peloton* rode the stage in a bunch, at
a pedestrian crawl, a punishing ride in torrid heat – many riders
abandoned – and, at the finish, Casartelli's Motorola team led in
the cortège. The riders donated all the *primes* for the stage to
Casartelli's widow; the Tour officials matched the total from
their own coffers. In what other sport . . . ? It was a moving
testimony to this extraordinary fraternity of cycling, even in the
ranks of the race-hardened professionals. Save that Rijs called the
truce on racing an absurd and inappropriate memorial, if that's
what it was, to a man who had dedicated his short life to racing.
He added that it gave Indurain time to recover and that had he

not had the respite he'd have lost the Tour that year, to Rijs.

Casartelli had pitched headfirst into a wickedly sharp-edged granite bollard marking the verge. The stone, like the blade on an axe, split open his skull and he died soon after. No helmet could have saved him. The frail mortal frame of the human body mounted on a flimsy racing bike rides a precipice of danger in head-over-heels descents at breakneck speeds on surfaces often skiddy with stones, a slick of wet, the camber uneven and treacherous, always with the hurricane of competition blowing from behind.

Simpson crashed once, tumbled down an embankment and crawled back up to find his bike, apparently undamaged, lodged in a tree. He pulled it out of the branches, remounted and set off down the descent only to find that the crash had, in fact, compacted the front forks so that the bike was now too small and a brute to control.

The Tour officials tried to impose the obligatory wearing of helmets some years ago. The riders protested. In the mountains, especially under a baking sun, even the latest aerated designs of crash-hat were intolerably uncomfortable, even if they didn't cook the brains. Fines were imposed. The riders held out. The helmet law was repealed.

An early proponent of helmets was Jean Robic, the 1947 winner whom the Italian *tifosi* nicknamed 'Glass Head'. He was endlessly prone to falls, ancestor to the vulnerable Alex Zülle, whose new Festina boss reckons that it's his posture on an ill-fitting bike which makes him come off it so easily. Robic turned up for the 1953 Tour with a white rubber helmet, a sophisticated version of the string-of-sausages hat he'd previously worn. This occasioned much hilarity and mirth, to Robic's extreme irritation. Furious, he proffered François Mahé a screwdriver and said: 'Go on, whack me on the head with the handle. Give it everything you've got.'

Mahé needed no persuasion and gave Robic a sound thump. Robic swayed around a bit and said: 'See? Completely resistant.' And walked off with a trickle of blood running down his nose from a split in his head.

On that Tour, Koblet fell on the col du Soulor in the Pyrenees,

Robic went down in the Fauremont and the race was left to the other Bretons. Mahé passed the yellow jersey to Mallejac who gave it up to Bobet after his solo exploit through the Casse Déserte.

'This is a tough profession,' said Anquetil, 'and we're not in it for pleasure; it is hard and dangerous; we risk our health for many reasons. I consider myself a professional: I do my job, just like anyone going to an office or a factory.' His career spanned 16 years and his great successes came in the big Tours: first Frenchman to win the Giro d'Italia, 1960; five Tours de France and the Giro–Tour double, 1964; Spanish Vuelta, 1963; five Paris–Nice, first stage race of the season, the 'race to the sun'. His great expertise was in the time-trial and he won the only classic race against the clock, the Grand Prix des Nations, a record nine times. From the other one-day classics, he stayed clear; he called them lotteries, not races. It was a judgement tailored by defeat. He trained hard for the 1958 Paris–Roubaix, punctured 12km, from the finish and never bothered again, though he won the Ghent–Wevelgem in 1964 and, in 1966, the Liège–Bastogne–Liège by a hefty five minutes. He held the hour record twice.

Rivière had beaten his first mark by some 1.2km and it was Géminiani, now his sporting director, who persuaded him back onto the track in 1967. (Gém it was who had prompted the 'stupid bet' on the Bordeaux–Paris immediately after the Critérium Dauphiné Libéré.) Anquetil was reluctant. Gém knew his man, however. 'Your name is Jacques Anquetil,' he said, goading that prickly Norman pride and, 11 years after the first record, Anquetil, now 33 years old, turning a massive 52x13, rode 47.493km, almost 347m further than Rivière. He presented the record-breaking bike to Jeanine, wife of his doctor and his own – as they say – 'constant companion'. She eventually left her husband for Jacques.

After the record ride, Anquetil failed to turn up for the routine dope test within five hours – stipulated by the sport's ruling body – and instead went home. He eventually pitched up to a local doctor in Normandy some two days later. His record was, therefore, not ratified, although his supporters claimed that, since he'd ridden under the same lax conditions as Rivière, the time should be allowed to stand. Compromises were proposed –

records with and without drugs control – all to little avail in Anquetil's case. Ferdinand Bracke beat his record a month later *and* produced his bottle of urine on time.

Anquetil's last Tour – 1966 – ended in retirement on the côte de Serrière in the Ardeche; once more a stomach infection. Beaten by Poulidor in the time-trial at Vals les Bains, Anquetil knew he was done but held on and abandoned only when he had ensured the victory of his protégé Lucien Aimar over the old foe, Raymond. Three years later, Eddy Merckx burst on to the scene, beat Poulidor into second place *again* – a new *bête noire* dogging the luckless Poupou – and Anquetil into third on the Paris–Nice. True, the *maître* did beat Merckx in a post-Tour track omnium, but it was over. Anquetil quit racing altogether, saying that he'd rather give up before the strain of combining an indulgent life style *and* racing killed him. The cycling must never be allowed to inhibit his gourmanderie. Just after he turned pro, he polished off a whole lobster in white wine as a pre-race snack, a flourish of bravado. The veteran Lazaridès, he who feared the Izoard bears, remarked: 'He may be starting as a bike racer but he's not going to last long.' How wrong he was.

Just over 20 years after his retirement, Anquetil died of cancer of the stomach. Doctors had removed his stomach and put him on a minimalist diet. The *bon viveur* went home and carried on as he always had: champagne and caviare. He and Poulidor had become friends at last: the rivalry was buried, irrelevant now. But, in the hospital, saying goodbye, Anquetil turned to Poulidor and said: 'Sorry, Raymond, you'll come second again.' He died next day, 18 November 1987.

He was never popular with the French public, who found him too distant: he seemed simply not to need their good opinion. Goddet called him 'yellow dwarf', refusing him the accolade 'giant of the road' that his feats ought to have accorded him. Yet time has mellowed remembrance of this great rider. His outright genius can, finally, stand clear of the brooding complexities of his character, the chilly hauteur, the steely scorn of his tongue. When Rouen, in his native Normandy, hosted the Prologue of the 1997 Tour, a dockside road by the Seine which cuts through the town was named Quai Jacques Anquetil. For the civic-minded French this represents true acceptance. Anquetil won his first Tour stage in Rouen in 1957. It marked, too, the tenth anniversary of the master's death and on the morning of the Prologue, Merckx, Hinault and Indurain, the surviving quintuple winners, laid flowers in the cemetery in Anquetil's home town, Quincampoix, where the first Hot Spot sprint of the Tour was to be contested next day. The Tour pays its respects and due heed to history. This Tour also marked the 50th anniversary of the first post-War Tour, in which Robic sealed his victory on the Bonsecours hill . . . just outside Rouen.

The racing cyclist faces a long and arduous season beginning in late February and continuing until early October. Added to that, some riders compete in a full round of six-day track races in the winter off-road season. Racing day by day, nearly all year long; then the enormous strain of the stage races. There is virtually no let-up. The Tour de France is the high point and the day after it finishes in Paris? The riders plunge immediately into the whirligig of one-day criterium, here, there and everywhere; operating as independents for the most part, team obligations suspended, on direct contract – so that local races can bill the Tour heroes – putting money straight into the bank, but having to make their own way to events how they will or can. Pedal all afternoon, drive through the night to the next venue, little or no sleep and off again. After one such post-Tour appearance race, Anquetil said to the newcomer Merckx: 'You'll see, this is no piece of cake, this criterium riding.'

In such a context, the temptation to stave off the encroaching exhaustion is probably outweighed by the sheer necessity. I make no apology for performance-enhancing drugs; but medication to mask or numb extreme fatigue?

Riders would arrive at the post-Tour criteriums, it was common knowledge, with two suitcases: in the smaller one, a clean change of clothes; in the larger, the pharmacy.

An eminent physician remarked to me, 'There are winners and racing cyclists.' Implying that the whole *peloton* is using medication – not all of it junk – of greater or lesser potency, of one sort or another; and young hopefuls, what the French categorise as *espoirs*, on the fringes of a pro contract, are keenly aware of the choice that will face them sooner or later: to take dope or not to

'This Pélissier does not know how to suffer,' said Henri Desgrange,
'he will never win the Tour.' Here is Henri Pélissier on his way to
proving him wrong, 1923 (*L'Equipe*)

Col d'Aubisque, 1932 (Flanagan)

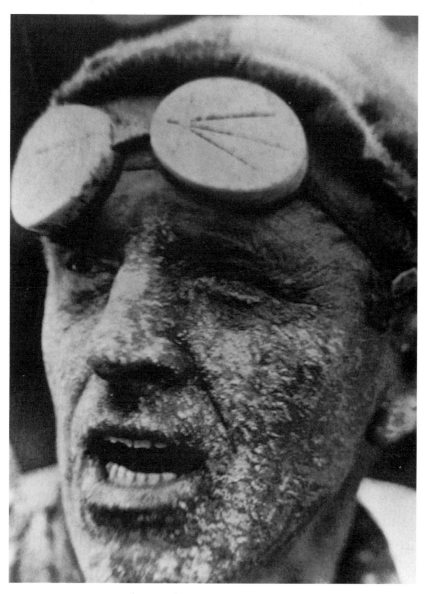

Hans Staub at the finish of the Championship of Zurich,
22 May 1932 (Author's Collection)

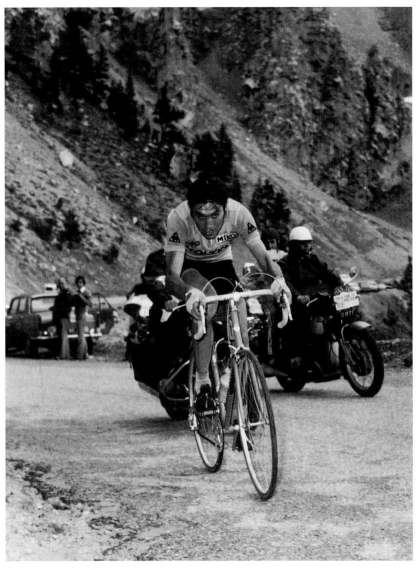

Eddy Merckx out on his own in the Casse Déserte, heading for the col d'Izoard, 1972 (*L'Equipe*)

TOP: Enjoying a picnic and the spectacle of the
Tour de France, 1954 (Robert Delvac)
BOTTOM: Departure of the second Paris–Brussels race, instigated by
Henri Desgrange, from Villiers-sur-Marne, 1906 (Author's Collection)

The *peloton* rides out of Biert, past chez Flanagan towards the col de Port, 1997 (Flanagan)

The *peloton* riding along the corniche towards the
col d'Aubisque, 1998 (Graham Watson)

take dope. And if all of them are taking dope are they all then guilty? One prominent athletics coach has recently voiced the opinion that the wholesale ban on drugs in sport should be revised; the interdiction is ludicrously punitive on men and women exposed to the stresses of top-level sporting competition.

The situation isn't helped by fuzzy statements from the authorities. Thus, Juan Antonio Samaranch, president of the International Olympic Committee said: 'We really must produce an exact definition of doping. The existing list of what are labelled dope products should be drastically reduced. In my view, nothing which does not impair the health of an athlete should be called dope.'

Desgrange's regulations for his Tour had been draconian from the start, but the official attitude to the use of dope has never been less than vague and equivocal. In 1975, Thévenet, *en route* to the famous defeat of Merckx, tested positive, but the President of the French Republic was waiting on the Champs-Elysées for the first time to welcome home the first French winner in eight years . . . Following his victory in 1988, Pedro Delgado tested positive for probenecid, a substance which, argued the officials in exoneration, had not yet found its way on to the banned list. Probenecid is a diuretic which Delgado said he had to take because he sweated so much on the mountains he found it difficult to micturate and thereby void the acids (lactic particularly) which build up in the urine. Probenecid dilutes the urine; this has the useful effect of masking the presence of any stronger, performance-enhancing drugs such as steroids. Delgado was, controversially, confirmed as winner. The next year, he dithered up to take his mark in the Prologue time-trial fully two minutes late and his chances for the Tour were sunk. What the dope test made of that, we don't know.

Athletes have been using performance-enhancing herbal juices for millennia. The ancient Greeks, who invented athletic sports in devotion to a physical – masculine – ideal, also as training for war, then formalised them in sacred games as a forum of state rivalry, were no strangers to the pharmacopoeia. Their oracular prophetesses were doped up to the eyebrows in the mephitic fumes of burning laurel leaves; the magic herb moly (either the mandrake or a species of garlic) given to Odysseus to ward off the enchantments of the sorceress Circe, testifies to the use of pain-inhibiting herbal decoctions such as the hellebores which have strong narcotic effects. Nor were they averse to banning ingested substances. An athlete was disqualified from one of the early Olympic Games. His crime? He'd been training on a diet of dried figs. The judges ruled that an honest athlete should stick to fruits available in their season, only.

Soldiers have always had recourse to stimulants, though not so frequently in such outfits as the highly drilled professional Roman army. The barbarians who met them in battle were rarely short of fighting spirit, Welsh *hwyl*, fuelled by alcohol often as not. Henry V's army came to Agincourt field riddled with dysentery, soaked to the skin, starved and weary; but roaring drunk. Frightened men going into battle craved lavish slugs of artificial (bottled) courage – Dutch courage was gin – to steel them to face what, even in an irrational mood, is a thoroughly terrifying, awful business. Rum to fire the stomach and devil the nerve before the great gun encounters on the wooden ships or in the hellish trenches of the First World War . . . whisky to quell the overshot nerves afterwards . . . hashish to calm and embolden the Old Man of the Mountain's deadly assassins (Arabic '*hashhashin*') . . . South American coca leaves chewed to prolong intellectual concentration or for a brave high . . . the hallucinatory mushroom . . . opium, and its derivative laudanum, to deaden the agony of table-top surgery and numb the senses to life in the Dark and Middle Ages which was nasty, brutish and short . . . the list could go on.

The principal sources of drugs banned by the International Cycling Federation are ephedrins, amphetamines, anabolic steroids. A brief summary therefore.

Apothecaries were known as druggists from Shakespeare's day, but 'drugs' was the late nineteenth-century medical student slang for a pharmacist, and this points to the origin of the distinction we make today between legitimate medicine – used on prescription to remedy or ease illness or infection – and a chemically prepared substance used, *mis*used, when there is no malady to cure. The slang is 'dope', an American word (from the Dutch for 'sauce') originally for any thick fluid or semi-liquid taken as food – e.g. a gloopy milk-shake bought at the drug-store soda counter.

Ephedrins were, until the early years of this century, prepared from an evergreen shrub *Ephedra*; and in ancient times by the Chinese who macerated its leaves in alcohol and water, then blew off the liquid to leave a speedy tincture, sovereign for the stimulation of a sluggish heart. In the 1920s, pharmacologists began chemical preparation of the same substance, and chemical preparation, more and more sophisticated in the modern age, lies at the root of drug abuse.

Thus, if a patient presents with a very low blood pressure, ephedrin will counter by increasing the systolic rate. The systole is the contraction of the heart, by which oxygen-rich red arterial blood is pumped into the system. Diastole is the dilation of the heart as deoxygenated blueish blood courses back through the veins. The transfer of oxygen from the lungs into the bloodstream marks the beginning of the energising cycle; any substance which gingers up that exchange will, necessarily, enliven the system generally and, as a bonus, make the patient feel better. The moral factor is important. Ephedrins promote the release of nor-adrenalin, a neurotransmitter which relaxes the muscles round the airways, complements the inflation of the lungs and aids respiration; the greater the intake of oxygen, the more efficient the human motor. Blocked nasal passages dry out through the action of ephedrin. And how does a cyclist suffering congestion from overtaxed lungs and famished gulping at oxygen-thin mountain air, oppressed, what is more, by the petrol fumes of team cars, choking dust and furnace heat, cope? Many hay fever remedies contain ephedrin: the dope controls insist on those which don't.

Whereas a drug like laudanum had a dual use – social and medical – from the beginning, the ephedrins have, all along, served only in the medical context, whether unlicensed or for illicit use. From ephedrins are derived amphetamines which stimulate the central nervous system. Alcohol is a simple amphetamine and it can promote a temporary energising stimulus. Here before me is a picture of the Swiss riders Colle and Parel, the 1921 Tour: they are sitting on steps in a doorway in some rural back-water, a baking hot day, by the light. Their bikes parked by them, a gaggle of admiring boys gawp at the supermen as they sink a large stein of beer apiece.

The effect of amphetamines is to boost the action of excitatory chemicals in the brain to render the taker more alert through speeding up the breathing and heart-rate. The problem with them – speed, bunnies, uppers – is that the body soon develops a tolerance, so that for any appreciable effect the dosage has to be steadily increased; this risks dependency. Long-term side effects are muscle damage, weight loss, constipation, all deleterious to a racing cyclist, of course.

The zingy effect of drinking strong black coffee, for instance, is to make you think you're doing better than you are; but also to inure the brain to protracted stretches of deeply boring, routine activity. Many Tour riders take belts of espresso before the start of every stage. Even smoking can be an aid to physical exertion: chewing tobacco doesn't release the nicotine very fast, but inhaling charges up the flow of adrenalin and prompts the flow of blood sugar out of the liver into the bloodstream quite rapidly. Another picture: 1920s, on the road, the *peloton*, riding four abreast, forges on; in the front row Vervaeke and Geldholf light cigarettes.

Muscle-building drugs, such as anabolic steroids, are tempting to cyclists in need of raw strength. A drug called clenbuterol was developed in East Germany for cattle: its effect is to reduce body fat and produce a leaner animal with more saleable meat on it. Body fat is one thing cyclists can well do without – useless kilos to heave up the big climbs – and it is known that wrestlers have used it. Reduce your body fat and you achieve a body more or less packed full of muscle with the added advantage that, now stronger, you are also lighter, allowing as much as 5 per cent, even 10 per cent power, to bodyweight advantage over an opponent still carrying some fat.

A drug called erythropoietin has come to the fore recently; EPO. Literally 'red-making', it increases the number of red blood cells, the oxygen carriers, in the bloodstream. That is to say it's an artificial haemoglobin, supplementing the vital work of the kidneys. In the mountains this happens anyway, so the result of taking erythropoietin is to mimic the effect of high-altitude training/riding where, granted an optimally high resource of

164

oxygen, the athlete is less likely to enter the zone of anaerobic effort, when the build-up of lactic acid in weakening, oxygen-starved muscles begins to increase rapidly. EPO is used medicinally on anaemic patients. When injected, it is completely untraceable; only in the exaggerated performance it underpins can suspicion arise. A number of Dutch cyclists who had used this substance were riding in extreme heat; they became dehydrated; one of them, suffering from a bout of gastroenteritis occasioned by food-poisoning, vomited which exacerbated the dehydration. His blood, already thickened by the effect of the drug, was further drastically coagulated by the loss of body moisture. The dangers of drug-abuse in sport are all too apparent.

When the Pélissier brothers abandoned in 1924 – as aces they were comparatively well looked after – they said: 'We are treated like dogs.' Henri went on to describe the Tour as a road to Calvary, *un calvaire*, except that instead of 14 stations it had 15. 'And you want to know what keeps us going?' He pulled a small bottle out of a bag containing numerous other small bottles and canisters. 'Cocaine for the eyes,' he said. Another bottle. 'Chloroform for the gums.'

Maurice Ville emptied his musette. 'And this is pomade [liniment] to warm the muscles. And pills? You want to see the pills?' They each tipped out three bottles.

'In short,' said Henri, 'we keep going on dynamite. You've seen us when we come in at the end of a stage? When we've washed the mud and grime off, our flesh is as white as a winding sheet, we're empty from diarrhoea, our eyes are swimming. Every night we dance the jig like St Guy [French St Vitus] instead of sleeping . . .'

They omitted: wine laced with strychnine and ether-soaked handkerchiefs to dull the fatigue.

Rubbing chloroform into their gums was a crude method of absorbing a painkiller. Cocaine masked pain, sharpened reaction and response to stimulus and accelerated the pulse rate, and thus the oxygenation of the blood, but pump too much into the bloodstream, by intravenous injection, for instance, and it could prove lethal. I myself remember the effects of cocaine injections from the dentist's chair in the '40s and '50s. Very pleasant, given the gruesome nature of the rest of the experience.

A revolt led by Anquetil in 1966 centred on the matter of drugs. Earlier in the year, he had decided the time had come to speak out. He even roped decent old Poupou into the arena, declaring that he was on drugs too, 'Everyone's doing it, no exceptions.' A few months later, Anquetil repeated his accusations and added: 'You think you can race Bordeaux–Paris on mineral water? First you eat a sugar cube, then you take some coffee, then chocolate and from then on you go crazy, you're doped to the eyeballs.' Challenged, he replied: 'Small trees don't grow in the jungle.'

The first open drug tests were carried out on that year's Tour, under the direction of a French law passed in June – 12 months earlier – making illegal the consumption or prescription of a list of drugs with the aim of enhancing any athlete's performance. The first enforcement of the law by the Tour organisers caused uproar. Poulidor very reluctantly provided a urine sample and the next day the riders, Anquetil at their head, protested against the dope controls and the inconsiderate methods of applying them. As the French journalist Antoine Blondin wrote: 'Four men in raincoats hammer on the door of your hotel room, they barge in and demand a urine sample and your papers; then, without a by-your-leave, they rummage through your suitcase. This is more like a police raid than the Tour de France.'

When they were 5km out of Bordeaux on the stage to Bayonne, the entire *peloton* slowed down to a halt, dismounted and walked 200m *en masse*, chanting '*Merde*', which is what Marshal Ney shouted back at the English when they called on him to surrender at Waterloo. The *peloton* then remounted and proceeded with the race. Poulidor's urine sample was conveniently forgotten.

Geoffrey Nicholson, the distinguished cycling journalist, points to the paradox at the heart of this question by recording the remark made by a French colleague who gazed over the dinner table they'd just vacated. There had been a long day's racing, a morning stage and an afternoon stage. All the scribes had done was sit in the car, write up the race and eat and drink. The table was strewn with 'crab and oyster shells, empty wine bottles, full ashtrays'. What stimulation could they reasonably deny the riders who'd actually raced the route and faced another trial the next day? (In the old days, even journalists had it harder. Desgrange insisted they turn up to dinner in *un smoking*, dinner jacket.)

Riders are occasionally caught cheating the dope control, though given the expertise of modern team doctors they say only an imbecile gets caught these days. Yet, one rider was told that his urine sample was negative but to take special care of himself because he was pregnant. Other times it's not so funny.

On Monday, 17 July 1978, the Tour de France was riding from St Etienne to L'Alpe d'Huez. Jos Bruyère (formerly Merckx's lieutenant) was in yellow, followed by Zoetemelk at a minute and three seconds, Hinault, a minute and 50 seconds, and Pollentier. On the first category col Luitel, 1,262m, Pollentier attacked and, at the summit, led by 22 seconds a strong group containing all the main men. He decided to risk the escape: 50-odd kilometres down to the valley and the final climb to the angry alp to conclude. His lead built to three minutes and 20 seconds but, as the chase picked up, he had only a minute and 58 seconds at the first of the 21 hairpins. He is no stylist on a bike; he is to elegance of pedalling what a dishcloth is to a silk scarf, but he hung on, lashing himself and his bike up the unforgiving mountain and took the stage by 37 seconds over the next man in, Kuiper (another ibex from the flatlands), and enough over the rest to put him in yellow. Bruyère trailed in eight minutes down.

The daily dope test is levied on the overall leader, the stage winner and runner-up, plus two other riders chosen at random. Pollentier had peed in his shorts on the way up the climb and had none left. He missed the dope control and cycled directly to his hotel. He had, in fact, taken a fairly innocuous adrenalin stimulant, alupin, to aid his breathing. It's a common drug, sold over the counter in Belgium but Pollentier took fright: his lead was narrow, the yellow jersey wouldn't give him immunity as it had Thévenet.

He stuffed a length of tubing and rubber bulb containing what he knew to be clean urine into his shorts and set off for the dope test. Meantime, one of the other riders, Gutteriez, was trying hard to produce a specimen. Extreme fatigue and dehydration inhibits the flow, of course, but a trickle appeared. Then the doctor spotted that the urine in the test flask wasn't coming from Gutteriez's penis but from a length of rubber tube. The doctor checked all the riders in the room; Pollentier took off his shorts and the ploy was exposed. He produced a genuine sample of his own urine and returned to the hotel.

At 8 p.m., Félix Lévitan, co-organiser of the Tour with Jacques Goddet, announced that Pollentier had been caught red-handed trying to cheat the dope control. Under International Cycling Union (UCI) rules, he was forthwith suspended for two months and fined 5,000 Swiss francs. Seven other riders, three from the Peugeot team, were also disqualified for taking over ten pushes from spectators.

Pollentier was stunned; after all, he'd eventually provided a fair urine sample and the doctors had signed him out clean. Why the protracted delay in declaring him a cheat? Moreover, he hadn't tested positive in any other race that season.

Pollentier's Flandria team, including his close friend Maertens, talked of quitting the race *en bloc*. (It had happened in 1950: the Italian team walked out in the Pyrenees. On the climb of the col d'Aspin, crowds had swarmed so close in on the riders that Robic and Bartali fell in the scrum; then the luckless Italian was set on by drunken French thugs spoiling for a fight. Bartali was kicked and punched but escaped and made it to the finish. But, even though their man Magni had the yellow jersey, the Italians quit; Kubler refused the yellow jersey next day, but took it into Paris.)

Like Kubler, Zoetemelk found himself in yellow by default and publicly castigated Pollentier for taking unfair advantage: his use of stimulants had put his pursuers on the rack; they had to fight merely to limit their losses; any thought of attacking was out of the question. This sounds rather pious.

Hinault couldn't credit that a rider of Pollentier's class should need to take drugs or make such a crass mistake as to try to cheat the control. However, the exclusion of Pollentier cleared the way for him – Zoetemelk packed a much lighter punch and the coming time-trial would probably see Hinault leap-frogging the Dutchman into yellow.

The hapless Pollentier wrote to Lévitan and Goddet. He apologised; said that he was no more guilty than the majority of other riders and asked why Gutteriez had not also been punished.

(They would probably say that the wearer of the yellow jersey bears extra responsibility.) He had given a sample of his own urine and, besides, was in such a confused state after the debilitating ride up the alp that some mitigation might be in order. He pleaded for clemency and concluded: 'Believe me when I say that hardest to bear is the charge of sullying the standing of the Tour. You know how I have committed myself to the racing on the roads of the Tour. This should have been the finest day of my career. Unhappily it will be the saddest. Please accept my sincere expression of regret.'

He was, in the circumstances, dealt with harshly; another of the Tour caprices; what a miserable thing to have to live with.

The fingerpost indicates col de Vars 19km. On the first bend the rain starts. I decide to remove the silk long johns I'd put on to keep my legs warm. Wet, they'll be no use anyway. This change means a full strip, waist down, at the side of the road. I'm just putting my shoes back on when a police car drives by. Tour riders are fined for relieving themselves in built-up areas, but not behind trees or (to the side of the crossbar) on the move in open country or, like Pollentier, let free in full throttle.

I hated the col de Vars. It had little to commend it at the time and I can't stir much charm out of it in retrospect, either. One Tour rider, asked what his objectives were for that day in the mountains, retorted: 'To survive.' Absolutely. The weather didn't help: the day had already cried itself to a standstill, given up and turned its face to the wall of the mountain. There was nothing besides wet trees, wet roadsides and wet mountain slopes to look at. The water of the River Chagne might be tumbling over itself down the gorge in a chattering giggle of foam but I can't take to cheery babbling about being cold and wet. I've got water on the soul.

On 14 July, Bastille Day, 1975, Merckx, whose powers of recuperation were miraculous, put the misery of the previous stage into Pra Loup behind him and attacked down this very climb *en route* to the Izoard. He was hitting back as hard as he could; Thévenet was adrift, his first day in yellow. But the long haul up to the Casse Déserte lay ahead; Thévenet kept his nerve, reeled the Cannibal in and left him to ride alone through the lunar landscape past a young girl in a swimming costume with a placard which read: *Merckx, the Bastille has fallen, Thévenet has won.*

Thévenet hadn't sprung out of the *peloton* overnight. Débutant in 1970, he came fourth in 1971, winning that telling stage into Grenoble ahead of Ocaña's group, and second overall in 1973. His victory initiated a renewed French domination of victories. Merckx's own first win put an end to a Belgian drought which had lasted from Sylvère Maes's win in 1939.

The town of Vars itself, a ski station flung together out of quick-drying concrete, may be a jolly place on a sunny winter day when the snow is crisp; in rainswept September, draped in a fog that leans like a morning drunk against a side wall, Vars is as unattractive as a waste bin. And it seems to go on for miles. There's Vars this and this de Vars and Vars the other. Home, what's more, to no fewer than three saints: Marcellin, Marie and Catherine. Says a lot about the place that it needs such heavy canonised insurance.

The guidebook says that the time to come to Vars is in June when the flowers are out in gaudy profusion. And when the Tour comes through, in a profusion of lycra.

Placards as big and flimsy as Hollywood film-set façades exhort me to sample the delights of cross-country skiing, bobsleighing, snow-biking. The cash kiosks stand empty. The ski lifts creak, gaunt and immobile, like pit-head winding gear all across England now. The boutiques sulkily *fermé* for business. The restaurant menu boards hang out like self-conscious schoolkids, full of chips and 'look-at-me' self-advertisement.

At the far side of Ste Marie de Vars, halfway through the Vars holy triple jump, at 1,658m, from the 1,000m at Guillestre, the road suddenly springs up in my face. I groan, snarl and get stuck in. The Vars conurbations behind me, the rain changes to snow.

The col de Vars was first included, as was the Izoard, in the 1922 Tour, and ever since generally put in tandem with it. The road is vastly superior to what they climbed then, but it is still a rough gutter for debris off the mountain, its wrinkled surface littered with stones. Belgians had won every Tour since 1912, and now Lambot, the winner in 1919, lined up again to challenge for a second victory. His relegation at Le Havre seemed to turn the tide, but everything changed on the Nice–Briançon stage, over the Vars and Izoard – a combined altitude gain, *dénivelation*, of 5,347m.

A formidable group of Belgian riders led the way: Philippe Thys, first triple Tour winner 1913–14, 1920, tracked by the only Frenchman who could stay the pace, the great climber Alavoine; then Lambot and Heusghem. Alavoine cracked; Lambot and Heusghem moved up and caught Thys. Heusghem seemed to be the strongest and was heading for yellow which he must then surely keep till Paris – he'd come second in '20 and '21. But he committed some minor infraction of the rules, was docked an hour and Lambot took yellow.

In 1933, Speicher rode up the Vars heading for victory in Paris with the aid of a new secret weapon: a rear brake working by the same method of clamping to the wheel rim as the front brake.

The first crude braking system – augmented by applying foot to wheel – often caused the bike to rear up if applied too abruptly which added to the perils of descending. This harked back to the penny farthing or 'ordinary' and many riders came a purler over the front wheel. Technical innovations were advertised by Tour riders, of course.

Watching the 1935 Tour *peloton* containing Speicher, Leducq and Vietto as it passed through his home town St-Méen-le-Grand was an apprentice baker, name of Louison Bobet. Three years later, Speicher came to an ignoble end: eliminated for taking a ride up one of the Pyrenean cols, hanging on to a car door. It was Bartali's Tour, his bike fitted with the *dérailleur* whose use Desgrange had finally permitted; the Archbishop of Reims sent Bartali a photograph dedicated: To a champion of the Catholic faith and of the pedal.

I feel as the specialist sprinters must feel when they are on the mountains, except that I can't join their *autobus*. On Van Impe's triumphant day into Pla d'Adet in 1976, the time limit for the stage was set at 10 per cent of his winning time. Only 52 riders made the cut – approximately 28 minutes deficit; the remainder, 43 members of the *autobus*, faced disqualification, thus reducing the Tour to a pitifully small field. The officials decided to relax the rules and allow the men who came in under 40 minutes to stay in; the remaining nine riders, down to 46 minutes, would be eliminated. Five of them belonged to the Raleigh team who had dropped temporarily out of the race to nurse their leader Kuiper after a fall. He was too badly hurt to continue, and so he abandoned – by which time the loyal *domestiques* were miles behind the race. In fact, only one member of the Raleigh team – Pronk – had beaten the guillotine and the manager threatened to withdraw him if the others weren't reinstated, especially since they lost so much time waiting for Kuiper, as it was their professional duty to do. After a heated argument, the officials relented. The spirit of Desgrange the pragmatist lives on.

By the time I reach the top my hands are frozen. I had hardly noticed while I was riding; I arrive without any sense of jubilation; dismount without fuss and at once feel the extreme pain throbbing in my hands.

Benoît Faure described how on a 200-mile stage in the 1926 Tour, across the Tourmalet and Aubisque, they were sobbing through the cold: fingers locked and stiff, unable to brake on the descents; spectators rubbing life back into their frozen legs and bodies, plying them with cognac. Faure swore this first Tour would be his last. He was a tough farm boy, used to privation and exposure, but this was unbelievable. Worse for such as him, being a *touriste-routier*, of course – the *ténébreux* 'shadow men' as they were known – was that, unlike the stars, he had no hotel room booked, no back-up or team support, no comforts laid on. He vented his spleen in an article about the miseries of this Tour de France for the magazine, *Match*. Torture on the roads and bedbugs in the sleazy hotels. Desgrange was not amused and fined him 4,000 francs. (First prize for a stage win in those days would be around 5,000 francs).

Iron man Eugène 'Cri-Cri' Christophe described the 1910 Milan–San Remo:

> That was a race. Mid-March. It was bitterly cold from the start and as we began the climb of the Turchino pass [532m in the maritime alps above Genoa] we ran into snow. I was leading but I was shaking with cold and the road was so rough I could hardly control the bike. I fell into a ditch. Some bystanders carried me into a cottage, gave me hot drinks and rubbed me all over to restore my circulation. They gave me a pair of long trousers to wear over my shorts and I pressed on. Meanwhile I'd been overtaken, but with about 130km to ride, I chased and caught the leaders and finished the race alone.

Some understatment. He beat Ganna by 20 minutes but Ganna had taken a tow from a car and was disqualified. Next man home, Cocchi, was an hour and ten minutes down on the Frenchman. Even Christophe's abnormally robust constitution took a beating from that race: he was so weak he could barely walk, had to spend a month in hospital and lost the rest of that season and much of the following one.

Imagine puncturing in such circumstances – at night, in the snow, trying to peel the tyre off with fingers frozen numb. Poor Léon Scieur on that day of eight punctures: one minute and 30 seconds to repair each one, then stitch up the regulation tyre and off again, pulling on the bulging mica eyeglass goggles the Belgians favoured, which gave them the look of frogs. And victory in Paris.

The snow is driving in at 45 degrees. I park the bike against a noticeboard and fumble at the fastenings on my saddle bag, fingers like vulcanised rubber, hands pulsating with cold. I windmill my arms to try to restore the circulation and resume the fumbling. The café across the road does not tempt me in the slightest. The col de Vars has drawn the fight out of me and I am not ready to let the fight slip back inside. Sitting in artificial heat and having to step back out into the cold is no pleasurable prospect. My every instinct is to press on and work up my own heat.

It was on the col de Vars, the day before their great solo ride to l'Alpe d'Huez, that Hinault came very close to breaking. He was in fearful pain from a pulled muscle in the knee. It was, he said, the only time he ever cried on a bike. Urs Zimmerman and Lemond were ahead, Lemond heading for yellow, when Hinault, in awful trouble, heard a moto-cameraman say to his driver who was setting off to follow the rest: 'Stay with *him*, he's going to abandon.' It was every cliché you like to deploy; start with a sting of the whip. Hinault reacted with pride; there was little else left, but those words rang in his cars like the final voice of shame on doomsday when there's no redress. He fought back, so far beyond any present thought of pain and discomfort that he limited the day's losses to four minutes on Lemond, who took over his yellow jersey. He started the next day still in considerable pain, but if pride is no great cure it's a powerful anaesthetic. The pain eventually left on the Croix de Fer and a Calvary had been endured.

On his first ever climb of that col de la Croix de Fer, during the 1977 Dauphiné Libéré, his assistant manager handed him a bottle filled with champagne which he guzzled to the dregs and finished the highest pass he'd ever ridden 'half blotto' he said. That same race, when he'd been dropped by Thévenet, Van Impe, Zoetemelk and Martin, it was Merckx who urged the struggling newcomer on. 'Come on, stick at it, go on, you're still winning, don't give in.'

Such banalities the words may frame on paper, but uttered by an established rider of such class to a new man of obvious talent, then the banality achieves the simple moral direction of the epitaph, the crack regiment's motto, the family blazon. And that is what it comes to: the moral imperative. As Hinault said: 'No technology can increase the energy or the willpower of the rider, nor can it lessen the doubts which sometimes overwhelm him.'

Anquetil said of the 1986 Tour won by Lemond that it was fantastic and, 'We owe it all to Hinault. Even if he didn't win, it was his Tour.' He *dynamited* it, as the French journos say. Testimony to that comes from Robert Millar, too: 'This was my fourth Tour and by far the hardest. I don't think we ever climbed the mountains so fast.' This from a specialist climber is praise indeed.

That moto-journalist may have been instrumental in the Hinault fightback; it's impossible to say. But journalists, even highly experienced ones, certainly get things wrong. The truth can be so swayed by subjective interpretation. What seems, on the face of it, a dull, uneventful stage may have been seething with tactical jiggery-pokery inside the *peloton*. On the '74 Tour, a television crew set out to station themselves at Besançon to catch the demise of Poulidor, now 38, and matched, after Anquetil, with Merckx. Nobody gave him a chance once the mountains had dug their teeth into his legs. The cameramen got there in time to see Poulidor dump Merckx on the climb of the Relais du Chat. Next day, the buzz amongst the journos was that maybe this was Poupou's year at last. And from Monsieur Eddy, too. Alas, on the

Galibier, Poulidor caved in, the pressmen started scribbling about irreparable losses, luck running out, once more defeat only to watch, amazed, as the veteran trounced Merckx over the Ventoux and led him a dance in the Pyrenees.

The one thing you do learn if you ride the mountains is that nothing is ever certain. Often a rider with no obvious pretensions at even a stage victory will overturn expectation. On stage five of the '97 Tour, Cédric Vasseur, not a fancied rider, made a brave solo attack of 147.5km to take yellow. Four days later, he was still in the lead but none of the pundits gave him any prayer of holding it that day, over the cols du Soulor, first category; Tourmalet, super category; Aspin, second; Azet, first. He surprised them all with a wonderfully gritty ride and held on to yellow, even if he ceded it next day.

A team rider will sometimes perform extraordinary feats in the service of his leader, though never able, seemingly, or inclined, to put such audacity into riding for himself. This is part of the racing ethic: a strict pecking order of jobs and status. The *domestique* is paid to obey orders and if the orders require him to ride like a star for a day, very well. Sean Yates did it frequently. On the sixth stage time-trial on the Tour in 1988, 52km, the strong man ('Animal') from Sussex won at one hour, three minutes and 22 seconds, the fastest average speed hitherto recorded; yet, he always maintained that he'd been lucky in his career, no more. This is over-modest. He was, in many respects, the *domestique* of *domestiques*: a tireless worker, self-effacing yet unpitying with his own energy and efforts in the team's cause. He never complained and was never wanting in a ride. His *palmarès* boasts wins in several of the big-stage races and his entire professional career compels admiration. A complete sportsman, a pro to his shoe plates.

In Barcelonnette, I squelch into a small bar/resto in town, eat an omelette, bread, green salad with half pitcher of red wine and an espresso, and by 1.45 p.m. I am back on the drenched road, saturated from the neck up and the waist down. I ride past the turn off to Pra Loup; I had wanted to ride up that fateful climb where Thévenet left Merckx for dead; but in teeming rain, an added ten miles with hard climbing does not appeal. I still have 40-odd miles ahead of me to put me within strike of Ventoux. Another time.

When I returned to England, John and Angela told me that they had ridden into Barcelonnette at about 2 p.m. and called it a day. John said he'd never been so cold on a bicycle. (Merckx said that in severe weather they'd sometimes get off the bikes and run 200m or so just to get some circulation back into their legs). They discovered a fresh pasta restaurant round the corner which serves portions so big they couldn't finish them. In fact, you could have served Angela's leftovers to a party of four. Not that she is no trencherwoman. She once ate three pasta courses on the trot in a trattoria in Vietri, Italy. The *patrono* was so impressed he brought out a fourth plate, which she tucked into heartily.

I must have missed them by a whisker. 'We'd have tried to persuade you to call it a day,' they told me afterwards. But I was spurred on by the challenge of Ventoux.

'I aim to enjoy Ventoux,' I'd said.

Angela gave me a wry look and said: 'You don't really *enjoy* Ventoux', which was odd, even cautionary, coming from her who had called after me on the first ramp of l'Alpe d'Huez: 'Enjoy it.'

Mountains have their summits and there is no obligation, no exterior compulsion, other than pride, to finish the climb. We can at any moment choose not to. A good lesson, then, to stay in the moment. When you get to the col you do not cast off the frailties of halfway up, you absorb them and carry that weakness into the triumph of getting there, the triumph which owes more to patience than to effort. Statistically, the demands of the mountains can be expressed like this: riding flat out on the flat, or at speed downhill, up to about 82 per cent of the resistance to forward motion comes from the air. Riding in another rider's slipstream reduces that by nearly two thirds. On a climb the air resistance falls to around 6 per cent; everything else that gets in your way is provided by gravity – about 78 per cent – and grip of tyres, tendency to roll back and so on. Applying the same effort to 30kph on the flat, a rider will make only about 10kph on a one in 16, and less, obviously, as the incline steepens.

Everything we do may teach us something about ourself. *We are part of all we have met.* And if we do not know ourselves how can we know others? Those who know – or admit – less about themselves have little capacity to think of anybody but themselves.

Too often our experience of the tedious routines establish our value of life. As a result, transcendent feelings tend to become as uncommon as they are untrustworthy. Life isn't like that, will go the complaint. Whatever these mountains have taught me it is that there are different strengths to uncover in our spirit, beyond the commonplace of head down and run at it. And I am very conscious that from this new encounter I have drawn a singularly limited experience; just how limited that experience was I would find out on the slopes of Ventoux. Even to label them slopes makes it sound risibly chummy and casual.

Merckx out on his own for 60km into a vicious headwind on the 1971 Liège–Bastogne–Liège; his sporting director Driessens told him it was pure madness. Merckx didn't even bother to look at the man. When he was 3km from the finish he was rejoined by Georges Pintens but refused any relays from him, simply hooked him on behind and took the sprint from the front. He was hardly off the bike when Driessens was all over him, hugging and kissing him, saying what a great idea he'd had to advise Merckx to attack when he did.

Towards evening, in drenching rain, I can't find anywhere to stay. The way I feel I could cycle another 40 miles without concern, but this is being pig-headed. Just beyond the junction with the N85, which, like Napoleon's army in 1815, forges straight along the valley of the Durance, I turn off to La Saulce on a whim; see a signboard. I ask for a room; they have a room.

My bike is in a filthy state but there is nothing to be done except oil it next day when it is dry. Vietto would have been cleaning it and polishing it like a gold watch, shoes too. If Christophe had only checked and cleaned his bike after 17 hours in the saddle, those forks might not have snapped. But I leave my cherished Alan Shorter unwashed, untended, in the corridor and clump up to the room in shoes aslosh with rainwater.

I have a glorious warm shower, wash every stitch of my wet gear, pat and roll it dry in the spare towels (a pro's trick). There is a knock on the door: the *femme de ménage* to take away all my wet gear for drying.

Down in the bar, I drink several *demis*. The place is fuggy-warm and crowded, men stopping for a drink or two on their Friday way home from work, followed by men and women taking *apéritifs*. They shake hands as casually as we say hello. The air is loud with conversation. Four card players – two men, two women – unroll a strip of baize at the table next to mine and play a noisy rubber of piquet.

I order the set dinner – menu scrawled in chalk on a slate – for 7.30 p.m. *Hors d'oeuvre* of leeks in olive oil, *pâté en croute* and bread, red wine. Then rosé for the baked hake, baked red peppers and a mountain of rice. A board of cheese, as much as I want. Rum baba – the only disappointment: sponge the texture of wet bread and cream from a grease gun. Shop-bought. The rest of the meal is home-cooked and entirely delicious, 65 francs all in, prepared and served by the *femme de ménage*.

By 9 p.m. the café has all but emptied. Dry, glowing, nicely plump, I take a stroll through a dark maze of tiny streets – the rain has stopped – and at 9.30 p.m. go to bed. My dry clothes, the purple jersey of leader in my own tour among them, lie folded on the chair.

CHAPTER SEVEN

MONT VENTOUX

The British Riders

The col de Macuégne, scarcely more than a pimple after the high passes, 809m to 1,068m in 4km, leads me to a crossroads. I consult the map. The road to Montbrun les Bains plunges off downhill to the right in what looks like an attractive scenic ride. Above me rears the Montagne d'Albion and its pass, the col de l'Homme Mort at 1,212m. That way I have to go. This day has death brooding over it.

Albion was the ancient name for Britain before King Arthur came to Camelot, but Albion is still in the French dictionary for 'Britain'; and the col of the Dead Man? It's not a wholly unusual name in these parts, but here is a chilly coincidence.

I had written a sequence of seven radio plays (and a book) about King Arthur. The man who was to have written the series died of cancer while he was working, at desperate speed, to finish them. The illness had advanced so far that what he wrote was degenerating into distracted incoherence. The spooky thing was that as soon as I heard he was writing the plays, just before I met him – he acted in another play of mine, coming out of the hospital ward to the studio each day, ill as he was – I had a premonition that I would be doing the job, not he. Nothing I could do, however squeamish I felt. He did die and, in his memory, I started my own work from scratch. In the final play, Arthur leaves the field of the last battle to fulfil the prophesied end, by restoring the sword Excalibur to its true owner, the Lady of the Lake. Mortally wounded, imbrued with blood, he said to Sir Bedivere: 'Put me on my horse. Put me on my horse.' There was almost a fearful row about that on the last day of recording; the producer insisted on 'Set me on my horse'. Amenable on most changes, I refused point blank on that. At the time, I thought it was what a dying man *had* said, as you will see.

Only 20 British riders have finished the Tour de France. The first British riders to enter the Tour were Charley Holland and Bill Burl, in 1937, first year of the *dérailleur*: 20 stages, 4,415km, six rest days. (The *dérailleur* mechanism comprises a dolly-wheel on an articulated arm, extending below the chain-ring, through which the chain passed. Worked by a simple switch lever, it shifts another mechanism below the freewheel cogs back and forth.)

The bold duo formed a three-man team with Pierre Gachon, a French-Canadian. Gachon missed the time limit on day one, Burl crashed twice and abandoned after stage two, so Holland lined up for stage three on his own. He rode well, finished in the top 30. On the Ballon d'Alsace, 9.5km to verdant pastures at 1,247m, the officials decided that Holland had taken a tow from one of the cars and relegated him to final place. Holland spoke of the endless drag up that climb and the choking fug of car fumes which made breathing that much harder. The Tour reached the Alps. At the start of the Galibier, Bartali attacked; Holland and the others grabbed some food bags and rode on into snow, Holland's first taste of the big mountains. On to and across the Pyrenees and the end of his Tour, on a technicality. He punctured twice, carried only the regulation two spare tyres, so had to wait for someone to come along who'd give him a third spare. A priest gave him a bottle of beer, but his sacristy did not run to bike equipment. Finally, a tourist cyclist gave Holland the wherewithal – an oversize tyre, but a tyre – and he rode on; the tyre kept slipping off the rim; he searched out another but when he reached the checkpoint, the officials had packed up and moved on. Holland had no option but to peel off his number and retire.

In the Alps, Bartali seemed to have the race secured. He'd been required by Mussolini to ride the Tour instead of the Giro and to dominate it for Italy. Shades of Hitler's 1936 Olympics. After the Galibier, he arrived in Grenoble with eight minutes' advance on Maes of Belgium, 16 minutes on the French hope, Lapébie. Next day he added to his lead over the col du Laffrey and began the descent, guided by his team-mate Rossi. But Rossi fell, Bartali hit the parapet and flew off the road into the torrent below. Stunned, he was hauled out of the icy waters by another team-mate and remounted. But the shock of the crash and the chilly drenching had bitten him to the bone. He couldn't get warm; the cold had seized up his lungs and muscles. Over the Izoard, Vars and Allos he lost 20 minutes. Maes took yellow and in sunny Marseille, Bartali shook Desgrange's hand and abandoned. He was ready to regain yellow from Lapébie but the Italian Federation had ordered him to quit.

In the Pyrenees, the bitter rivalry between the French and Belgian teams got nasty. Setting out from Luchon, Lapébie's handlebars broke: they'd been sawn through. A change of bikes; no *bidons*. Tension mounted. The Belgians accused Lapébie of taking extra – illegal – food from his brother Guy, Olympic champion in the '36 Olympics. Dropped on the Peyresourde, Lapébie reached the foot of the Tourmalet five minutes behind Maes. He saw, by the side of the road, Antonin Magne watching the race. 'Tonin,' he called out, 'I'm pooped. What do I do?' Magne didn't reply.

A bit further on, around a long bend, flagging now, Lapébie saw Félix Lévitan, later race co-director. Their eyes met. Lévitan saw what was what and, hidden from the other riders by the bend, gave Lapébie a long push, two-handed. It was sufficient to launch the revitalised Frenchman in pursuit of the Belgian 'Black Squadron', so-called from their all-black strip.

Lévitan dutifully owned up to the push: it cost Lapébie a minute and 30 seconds penalty. Next day, 40km from Bordeaux, Maes lost a minute and 33 seconds with a puncture, and in the race to get back accepted help both from his own team *and* independent Belgian riders. He was penalised 15 seconds. Lapébie's deficit was reduced to 25 seconds.

The Bordelais fans mobbed the Belgians, however, and threw

pepper in their eyes. It was disgraceful and the Belgians decided to abandon the race in protest. Lapébie won.

The unfortunate Holland was not forgotten: he became a popular hero in France – the plucky Brit who'd ridden so well, against the odds and without any support, human or material. The partisan French may enjoy hating the English, *de rigeur*, but when it comes to riding their Tour, every rider who shows exceptional pluck is a hero deserving of respect.

One such was the Briton Brian Robinson. In 1955, he and Tony Hoar were part of a ten-strong British team which competed in the Tour. Robinson and Hoar alone finished, the first British riders to do so; Robinson 29th, Hoar as *lanterne rouge*, six hours five minutes and 37 seconds behind the winner, Bobet. In 1956, riding on Charly Gaul's team, Robinson came third on the first stage and arrived in Paris a very respectable 14th in 1956. In 1958, he won the seventh stage, into Brest, controversially: the winner Arrigo Padovan was disqualified for dangerous riding in the sprint. Alas, he was forced to abandon and didn't see his leader Gaul take yellow in Paris. After an epic, and record-breaking, solo ride of 140km, Robinson took the 20th-stage victory at Chalon-sur-Saône by 20 minutes and six seconds, in 1959. Another Briton, Vin Denson, also finished – 37th – that year. Robinson's example undoubtedly drew Tom Simpson to the continent. For any amateur with serious ambitions to make road-racing a career, there was no option but to cross the Channel. Track-racing flourished in Britain, but the legal ban on road-races continued until well after the Second World War. The racing code was rigidly amateur; illicit time-trialling took place at crack of dawn, riders wearing black alpaca tops to ensure invisibility.

During and after the War, the British League of Racing Cyclists campaigned for open road-racing in Britain, but even after the inaugural (amateur) Tour of Britain, and its reincarnation as the Milk Race in 1955, official attitudes were not malleable.

Moreover, British cyclists were, and remain, obsessed with time-trialling: one man and his bike on the dual carriageway, shaving fractions of seconds off last week's time over 25 miles, 50 miles. It is insular, introspective, self-serving and no preparation, mentally or psychologically, for road-racing. It is a useful exercise only to a very limited point; it reminds me of what Anita Roddick, of the Body Shop, said about basing commercial strategy on market research, that it's a bit like driving a car looking only into the rear-view mirror.

In his début year, Simpson entered the eight-day Route de France stage race for under-25s. Here he encountered the mountains for the first time. His French was still patchy; the team mechanic was trying to tell him to ride within his capabilities, to keep something in hand. Simpson couldn't understand until the guy started making slow pedalling motions with his hands and saying '*touriste, touriste*'. Simpson cottoned. He rode the approaches to the Tourmalet in the leading group and, at the start of the climb proper, changed into his lowest gear. He said: 'It was awe-inspiring going up the Tourmalet. There were great banks of snow piled at the side of the road for miles . . . I felt very small and insignificant. Still, I was learning fast, although I still had the dread inside me that I would not finish: a disgrace which I could not face.'

He managed the climb comfortably, crossed the col feeling good, not even sweating, ten minutes down on the field. He was on his way. Next year he won the Grand Prix Mont Faron, a mountain race, beating the great Charly Gaul and several other renowned *grimpeurs*, and that summer lined up for his first Tour: he finished in 29th place; his talent was solid enough, but the demands of pro racing, as of any professional activity, go way beyond mere talent. Like all foreigners seeking to break into the continental racing scene, Simpson had a hard fight on. He was nervously ambitious, driven by the need, the desperate need even, to make a mark, to make money, not to take the boat home with empty pockets and a failed career behind him. The Tour de France was where a reputation could be made, and a reputation led to bigger contracts and the happy possibility of retiring with enough money to live on. In spring 1961 came his first major victory: he won the Tour des Flandres, a Belgian classic, and in the '62 Tour became the first Briton ever to wear the yellow jersey; for only a day, yet he had pulled on the golden fleece of cycle racing and his desire to do even better in the Tour tightened its grip on his senses. He came sixth that year, the highest placing ever for a British rider. Simpson was a natural one-day racer – victory in the Milan–San Remo, 1964, followed by a majestic win in the World Road Race of 1965 proved that – but his physique was not ideally adapted for taking a daily hammering and producing the kind of dominating performance he yearned for in the stage races. True, he won the Bordeaux–Paris, but the Tour is the Tour. (Ironically, before the inaugural Bordeaux–Paris in 1891, the great Charles Terront, winner of the Paris–Brest–Paris that year, the poor working-class boy who began his starry career on hired wooden bikes – together with all the other French riders – was refused entry by the British amateur contingent because they were professionals.)

On 13 July 1967, 13th stage, the Tour riders faced a ride of 136km from the overnight stop in Marseille to the town of Carpentras and a further 75km, thence, over Ventoux and back to Carpentras. Riding with Simpson in the British team were Barry Hoban, Vin Denson, Colin Lewis and Michael Wright. The French called Simpson 'Major', from the publicity photos of him sporting a city-slicker suit, bowler hat and umbrella, in teasing mockery of the stodgy '*rosbif*' image. He had a lively good humour, unlike most Brits whom the French found impossibly dour, never allowing any emotion to set the stiff upper lip aquiver. Simpson was also a fine racing cyclist with a touch of steely class in him: the continental fans not only liked him, they admired him, too. If Simpson could make a good showing in this Tour – he was 29 years old and not kidding himself that he had time in abundance at his disposal – a round of fatly paid post-Tour appearances might see him clear for his future. It was the basic insecurity of all professional sportsmen and women, made more acute as physical powers decline and anxiety about the future increases in proportion.

This Tour promised success. Simpson was climbing well; a brave ride on the Ballon d'Alsace lifted him to seventh overall, the position he held that morning in Marseille. He'd been sick on a hard stage in the Alps but seemed to have recovered.

Of the first time he rode Ventoux, Simpson said: 'It is like another world up there among the bare rocks and the glaring sun. The white rocks reflect the heat and the dust rises, clinging to your arms, legs and face. I rode well . . . doing about five miles to the gallon in perspiration. It was almost overwhelmingly hot up there; my pants were soaked and heavy with sweat, it was running off me in streams.'

At the start of the climb to Mont Ventoux, in Bédoin, Simpson darted into a bar with a few of the other riders and is alleged to have drunk a small cognac. (One witness says it was more like a full glass; another rider, Riotte, downed two glasses of red wine.) This practice of raiding local cafés and bars on passage, an immemorial tradition of the Tour since its inception – in the absence of organised water supplies by the organisers – is strictly forbidden nowadays.

The heat was intense: 131°F. Poulidor and Jimenez attacked, the pursuit splintered and strung out along the climb; Simpson was in the main group of chasers. Bédoin stands at 275m altitude, Ventoux's col des Tempêtes at 1,829m; the distance between them is 21km. The record stands at around 45 minutes. Simpson was going badly. The road was lined with fans cheering him on, cheering them all on, but 3km from the top, Simpson faltered to a dead stop and toppled sideways, the bike under him, pedals gripped fast to his feet by toe-plates and straps. He was by this time delirious, incoherent. (In his excellent new book *Put Me on my Bike* William Fotheringham suggests he mumbled 'on, on, on'; the more dramatic plea was invented by a journalist.) A spectator helped him remount and he wobbled up that cruel slope in furnace heat enduring who can imagine what mad torment to stay on the bike somehow and reach the top for some relief on the downhill. He faltered up another kilometre of that brutal climb; 1.5km from the summit, he slumped to the ground a second time, all but unconscious now. A spectator gave him the kiss of life; the Tour doctor Pierre Dumas arrived with oxygen, radioed for the police helicopter and tried to revive the dying man. Airlifted to Avignon hospital, Simpson was pronounced dead at 5.40 p.m. The attending doctors also announced that there would be an autopsy of his body: a clear indication that they suspected he had taken drugs. Indeed, in the team baggage van a box belonging to Simpson was found to contain various stimulants, including two kinds of methylamphetamine.

The dose of amphetamine that he had taken had not been large enough to kill him; it did, however, allow him to push his body way beyond normal endurance. His overriding concern had been to dull the pain he knew he'd go through in the supreme – the mortal – effort he needed to stay on the leader board. The night he died, Jacques Goddet said that he thought Simpson was a 'great guy who was probably scared of losing'.

Three days later, Anquetil dismissed any moralising about the dope Simpson had taken. He said that no rider could have climbed Ventoux in that asphyxiating heat without the aid of some decongestant simply to be able to breathe. The likelihood is that Simpson ignorantly used an unproved brand instead of one that any doctor would prescribe to anyone else other than a racing cyclist.

The British team were poleaxed by the news. Their manager Alec Taylor persuaded them, numb with grief and shock, to ride on in Simpson's memory. They went to the start line next day wearing black armlets; the crowd applauded. Denson, a friend of Simpson's for 14 years, was in tears, so too Hoban. A short speech, a brief silence before the race drew out on to the road; Denson was asked to go ahead and take the stage as a tribute to his friend; he couldn't do it and the doleful honour went to Hoban instead. Denson abandoned soon afterwards; the remaining three riders continued to Paris.

The following year, what they christened the Tour of Health started in the spa town Vittel, home of the mineral water. Goddet said that since doping had been forced out of the shadows it could now be controlled. The riders seemed united in their determination to purge the sport of drug abuse. 'Dear Tom Simpson,' said Goddet, 'your death in the stony desert of Ventoux will not have been in vain.' But the racing was lacklustre, the event a bore from start to finish.

Simpson had been promised a lucrative contract with one of the best Italian teams – Salvarani – riding for its leader Gimondi, if he finished the Tour. But the long stage race had never been his forte and, at this end of his career, his strength was naturally depleted. A three-week race was probably beyond him, but the twin imperatives of all riders – money and racing instinct – forced him on. He was dosing himself with extra glucose during the Tour, but the effect on his alimentary system was disastrous and he could hardly ingest more substantial food. It is almost certain that, even before Ventoux, he had already driven himself beyond the limit of physical punishment that his body could absorb. As for the amphetamines, this was nothing out of the ordinary. US Airforce pilots took them *de rigeur* to obviate drowsiness on missions. Simpson, it can be said, broke his own heart on that mountain.

It was – still is – a tough world that all amateur English riders faced when they crossed the Channel, hoping to succeed in a harsh profession, contending against continental riders whose traditional *métier* is road-racing. The training and competition was, is, unforgivingly hard, the homesickness often worse, and until they secured any sort of reputation they remained the outsiders. Add to that the gnawing anxiety that they will have to give up and go home penniless failures. The crushing sense of waste; self-confidence chewed out: racing for a living in the one race they can't win, against time. But: 'Half the failures in life arise from pulling in one's horse as he is leaping . . .' (Julius and Augustus Hare) and Simpson wasn't one to flinch from the risk.

As Dr Johnson said of another cruel profession: 'Sir, he who would earn his bread by writing books must have the assurance of a duke, the wit of a courtier and the guts of a burglar.' I would add: 'and the staying power of a *touriste-routier*.'

Britons have made the trip across the Channel and succeeded: their tally of stage wins in the Tour gives some indication. Adding to that melancholy stage victory in Sète that day, Hoban, a rated sprinter, took seven others in 11 Tour appearances (1964–68) and was a valued *domestique* of both Poulidor and Zoetemelk. Michael Wright, born in England but brought up in Belgium, won three stages between 1964 and 1974. Robert Millar rode every Tour between 1983 and '93 and finished eight, but in 1984 achieved the highest placing yet of any Briton when he took fourth and the Mountains Prize. Wins at Luchon, '83, two summit wins – Guzet Neige '84 and an elbow-to-elbow with the '88 yellow jersey Pedro Delgado in 1989 – reinforce the reputation of Millar as a climber of exceptional class. A consistently fluent and strong example of that rare breed of rider who loves to see the Alps and Pyrenees ahead, he has crossed a whole clutch of cols ahead of the Tour *peloton*. In a later Tour, climbing to that same finish on Guzet Neige, Millar inexplicably took a wrong turn 2km below the summit, following the signal of a gendarme waving the cars into a car park. He missed what might have been a second victory up there. A case of bad luck, perhaps. Millar attracted bad luck.

In 1985, he was well placed to win the Spanish Vuelta but found himself racing virtually unaided against the entire *peloton*. He went into the penultimate stage with ten seconds on the Colombian Rodriguez and a hefty six minutes and 13 seconds over the Spaniard, Delgado. His Peugeot team were exhausted; a wholesale effort to protect their leader had overextended them and the manager, Berland, had, reportedly, refused an offer from Luis Ocaña, now manager of the Fagor team, to sell his men's services to protect Millar's jersey. A case of French hauteur: Peugeot, said Berland, didn't need help.

The attacks came on the first climb of the day; the Peugeots were all over the road, in the parlance, even the ultra-hard man Yates climbed off his bike. And the attacks kept coming: this was a concerted effort by the home riders to rip the Peugeot challenge apart. Millar punctured. Delgado was off the front in a breakaway group; Millar in a chasing group of 20 riders, none of whom would work with him; why should they? At 23km from the finish, Millar's original lead over the Spaniard was down to one minute and 17 seconds. Millar tried vainly to enlist support for his pursuit. 'But there was no chance,' he said. 'They all knew what was happening. They just sat there and laughed at me.'

He was 400m from the arrival line when the crowd roared: the ticking clock had swallowed up the remaining seconds of the deficit and Delgado pulled on the amarillo (yellow) leader's jersey. Millar complained about a coalition against him that day; Merckx rode against such coalitions throughout his career.

Max Sciandri, another Brit with a continental education, won the flat stage into St Etienne in the '95 Tour and miffed the parochial British cycling magazine editor by conducting his post-victory press conference in Italian.

The British domestic scene is a backwater, no proving ground nor efficacious preparation for that big league. Short on money, contacts, social habituation, language and, above all, professional nous, the Brit abroad, however highly gifted, finds himself matched with comfortably paid rivals – even the amateurs – born into and shaped by a tough system. It's hard to acclimatise; the transition to pro is hard enough anyway. The problem of language, first of all. Simpson records being in a restaurant early on and the waitress asking him:

'L'addition, monsieur?'

Thinking she was asking him if he wanted more, he said: 'Non.'

She asked him again; 'Non' and so it went on. She was actually asking him if he wanted the bill. Another time, at a hotel in Pau, he asked the French riders how to ask for the toilet. They told him to say: 'Avez-vous un chiotte, s'il vous plait?' Do you have a shit-house, please? and stood back to watch the fun, when he strode up to the receptionist. Part and parcel of the pro job, laughing and making people laugh, an old pro told Simpson.

Unless a foreign rider can somehow make himself at home, like Sherwen who not only learned to *speak* French but, as it were, to *do* French and ditch all preconceived ideas about the way to do things, the *peloton* will give him an extremely rough ride and, like as not, he'll go under. Over there, they do things differently. A rider finds himself in a sort of feudal organisation, a tightly closed shop observing and imposing quasi-masonic rituals of duty, status, loyalty and what is and is not permissible. Riders untutored in the rigid team ethic will simply not survive. Robert Millar, who has recently undertaken an experimental role as national coach in continental bike racing, has found the home-based British riders unruly and self-centred, driven by personal ambition and to hell with anyone else. No lack of talent or basic motivation; almost complete ignorance of the need for unquestioning co-operation, the anonymity of the individual within the team set-up. A wholly insular attitude, in fact.

Simpson records an example of how the hierarchy works. He entered the 1964 Paris–Nice intending to use is solely as preparation for the Milan–San Remo, first classic of the season, the 'race of springtime'. On the last stage, Anquetil wore the leader's jersey. Simpson, sticking to his own private plan, with no interest in the race, and chuckling at the thought of stirring up the pack, attacked on the big climb of La Turbie near the start and flew away at such a speed that the *peloton* peeled off in all directions. Anquetil sent Altig after him. He caught the Briton halfway and gave him an angry scolding: this was no way to pace a stage. Simpson ignored him and attacked flat out; Altig was dropped, chased, caught up again. Once more Simpson leapt clear and was gone, over the top and down towards Monaco, leaving the field behind him in ribbons. The Philco team abandoned *en bloc*. 'Everyone hated my guts, but I didn't give a hoot.' He stopped, and watched the *peloton* as it rode by, calling out cheerily: '*Ciao*', before riding along the coast road to Nice, having ridden only 40 of that day's 180km.

He won the Milan–San Remo and later that year was in the lead on stage two of the three-day Tour du Var. 3km from the finish, he came to the bottom of a sharp hill which he'd failed to spot on the course map and took sudden fright. Anquetil and Henri Anglade, deadly rivals in normal circumstances, launched a fierce attack in tandem. Anquetil took the leader's jersey and Simpson cursed the pair of them. Anquetil took him on one side, smiled his quiet smile and said: 'The coin has two sides you know, Tom. Good deeds are always repaid and bad ones, too.' Simpson was puzzled. Anquetil explained: 'If you hadn't made such monkeys of us on La Turbie, you'd have won this race.' Hard lessons.

Sean Yates and Paul Sherwen, for instance, both typify the solid reliability and ability, if not blue-chip, star quality of those handful of British riders who have made an indelible mark on continental bike racing. They also epitomise the willingness to embrace the continental ethos wholeheartedly. Sherwen's own record is respectable if not outstanding. Now a respected Channel Four commentator, he completed five Tours (started seven); never won a stage, but, testimony to the high regard in which he was held is the fact that when he crashed heavily on an Alpine stage in the '85 Tour and missed the time limit, he was generously reinstated on merit. The caprice of the race organisers isn't always ill-natured.

The story deserves full recall. Just 4km out from the start in Epinal, Sherwen spotted one of his La Redoute team-mates heading for a collision, grabbed his jersey and held him upright; the unselfish deed cost him his own balance, though, and he slammed into a metal barrier at the side of the road. He came off, his back badly bruised and, even as the race doctor was tending to him, Bernard Hinault launched a ferocious attack: softening up the *peloton*, no doubt, showing them who was the *patron*. Sherwen remounted already five minutes behind. Hinault was still head down and the chase was hotting up to a frantic speed. Two of Sherwen's team men, Regis Simon and Alain Bondue, had pulled back to help him rejoin, and though *Le Blaireau* was reined in after 15km, the *peloton* had decided to keep him at it and were still thrashing the big gears. Sherwen – his back in such agony that he could hardly sit on the bike – simply could not match the pace, even relayed by his men. The bunch were cruising at fully 3kph faster than their best. It became obvious that he probably wasn't going to make it: he told them to leave him, not to risk elimination themselves. They were professionals; there was no refuting the imperative of duty and so, 20km into the stage, Sherwen was left to his fate, flanked by the backmarker motorbike gendarme and dogged by the sinister broom wagon, those two engines grinding in his head like a dentist's drill. 'Having that truck behind me all day actually helped,' said Sherwen. 'That would be a very undignified ending . . . going out of the world's greatest bike race by the back door.'

Three and a half hours later, 66km from the finish in Pontarlier, Pedersen launched what proved to be the winning break; Sherwen was an hour down, excruciating sharp pains shooting down his back with every turn of the cranks. When Pedersen crossed the line at 4.20 p.m., Sherwen was 40km adrift, facing a long weary climb to the finish at 1,200m. The punishment of that cruel day's pursuit, driven only by pride through pain and the yearning for it just to stop, can only be guessed at.

Sherwen reached the line 26 minutes outside the elimination time and it is a mark of the esteem in which he was held and the courage he showed that day, that in a gesture of flamboyant generosity the officials simply waived the rules and reinstated him. Never had a prize for the day's most combative rider been more richly deserved. And next morning? Back on the bike, Paul.

One British rider, Graham Jones, was, in the opinion of many, more or less crushed by the system. He showed enormous promise on his début in 1980, yet, forced into the humble role of water carrier, he never emerged as the leader he clearly had the prowess to be. Anquetil, however, had no patience with such excuses.

A French rider who'd made a splash in the amateur ranks was asked by a journalist why he'd achieved so little as a pro. 'I'm in Jacques Anquetil's team.'

'So?'

'Well, we all have to work exclusively for him. If only I could ride for myself.'

Anquetil read this and told the man he could ride the Dauphiné Libéré and the Grand Prix du Midi so that he could 'express himself with complete freedom' while he rode the Giro. Even the French phrase 'express himself' hints at the very different attitude to this whole business of bike-racing; a difference of culture, even.

Merckx sums it up: Coppi first came to the fore in the Giro, when riding in the same team with the acknowledged leader Bartali. Pingeon's victory in the Tour owed much to the support of the established leader Poulidor. 'Being in a team with an out-right *leader* (French uses the English word) limits the possibilities for an individual, it's true, but a gifted rider can always find some way of showing how good he is. I never saw a man capable of taking victories sacrificing himself all year round. On the other hand, I do know of men who get unexpected wins solely because they were riding in a champion's team and every rival in the *peloton* was concentrating on *him*.'

In the end it is a matter of *will*. As Merckx says, you can test a rider's potential approximately with morphological and physio-logical tests, but no one knows what laws govern the will, nor can the will be measured. There can be no theory as to what constitutes a racing cyclist.

I'm wondering when I will catch my first sight of Ventoux. The fascination of its coming epiphany in the distance works on me. I know of its distinctive barrow-like shape by reputation. Its other characteristic reputation, too – '*Le Mont Ventoux ne tolère pas le surrégime* (Mont Ventoux takes orders from no one),' wrote

Marcel Bidot, who died on 26 January 1995, at the venerable age of 92. Can a mountain have a personality? Believe it.

My nerves are beginning to flutter, there's no denying, and on the 10km downhill into Ferrassières, a narrow road which eats too much ground, grows a big gut and opens out into the width of a boulevard, the wind starts to rip into me with dire force out of the north west, an onslaught so violent that it buffets me sideways now and then, like a lorry's slipstream. Manageable if you know it's coming, but dangerous in ambush. I nearly lose the front wheel a couple of times. And, suddenly, there, in what seems like another world, miles away, rises up a preposterously large mountain into a torn blue sky. Incalculably vast and aloof, a naked summit, white as monumental alabaster, the bloodless white of death, topped by a radio mast, like a steeple. So remote is it that I imagine any roads going up there must belong to different scales of tick-tock and map measurement, with time locks between them and the road I am riding. A real ogre with winter in its hair, a gale screaming out of its throat and an extremely uncomfortable way of staring at a body. I didn't want to believe this was Ventoux. I couldn't believe it wasn't Ventoux. It was Ventoux, all right.

At the bottom of the valley, in Sault, the wind is headed off round hidden breaks and I ride into the lull gratefully. A lovely peace, all at once. It was at siesta time in the town; baking sunshine, and I'm as warm as a pie. Here I have the option to stay, that choice like a newly minted fifty pound banknote tucked in my wallet. A trio stroll by; almost certainly on their way back from a long lunch. I slow without stopping and ask the time. Quarter past three.

In fine weather, feeling strong, in all practicality and honour I couldn't not go on.

From Sault, at 735m, to the top (at 1,829m) I face 26km to add to the 96km I have already done.

Overhead, the wind moaned like a bittern in mourning, a constant whine that occasionally altered pitch to a grumble or a howl.

The road emerges from the trees. Effulgent sun glares off the white shale of *lauzes*, chalk lozenges that litter the bald eminence of Ventoux and, like Mount Fuji, give an effect, from a distance, of snow. And towering aloft, 200m up into the sky, 6km away, the crest and the radio mast. And the wind, my God, the wind.

This is Mont Ventoux and in a stark fury, too. Briefly, its summit looks to me undreamable, beyond me. Only briefly; I can't admit such doubts. I know that this is going to be hard and steep. Not only is the mountain bare, the road has become no better than a nasty metalled causeway: broad, exposed, ugly, its ramps piled up like zigzags on an Inca pyramid and raked by a raging gale force wind.

Those meagre 6km make a horrible, unremitting, gut-wrenching, demoralising slog. I hate it; it nearly finishes me; it is cruel to a power beyond rational grasp. I cling on, literally cling on.

And here was what I knew I'd see: a granite stele on which is cut a polished intaglio of Simpson, hunched over the bike, riding at speed.

À LA MEMOIRE
DE TOM SIMPSON
MEDAILLE OLYMPIQUE, CHAMPION DU MONDE,
AMBASSADEUR SPORTIF BRITANNIQUE,
DÉCÉDÉ LE 13 JUILLET TOUR DE FRANCE 1967
SES AMIS ET CYCLISTES DE GRANDE BRETAGNE

Scattered in front of it lies a wrack of dry flowers and old tubular tyres like exotic seaweed from a flood tide. I have not a scruple of energy to pay for a stop, nor even to contemplate.

Merckx had ridden with Simpson in the Peugeot team at the start of his career. On his second Tour he crossed Ventoux in the yellow jersey and, as he passed the spot where his old *patron* had fallen, he removed his cap and clutched it over his heart, in silent tribute. Jacques Goddet lay flowers on the memorial stone as he rode by.

Merckx was one of the few continental riders who attended

Simpson's funeral. Years later, he paid him generous compliment: 'It's unjust that his name should forever be so indelibly linked with drugs. The controls in those days weren't systematic and I don't pretend that Simpson didn't use a prohibited substance; he was far from being alone. He was a great rider who boosted me from the benefit of his own experience in training methods, dietary regimes, racing nous and the study of race routes. Not all old pros would do that with younger riders; especially with a rider they could see posed a serious threat to them. Simpson was warm-hearted and open-handed. Nor was he the dope-head some people paint him as. On the slopes of Ventoux his ambition killed him. His pride had no limits. He never relinquished the belief that he could win the Tour de France. If he'd had the support of a sporting director in a commercial team, he'd never have been put back on his bike when he was so groggy. Nor was he a drinker, but on very hot days it's not unusual for a rider to take a glass of cold white wine or a beer offered by a spectator. That day was so hot: ten people died from the heat in Brussels.'

An example of Simpson's education of the young Merckx in racing nous. The 1967 Paris–Nice. Merckx had already won a stage and was wearing the leader's white jersey. On the stage over the col de la République Simpson attacked and wrested the *maillot* from him, reasserting his position as team leader. Two days later, the irrepressible Merckx was once again leading the race on the climb of Mont Faron, with the '66 Tour winner, Aimar, with Guyot and Simpson in pursuit. Gaston Plaud, the Peugeot sporting director drove up and told Merckx to wait for Simpson. He did so and relayed him 25km to the stage finish and overall victory in Nice.

This submissive loyalty, a sort of vassalage, is hard for the uninitiated to understand. It is taken to extreme lengths in Italy where if the *campionissimo* decides he wants an easy day the entire *peloton* conforms and any hothead who launches an unauthorised attack gets a roasting. Hinault was a known *patron* who could put the damper on a day of the Tour; but that must be seen in the context of the peculiar nature of the stage race, where, for the most part, the serious business of the day is concentrated in the final hour and the acceleration and jockeying for pole position in the sprint home. If the Tour takes in a rider's home town or, more poignantly, his village, he will be allowed to go ahead and lead the race through – on the proviso that he doesn't use the temporary release as the basis for an escape. Sean Yates had this honour in Forest Row, Sussex, when the Tour came to England in 1994.

The subservience of the young rider to the senior is no more than an apprenticeship; the newcomer has to earn his spurs, pay his dues and assimilate the rules which apply to team racing: that the individual ambition can only operate within the demands of overall victory and the success of the designated leader. This may lead to a clash of interest. In the 1997 Tour, the manager of the German Telekom team, Walter Godefroot, a great sprinter in his day, one of Merckx's most energetic rivals – a wonderful solo ride to beat the Cannibal in the 1969 Paris–Roubaix, for example – was diplomatic about his co-leaders: whichever of Rijs and Ullrich proved stronger would be *de facto* leader; time would tell. The road would tell.

On the first day in the Pyrenees, stage nine, over the Soulor, the Tourmalet, the Aspin and the Azet cols, Ullrich played the obedient second and Rijs struggled. Godefroot praised Ullrich's power but made no statement about the leadership. Next day, whatever decisions had been made in private, the event proved the fact: Rijs was weak – he always had a bad day on the first mountain stages, he said – and Ullrich showed his hand to the climbers, Virenque and Pantani. They held on but the young German took the stage, the yellow jersey and the leadership of his team. Rijs slipped back into the ranks.

Merckx's assessment of what makes a good team rider is revealing: he was careful to choose men to whom not even a suspicion of drug-taking was attached; they had to have an instinctive feel for a race, knowing when to control an attack without having to be told. 'I hate having to give orders.' However diverse their individual talents they were alike in one trait: total devotion to their leader, a loyalty which he repaid handsomely by converting their selfless support for him into victory after victory, the financial rewards of which they shared in. And their victories, too – Merckx sat up at the end of one race to let his faithful lieutenant Jos Bruyère ride through for the win. Merckx could afford it, but millionaires aren't notably free with their money and the gesture carried weight.

The Italians used to carry the hierarchical system to extreme lengths: the offer of lump sums in cash to a rival to throw a race. Very often this arose from bitter memory of a harsh childhood, as in the case of Gianni Motta who came from extreme poverty to the ranks of pro bike-racing. He left Simpson panting on a climb in the 1964 Tour of Lombardy and won on his own; on the descent of the Vars, next year, he tried to 'persuade' Poulidor to ride with him – if they reached the bottom of the Izoard in tandem, nobody would catch them and one of them would win the Tour. Poulidor refused.

I can see the radio mast and station overhead; only three bends and three ramps left. I turn into the first of the ramps, straight into the teeth of the Mistral roaring at me with appalling ferocity. I weave 30m, the handlebars twisting as the wind tries to take the wheels from under me, and come to a dead stop. I hastily kick one foot out of the pedal footplate – I might simply have toppled sideways like a tipsy Centaur passing out – and rest for a bit astride the bike, staring up this shortish climb, in what passes for the lee of the mountain; 200m to a bend, another similar ramp and the last bend at the top.

A lull in the wind; I try to ride on; 30m and I am blown to a standstill once more. This is a gale out of the invention of primal wind, an elemental fury. Aeolus or the god Vin Tur have unleashed the entire sackful of the hurricanes that howl through Chaos over this terrible rock. Impossible to ride in this. I clamber off the bike to walk and can hardly even do that. My shoes slide on a rink of wind, the bike leaps and bucks like a loose toe of canvas in a storm. Yes, time dies in my shoes. It isn't that I am out of strength; I have never had strength sufficient to cope with that wind's force.

On the 1969 Tour, the Mistral hit the *peloton* at 70kph throughout the stage in the Camargue. Goddet and Lévitan, the race directors, took pity and allowed the riders to tuck in behind the support vehicles for the last 50km. As Poulidor described it: 'An authorised *en masse* doping.' Little comfort to me.

I struggle to the dog-leg turn at the top and find a bit of shelter. The wind shrieks over the parapet embankment. I remount and cycle the last few hundred metres.

My senses have been turned inside out like a skinned rabbit. I have no room for elation, no room for joy, no energy to give it standing room in the foyers of my imagination. Nor is there any obvious sympathy with this demonstration of Nature's power, either. Nature has subjected me to an alarming spell in the rough house and I can't see this mountain in any but the terms of a screeching gale and a wild, steep place.

One thing remains to do: I pick up a stone from the scree near the radio mast, an unlovely iron tower set in soda-white concrete, and stuff it in a side pocket of my saddle bag – for my friend Ronnie's cairn. Cyclist, poet and piper, he'd died before his time of a brain tumour the year before. There is a lot of death brooding on this mountain.

Shuddering with rage, relief and jangled nerves, I struggle to the very top, the absolute summit, where nothing can be higher, and recoil with dismay. The road simply snaps in two and disappears over a precipice: no parapet wall, no safety barriers, like a fledgling's plunge from a nest into fresh air boiling with Mistral. I have to go over that?

For the moment I retreat back down from the summit to a café, a dodgy enough descent, all of 200m. The view which stretches beyond, in a gaseous haze south, across the sprawling Plateau de Vaucluse towards the Lubéron catches my eye, but only for a few seconds: I have to concentrate on getting safely into the shelter of the café wall. I drink hot coffee and steeped sugar lumps. I ponder Simpson's passing and my passing of his memorial stone, and Yeats' epitaphic poem:

> Cast a cold eye
> On life, on death.
> Horseman, pass by.

The 30 miles from Sault to Malaucène over Ventoux is the more ecstatic, paradoxically, because even as I fly into town on the last wingbeats of that fantastic swoop off the mountain's summit, I am promising myself *Never, never, never will I ride up that mountain again, never, never.*

It springs from an indescribable cloudburst in my head of joy, relief and thanks due to whatever spirits guard us through adversity and when we are close to breakdown. In ancient times, stranded up on that inhuman pinnacle, I would have vowed my *own* votary cairn to Fortune who protected me and the god of the mountain who spared me.

I find a hotel in the main street, secure my bike in a sort of lock-up store room with a higgledy-piggledy collection of discarded furniture, electrical apparatus, boxes of newspapers, and go up for the shower of showers. My walking-out clothes on, and across the street for my reward: several beers and dinner in the same bar/restaurant. A bottle of Côtes de Ventoux, of course. I keep the bill for my scrapbook. I brim over with contentment; 140km and Mont Ventoux.

They called my hero Merckx, *Le Cannibale,* but the word was, it seems, first used in cyclist journalism of Poulidor in a stage of the 1965 Tour – another second place, to Gimondi by two minutes and 40 seconds. The writer said he swallowed up Mont Ventoux '*avec la voracité d'un cannibale engloutissant le mollet d'un archevêque . . .*' (with the voracity of a cannibal wolfing down a leg of archbishop.)

About a week after my return to England, I was going smoothly at a fair pace to the top of Highgate West Hill, that evil little pimple whose gradient sprang to mind on the first ramp of l'Alpe d'Huez, when a paunchy, oldish man on the far pavement yells: 'Push harder on the pedals.' No hint of a smile or cheer of encouragement.

In France they shout – pedestrians or cyclists, it makes no difference – *Allez! Courage!*

A month after the return, I did climb Mont Ventoux again, in a manner of speaking. The piece for the wind quintet arrived.

CHAPTER EIGHT

TOUR '98

The Tour is Dead, Long Live the Tour

At 5.30 a.m. on the morning of Wednesday, 8 July 1998, three days before the Tour de France Prologue, French Customs officials in the town of Neuville en Ferrain, just inside the Franco–Belgian border, made a routine search of a Fiat car driven by Willy Voet, *soigneur* to the Festina team. In the Fiat, part of the official Tour fleet, were packed over 400 phials of human growth hormones and testosterone-based steroids, boxes of EPO, masking products, anti-hepatitis vaccines and quantities of syringes. Voet was taken to Lille police HQ for interview and later that same day a squad of French judiciary (criminal investigation) police searched the Festina base in Lyon and impounded more drugs. Bruno Roussel, the Festina *directeur sportif,* haughtily dismissed these events as a sick joke.

The following Monday, as the Tour rode out of Dublin, Willy Voet admitted that this was not the first time he'd ferried such a haul of performance-enhancing dope to big races, generally, as on this occasion, under orders from the Festina team bosses. Two days later, the 'sick joke' blew up in Roussel's face: after the stage finish in Cholet, he was taken in for police questioning, the Festina riders' hotel rooms were searched and the team doctor, Erik Rijkaert, joined Roussel in the local jail. Next day, the Tour de France organisers announced that Roussel had been banned, while the riders of the Festina team would be allowed to ride on.

Next day Roussel's lawyers issued a statement: the Festina manager had informed the police that within the Festina team controlled doping had been introduced to safeguard the riders' health and wellbeing. Rather than leave the matter of drug-taking to chance, team, policy was to monitor the riders' intake of chemical substances under strict medical supervision. The subtext of this was, naturally: we know all (or even most) professional riders take dope; we can't put our men at a disadvantage; it's our concern, our professional, *responsible* concern, to make sure they take safe dope in safe quantities.

The can of worms was open.

At 10.50 p.m. on the evening of Friday, 17 July, the eve of the individual time-trial, Tour officials announced that the Festina team would, after all, be expelled from the race. The French judiciary police had charged Roussel and Doctor Rijkaert with importing and circulating illegal substances. Ironically, the other teams would ride the race of truth against Festina chronometers but not the Festina riders. At a private meeting, Richard Virenque begged Jean-Marie Blanc, the Tour director, to reconsider the decision but emerged, in tears, to inform a press conference that Festina were out of the Tour.

In the Mosaic ritual for the Jewish Day of Atonement, two goats were chosen, one of which – the scapegoat ('escape' goat) was sent out alive into the wilderness, the sins of all the people having been symbolically laid on it. The other goat was appointed to be sacrificed. Festina had been cast out into the wilderness; the sacrifices were to come.

Virenque, protesting that he had never in his life taken drugs – abjuring declared team policy thereby – called for the Tour organisers to investigate all 22 sporting directors: 'then we'll see what conclusions to draw'. His lawyer declared that Virenque and the rest were being victimised. It is fairly clear that at this point the *peloton* wanted to quit the race *en masse*.

News leaked that as early as the previous March a TVM team lorry had been stopped by customs in Reims and quantities of EPO impounded. The Tour rapidly spiralled into near chaos: police rough handling, fresh revelation, dismissal and strike.

Festina riders' medical dossiers were seized; the riders were detained for questioning in Lyon. Virenque and Pascal Hervé protested their innocence of drug-taking 'with or without our knowledge'; for the time being, the others kept quiet. The TVM riders were hauled out of their hotel after the stage finish on 23 July and detained, without substantial refreshment, until midnight. Their hotel rooms contained cortico-steroids and masking agents. Next day, shocked by the ruthlessness of the police intervention and the ill-treatment meted out to the TVM men, the entire *peloton* sat by their bikes on the road at the start in Tarascon and, for two hours, the Tour de France ceased to be. One Italian rider, Gian Luigi Stanga of the Polti team, remarked that the Gestapo couldn't have done better than the French police, but hysteria of this sort was becoming a commonplace.

The riders eventually set out; Jalabert and two others launched an attack but, having 'made his point' he sat up on a big lead 60km from the finish. No one was interested in racing. The day's stage went for nothing. Interestingly, the Deutsche Telekom team (Ullrich, Rijs, Zabel *et al*) had been ill-disposed to the strike and joined only reluctantly.

Before the next day's stage, Saturday, 25 July, spokesmen from the *peloton* met the UCI president, Daniel Baal, to air grievances about the mishandling of the drugs affair. It has always been the case that the riders bear the brunt of any organisational foul-ups. In the summer of 1998 they were landed with the hardest consequences of the tussle between Tour organisers, UCI and French judiciary police. Some reacted petulantly, but when the so-called authorities were swaying and dipping in whatever breeze of controversy happened to be blowing, the riders, at least, showed a solidarity lacking elsewhere.

If the authorities knew about drug-taking, and when the leading team in the *peloton* had a policy of controlled doping it is inconceivable that they did *not* know, their failure to act is culpable, reprehensible. End of story. As someone said at the time: 'Intellectual honesty and solidarity have been rare commodities these past few days.' Except, I would add, amongst the riders; *de facto* guilty, most of them, but at least prepared to declare common cause.

Next day, three Festina riders – Armin Meier, Laurent Dufaux and Alex Zülle – came clean; they *had* taken EPO and so, too, had most of the other riders they raced against. Zülle, recruited from the powerful Spanish ONCE team at the beginning of the season as co-leader with Richard Virenque, the mountains ace, expatiated on his confession.

> Everybody knew that the whole *peloton* was taking drugs and I had a choice. Either I buckle and go with the trend or I pack it in and go back to my old job as a painter. I regret lying but I couldn't do otherwise. I had to think about my sponsors and people with family responsibilities who worked for Festina. I had no wish to be a traitor. It was my free decision to take EPO and I did so under the supervision of the Festina doctor.

It later emerged that every Festina rider was required – *required* – to pay a yearly subscription into a slush fund to finance the purchase of performance-enhancing drugs for the whole team. It may well be true, as Zülle said in mitigation, that EPO does not turn a donkey into a racehorse, but that is not the point. EPO may well turn an inevitable runner-up into a winner: and that *is* the point.

Zülle's confession is, in some aspects, touching. Arrested by the police in Lyon, he was strip-searched, his spectacles and watch confiscated, and held in a cell for 24 hours, given no sustenance but one glass of water. He was, he said, treated like an animal. He had been so keen to win the Tour that year that he'd been prepared to take a banned substance; to cheat. It's a horrible admission and one wonders how he will live with it. And how Virenque will reconcile in his mind the repeated disavowals he had made against the appearance of his name on the Festina doctor's list of the riders who have had EPO administered to them.

After the Tour, the directors of Festina announced: 'The Tour de France was sensational for our image and reputation.' A claim which the sporting paper, *L'Equipe*, described as '*ubuesque*', anarchic. In this business, cynicism comes dirt cheap.

Even the Canadian doctor who had devised tests for tracing EPO claimed that the UCI was simply not interested. He'd met officials from both the UCI and the IOC but they showed no enthusiasm for establishing tests – using antibodies – which could have proved the use of EPO. Their stated reason was that no such test would bear legal scrutiny. Of this professed nervousness about litigation, Dr Brisson said:

> It was too easy for them to say that, because then nobody can be accused of taking EPO. The arguments they used made it clear that they didn't want to catch athletes. That's always the situation when your responsibility is to promote a sport . . . The solution cannot come from the IOC. I'm sure that they will only act if they are forced to do so . . . But they have to test. Users will change their approach, the trafficking will become more subtle; but now everybody knows the problem is there.

The gradual unravelling of the scandal continued. Blood and hair samples were taken from the TVM team; a BigMat-Auber team lorry was searched and medicines taken away for analysis and the *peloton* reacted again. On Wednesday, 29 July, 32km from the start of stage 17, the *peloton* dismounted and sat in the road. Thence began to-and-fro diplomacy between them and the race organisers. When the riders eventually remounted, Pantani tore off his race number and the rest of the bunch followed suit. There ensued a protracted discussion *en route* between Leblanc and Bjarne Rijs speaking for all the riders. Rijs delivered an ultimatum: no more persecution from the police or we quit. Leblanc replied; Rijs returned to the ranks and the entire *peloton* dismounted a second time. More negotiations, a second restart, followed almost immediately by the abandon of the ONCE, Banesto and Riso Scotti teams. Laurent Jalabert, the ONCE leader, climbed off his bike and said he was finished with the Tour. Hard-nosed commentators said this wasn't moral outrage; Jalabert was going badly, now he was off the hook; but that's an indicator of what miserable depths current opinion was plumbing. The race rolled into Aix-les-Bains at walking pace and another big story broke. The police searched the ONCE team rooms and interviewed Jalabert; the Française des Jeux rooms and interviewed the manager Marc Madiot; and, as Virenque was once more reiterating his denials on French television, police emerged from a search of the Casino team rooms having detained one of their men, current leader in the Mountains prize, Rodolfo

Massi. (The new Mountains leader, Christophe Rinero, refused to wear the polka-dot jersey until he had won it on the next stage.)

Two days later, Massi was charged with selling banned drugs. The Tour de France had spewed out its first drug peddler. A suitcase full of corticoids, growth hormones, steroids, plus a large sum of cash were discovered in his room. He explained, somewhat lamely, that he needed the drugs for his asthma. The man who informed on him, Gilles Bouvard, formerly of Festina and now a team-mate in Casino, had fallen out with Massi earlier in the season. Not only were banned substances going down the pan, so too was loyalty. The ONCE team doctor, Nicolas Terrados joined Massi in custody (both were released on bail) two days before the Tour arrived on the Champs-Elysées where Pantani took victory, the first Italian since Gimondi in 1965 to do so and only the second Italian, after Coppi, to win the Tour and Giro double.

Public reaction to the scandal as it unfolded and as the Tour proceeded was generally in support of the riders. The tarmac bulletins, usually daubed with riders' names, carried: *Le Tour est mort. Vive le Tour.* The Tour is dead. Long live the Tour. And: *Le Tour est innocent. Faut pas toucher au Tour.* The Tour is innocent. Hands off the Tour. But there was this, too: *Ne vous dopez-pas. Faites-nous rêver.* Don't take dope. Allow us our dreams. And wherever blame might be apportioned, one message to the riders, the officials, all of them, individually, was clear: *Il y a de soi – c'est évident.* It's up to you – wake up.

Someone wrote: 'There's something rotten in this sport – the Festina affair is proof enough. But that does not stop one admiring the cyclists.' The magnificent, shattering solo ride of Pantani's up to Les Deux Alpes, in atrocious weather, wind, rain, fog, to trounce Ullrich by over seven minutes and effectively seal his final victory, was awe-inspiring and Ullrich's audacious attack the following day on the Madeleine, some 54km from home, a heroic strike to salvage pride worthy of the great champions. Only Pantani could hold his wheel and, at the finish, the two of them drove themselves over the line, exhausted, like two prize-fighters who'd slugged each other to a standstill. It was legendary stuff and put the whole dismal drugs brouhaha into a very squalid perspective. These were men still capable of riding into extremes of suffering. Ullrich's bravery gave Pantani a triumph worthy of the little Italian's own great courage. In such actions are the real champions revealed.

Even as Pantani and Ullrich were demonstrating that the basic instinct to attack at all costs and damn the consequences was still alive in some riders, the reputation of those who quit the race was sullied; not so much because they seemed to be dodging the issue of culpability on the drugs charges, but because to abandon is, without pressing cause, at very best undignified. When Bobet pulled out in 1959, he climbed into the car of *Le Parisien* and asked one of the journalists to lend him a hat so he could disguise himself. 'I'm ashamed to abandon,' he said.

Censure of the 1998 escapees was robust: 'Every rider who abandons is blameworthy because in that act they are destroying what earned them their glory.' (The glory of riding in the Tour, that is.)

Luc Leblanc commented: 'Jalabert should have stayed out of respect for the Tour, that is what one would have expected of a French champion.' (Jalabert was wearing the tricolour jersey as national road-race champion.)

A rider who abandons snaps something essential in his own spirit; he abandons an ideal. Lofty sentiments which had to be retrieved from the sordid detritus of post-Tour revelations and deal-mongering. Grubbiest of all came the announcement by the Festina sponsors that as a result of the scandal Festina had sold far more watches than any of their market forecasts predicted. Here is the real source of the evil: greed.

The Tour organisers handle an annual budget of 25 million pounds: 15 million pounds from the various corporate-backed sponsors, eight million pounds from television rights, two million pounds from the *villes d'étape*. Cycling teams dispose of between two million pounds and four million pounds per annum, and commercial imperatives drive the whole shebang. The ruthless profiteering of international pharmaceutical corporate firms is notorious; the financial rewards for highest-level success in cycling sport are exorbitant; the venality equally so. *Le Parisien* commented: 'We are all accomplices in this grotesque hypocrisy because we all know that drug-taking is prevalent in the Tour de France. Taking into account the fact that the race is dependent on high financial stakes, you realise it couldn't be otherwise. When you are in a team and have to earn a living you have no choice. For this reason, it is inconceivable that the Festina team is the only guilty party.'

Festina had the ill luck to be caught first. The UCI even considered forbidding the Spanish-sponsored Festina team from the national tour, the Vuelta a España but, in the upshot, took no action for fear of litigation from the Festina lawyers or individual riders seeking damages for loss of earnings. The Vuelta organisers, like those of the Tour, invite whatever teams they choose. Thus, the UCI has no legitimated power to exclude riders from a large proportion of the yearly racing calendar; much of what they do is no more conclusive than posturing and bold talk. However, pronouncements on the subject were sufficient to provoke a feud between the Spanish and French cycling federations. The route of the Vuelta was altered to remove a couple of stages which had been planned to cross the Pyrenees into France.

Nearly two weeks after the Tour, the UCI promulgated a list of measures designed to combat the use of drugs in cycling:

1. There would be no change in existing dope controls – classic blood and urine tests to be used.
2. From 1 January 1999, there are to be four annual checks on riders' health (both physiology and hormone levels), this to be the responsibility of national federations and conducted by an independent medical inspectorate appointed by the UCI.

    These checks will go much further than in the present checks on red corpuscle levels and produce a more general profile of the athletes' physical condition 'to verify that an athlete's organism is functioning well and to avoid accidents from the misuse of drugs'.
3. Responsibility is enjoined on team doctors:
    – to maintain regulations
    – to uphold ethics
    – to protect health and advise cyclists (who, if left to their own devices, face too many risks).

4. An anti-EPO programme, centred on laboratories in Lausanne and Cologne.

The issue of racing fatigue is addressed by ordinances which:

1. Limit the length of the racing season, whereby each rider might be confined to racing on between 90 and 120 days only. (This was put up for discussion.)
2. Reform the system of selecting teams for the major events. The present system is based on team rankings; but classification is derived from an assessment of performance in every single race in the calendar, so as to avoid losing the top teams and their star riders in the lesser races.

From 1999, there will be fewer qualifying events (two of the three big Tours, every World Cup race plus a few other senior events, such as the Dauphiné Libéré).)

Thus there will be a qualitative not a quantitative assessment 'to encourage the top teams to compete less often but harder.'

On the face of it, a genuine attempt to address the symptoms of the disease, at least. Except that less than two months later, on Monday, 5 October, the UCI issued a statement: The original eight-month ban levied on the three Festina Tour riders implicated in the drugs scandal (Meier, Zülle and Dufaux) had been reduced by one month, to allow them to ride in next year's Tour. The fines imposed – a paltry £1,346 apiece – stood. So much for the authorities.

It is the opinion of many – amateurs and professionals – that the penalty for taking drugs should be an immediate, unequivocal ban from the sport for life. It is a view implicitly supported by Bertrand de Gallé, for instance, the president of La Française des Jeux: a clause in his team contracts warns any rider caught taking banned substances of instant dismissal from the team.

There have been noises lately from riders about a new 'clean' *peloton*. In October 1998, the Festina sponsors vowed to take a lead in fighting the use of drugs and pledged a fund of $725,000 to wage war on dope-taking. They've even nominated a French doctor, Gerard Dine, to work as scientific consultant in analysing and monitoring the effects of industrially produced substances on cyclists. There may well be a huge collective relief attendant on this. However many pro cyclists take drugs, it is undoubtedly the case that many do so reluctantly, only because they know that if they don't they risk being consistently beaten by lesser talents. Commentators have adjudged Boardman's career in the pro ranks to have been so hampered; the promise he showed on the track having faltered, somewhat, in the long stage races. As the French paper *L'Equipe* put it: 'It depends, above all, on the determination expressed by the riders to show a genuine will to escape from a system of which, ultimately, they are victims . . . and then, finally, *happily* [my italics] there are the police . . .'

That great opponent of drug-testing, Jacques Anquetil, always backed the police as the only neutral authority whom he could trust. The calamitous events of 1998 rather endorse this view. Perhaps the very professional meticulousness of the French judiciary police, experienced as brutal and ruthless by the riders, delivered the harsh visitation of some kind of truth-telling – at last – without which the drug-taking would, once more, have simply been ignored by authorities whose attitude to positive dope tests was wholly in line with their own lack of positive action.

CHAPTER NINE

1999

The Tour of Renewal

With an irony even the French could not have foreseen, the organisers of the Tour de France chose to launch the last race of the millennium from Madman's Bluff – Le Puy du Fou – in the Vendée. The Festina affair had all but scuppered the '98 edition: it seemed to many cynics and ill-informed, sniping commentators an act of pure folly to run the race at all, mired as it had become in the drugs scandal. Examining magistrates in France had spent the winter trawling through grisly evidence of systematic doping in the professional *peloton*; riders who had owned up to the practice served their suspension; others kept quiet. Richard Virenque continued to protest his total innocence under judicial oath and in May, Willy Voet, the ex-*soigneur* from Festina, now out of a job, blew the whole gaffe with a book packed with 'revelations of 30 years of cheating'.

Massacre à la Chaîne ('Serial Murder' or 'Murder as a job requirement') is a shocking book, its gruesome candour fuelled by a distinct – and understandable – bitterness that its author has been made to carry the can for a whole phalanx of parties as guilty as him. Voet reproduces extracts from his notebooks recording the dosage of EPO and growth hormones dispensed to the Festina riders over a number of years. Names, dates, quantities. He talks of pills doled out like sweets, dope controls tricked by means of a urine-filled condom attached to a length of rubber tubing – 'a pipe up the arse' – of injections administered to riders on the move, once driving the needle in through a rider's shorts, a boost to carry him to the finish; of intravenous drips rigged in hotel rooms; and of one scene of grotesque farce when a visitor blundered into the Festina dope lounges and Virenque and another rider had to scoot into the bathroom, hauling the drips, still attached, with them.

Nor was it only the riders caught up in this routine drug culture. Voet kept himself going through endless car journeys and long séances of work as masseur and mobile dispensary with a heady cocktail of amphetamines, analgesics, cocaine, heroin and the occasional dash of corticoids known as *le pot Belge* – the Belgian slug, shot, pick-me-up.

Voet's confessions and the extensive testimony that the French judicial police drew out of him make depressing reading – one doctor was nicknamed 'Mabuse' (Self-abuse) from his readiness to dole the stuff out. What price enthusiasm, now? How can we not *all* be cynics in this seamy light?

So, whether or not one believes that Tour director Jean-Marie Leblanc really did not know to what extent drugs had dominated cycling, his announcement of this *Tour de Renouveau* was a brave call for a fresh start. There could be no eradication of suspicion – the scandal had been too traumatic – but in the true spirit of Desgrange, the real challenge was to demand that the Tour reinvent itself. This was, of course, greeted with derision by many. It had become horribly clear that the '98 Tour de France? Tour de Farce was too salacious a story for the muckraking journos wallowing in their own whited-sepulchre piety to pass up. No matter that the cyclists were, willy-nilly, bearing the brunt of the witch-hunt and that drug-taking was suspected in practically every other sport: if the Tour de France is not *all* cycling it is certainly cycling's enlarging mirror. If the Tour de France could not clean up its act, what chance for the sport as a whole? There was much to play for.

The Tour's renewal extended further than the elimination of drugs. Within a month or so of the Prologue, several of the main contenders were out. Jan Ullrich, the '97 winner, aggravated a knee injury in the Tour of Switzerland and withdrew. Bjarne Rijs, the '96 laureate, broke his arm in the same race and would not start. Laurent Jalabert, the world number one, who had enraged many by not only quitting the '98 Tour but persuading others to follow, had effectively exiled himself from France by going to live in Switzerland and refusing to submit to the new strict, even harsh, mandatory drug tests lately imposed by the French Cycling Federation. The 1998 yellow jersey, Marco Pantani, had been playing cat and mouse all year: he might, only might, ride the Tour. The course was too easy for a specialist climber like me, he said, but he said the same before his victory. And there is no such thing as an easy course: you just ride harder. Yet, cruising towards a second successive victory in the Giro d'Italia, a routine blood test revealed an abnormally high count of red corpuscles in his bloodstream, and he was eliminated 'for health reasons'. The implication – without incontrovertible proof – was that he had taken EPO; this he strenuously denied, but the UCI had set an upper limit of 50 per cent and Pantani showed 53 per cent.

This was bold of the Giro directors: to ban Italy's sporting hero, darling of the *tifosi*, on the eve of another triumph took considerable nerve. Whatever credit it did them, it inevitably complicated things across the Alps. Double Tour and Giro winner in 1998, the famously incendiary attacker Pantani was suspect of doping. Well, he wouldn't be riding the Tour: the field was being cleared of compromise.

At a press conference in Paris on 16 June, Leblanc (who rode the Tour in 1968 and 1970) posted warning that the new stringency would apply to everyone, no favours. Philippe Gaumont and Laurent Roux, who had both tested positive earlier in the season, were banned; Serguei Gonchar had been kicked off the Tour of Switzerland for a high haematocrit test (registering the proportion of red blood cells) and he and his Vini Caldirola team were expelled from the Tour. So too was Manolo Saiz, team doctor of Jalabert's ONCE team, for persistently making defamatory remarks about the Tour in the wake of the drugs scandal. The TVM team, who had mounted a very public protest after being rough-handled during the '98 Tour and then quit *en bloc*, were refused entry to the race because they had discredited it.

Controversially, Richard Virenque, darling of the French public, four-times winner of the Mountains Prize, baby-faced pinup the women swoon over, star of *Virenboum*, Virenque mania, made the start. Booted off the 1998 race, still protesting his innocence of any doping and due for trial, he was allowed to ride.

That, sadly, wasn't the end of it. The UCI intervened, pre-sumably having been leant on by Virenque's Italian team Polti (by racing in Italy he too avoided the draconian French régime), insisting that the Tour de France organisers had not given Virenque sufficient notice of disqualification. Virenque squeezed back in, ill-prepared, maybe, but ready to cut the rug in his chosen show.

The UCI, often in the person of its president, Hein Verbruggen, has been much criticised for playing the ostrich, and for its in-decision, lack of clear leadership and equivocation, but this latest fudge and job's-worth primping of strict rule and regulation was disgraceful. A shameful rebuke of an organisation trying hard to wipe the slate clean.

And so to Madman's Bluff.

Some pundits opined that, without many of the big names, this would be a Tour lacking in quality. Such opinions get in the way of renewal. The American, Bobby Julich, who unexpectedly took third in '98, started an obvious favourite. Zülle, restored after suspension and – surely – clean had come second to Indurain in '95 and boasts two Vuelta victories in his *palmarès*, '96 and '97. Here, too, are Abraham Olano, a master of the time-trial but yet to prove himself in the mountains; Pavel Tonkov, Giro winner; Ivan Gotti, Giro winner; Rinero, Mountains prize and fourth overall in '98; Michael Boogerd, the Dutch champion; and Lance Armstrong. The big man from Texas became World Road Race champion in 1993 and two years later was diagnosed with tes-ticular cancer which had spread to his lungs and brain. His being here at all, let alone at the highest level of bike-racing, he freely admits is a miracle. He has prepared for the Tour as 'Tonin' Magne always prepared: 12 days' seclusion riding the mountain stages.

Armstrong took the 6.8km Prologue by seven seconds over Zülle with a matchless display of speed and technical control. Boardman, the speed merchant fancied to take a fourth Prologue victory, was beaten into fifth place, by 16 seconds. This opening ride is no great indicator as to the shape of the race: the time bonuses on offer for sprint prizes and stage wins during the first week of racing tend to make tenure of the first yellow jersey brief, but there is no doubt that Armstrong's win was testimony of two things: his racing form and the intensity of his focus. His eyes are hardly blinking.

For the first six days the sprinters rule. Towards the end of each stage, the Telekoms drive for the line to bring up their man Zabel, aiming for a fourth green Points jersey (to equal Kelly's record); Rabobank wind it up hoping to launch their man McEwen to a win; the Red Train, the scarlet-shirted Saeco riders, Camesso, the young champion of Italy in the tricolour jersey at their head, blast through to shoot Big Mario Cipollini out of the maelstrom of the sprint. Except that Mario, the Lion King, is subdued this year. Saeco think he has had his day and aren't offering to renew his contract. 'They think I am a clapped-out banger,' he says, plaintively, 'and they want to send me to the breaker's yard. A group of friends is splitting up as well. I thought Saeco cared for me more.' The group of friends is the team devoted to getting Cipo onto the podium, and he is out to show his sponsors that his engine is still the fastest in the bunch. But not yet: the 'win merchant' from Estonia, Jaan Kirsipuu, takes the first stage. A historic day for his small country, as he puts it.

Riders take all kind of crazy risks to land a win so the sprint finishes, and the hectic run-up to them often provokes crashes. Recent Tours have been marred by some dreadful pile-ups: riders miscalculating the angle of bend and hurtling into the barriers . . . a touch of wheels in the close press of the accelerating bunch . . . narrow town streets, speed calmers, roundabouts . . . one rider down and the whole troupe behind him. Chris Boardman in '98 had a terrible fall which, had he not been wearing a helmet, would surely have killed him.

And in '99, before Stage Two, Boardman said: 'Today will be the worst day of the week. There's that causeway halfway through the stage and the race will split there for sure. It's so exposed . . . the race will fall to bits.' *That causeway*, the Passage du Gois, joins the Ile de Noirmoutier to the Vendée mainland; 5km long and no more than two cars wide, it disappears under every tide. Riding onto it, Boardman's front wheel skidded on some seaweed; he pulled over and counted to ten. Then, as another rider described it: 'A gust of wind suddenly went across the road; one rider fell and rest began to go down like dominoes.' The narrowness, the treacherous surface, made recovery very difficult. Ahead of the crash, a 75-strong group, half the field, containing Armstrong,

Tonkov, Julich and Virenque, were clear and whipping up the pace towards the finish. Behind it, Zülle, Gotti, Rinero and Boogerd eventually mounted a chase which trailed in over six minutes down. The crash had effectively denied them any realistic chance of winning the race, barring another accident. The demoralising impact of such a heavy loss so early on is cruel. It adds immeasurably to the threat of the mountains. One of Boogerd's team men, Marc Vauters, ended up in hospital, as did Armstrong's henchman, Jonathan Vaughters.

Cipo made history that week. His mood lightened and, whereas his racing had begun to look tentative, even nervous, he began to expand into his hallmark ostentatious flourish of power-sprinting. The Red Train came out of the siding of failed confidence as sleek as ever, threw the points and, on Stage 4, Cipo scorched in comfortably ahead of Zabel: a wondrous turn of speed, on Fagnini's wheel till it's the moment to say the word, Fagnini pulls aside and the man goes. Fagnini has agreed a contract with another team for the end of the season; that must have a lot to do with the glitch. But, four times in a row they worked the old one-two this year. Last man to do that was the specialist stage winner Charles Pélissier in 1930 (eight stages all told) and, before him, René Pothier in 1906 (five overall).

The day before, Cipo was beaten to the line by Tom Steels, the short-tempered Belgian rider disqualified two years before for flinging a bidon at another rider in the closing metres of a sprint. But, locking onto Cipo's wheel, Steels had shouldered the Czech strongman, Jan Svorada, into the barrier before jumping past the Italian. Had Svorada gone down there would have been carnage, and Steels was rightly relegated to the back of the field. He complained of injustice but had no claim and Cipo equalled the record held by his compatriot Gino 'the Pious' Bartali since 1948 when he achieved his three in a row across the mountains (seven stages all told and overall yellow). Cipo modestly discounted his effort in comparison to that of the great Bartali and then paid heartfelt and uncharacteristically self-effacing tribute to his team. His victory next day, in pure grace of speed, majestic style – invincible – catapulted him deeper into the record books. I warmed to him at last.

Back down the road, the luckless Zabel – no stage wins but

already in green – crashed and rode on with a bloody chin, lacerated knee and thigh and badly bruised testicles (run-of-the-mill stuff for these bruisers) slipstreamed to the finish by his team, among them Guerini, Ullrich's nominated mountain tow man, now promoted to team leader.

In the first major test of individual strength, 56.5km against the clock in Metz, Armstrong produced what he called one of his greatest ever victories, adding, 'I have never felt so tired, though.' He overtook Olano, who started ahead of him by two minutes, added nearly a minute to his lead over Zülle, and pulled on the yellow jersey. (Boardman went down by three and a half minutes.) It was a superlative show of time-trialling class: speed, will, concentration, deployment of power, control of the bike. Seconds can be lost on sloppy cornering, misjudged gear changes or ill-gauged expenditure of effort. Sadly, Bobby Julich crashed when his back wheel collapsed on a tight bend; he was taken to hospital.

Stage 9. The Alps. 213.5km

A couple of small climbs early on, one third, one second category, before the main agenda: col du Télégraphe, the monster Galibier, and Montgenèvre on the way to a sapping 12km climb to the mountain-top finish at the Italian ski resort of Sestrières, where Claudio 'the Devil' Chiapucci left the rest for dead and rode to a glorious solo victory in front of his home crowd in 1992.

The day began cold and wet, mountain fogs, thoroughly miserable: many riders hate these conditions, the chill gets into their bones, the roads are slick and difficult to negotiate. Armstrong actually enjoys them, or perhaps has learned to relish them, knowing that to do so gives him a physical and moral advantage over the others.

Armstrong and a small élite breakaway group – Zülle, the Spanish climbers Escartin and Beltran, Gotti, Virenque – led the race onto the final climb and, some 8km from the finish, under no pressure to make any time gains (indeed, more prudently advised to caution this early in the mountains), Armstrong attacked. Pedalling with superb fluency of rhythm at unfluctuating speed, he simply rode away and could not be caught. He went too soon, he admitted as much, and the last 2km were murder, but such spontaneity is innate in him. He felt good, so he went. 'Head-strong' they sometimes called him at the start of his career, but this was champion's style. Impetuosity is the kernel of what Merckx called 'the religion of attack', *le punch*, and though Armstrong didn't make huge gains in time (31 seconds on Zülle, 1m 26s on Escartin and so on down the field), the psychological blow was heavy if not mortal. Far from limiting his losses, that small-business principle upon which so many winners have based victory, he carried the fight to his rivals, to the specialist climbers on their ground. True, he might have a bad day and there were more Alps and even more Pyrenees to cross, but his audacity had secured him priceless advantage for the time being at least. Up to the rest to respond in kind, or not.

There were enough specialist climbers around still to make him suffer, but he had shown such impregnable confidence that it would take a bad day indeed to cause him serious grief. Never-theless, the Tour is the Tour: in 1998, Ullrich had suffered as never before, his face ravaged with the pain of a crucifying effort, when Pantani danced off through the damp chilly mists of Les Deux Alpes. He lost over seven minutes and the Tour.

Armstrong paid for his extravagant ride to Sestrières: on the ascent of l'Alpe d'Huez he left Zülle and Virenque floundering, only to be reeled in. They had kept their nerve and plugged away. Two brave escapees, Bourguignon and Heulot, had spent 150 of the day's 220km in the lead; Heulot went ahead at last but, 3km from the finish, exhausted, he watched Guerini and then Tonkov rob him of glory. His, and all France's, dream of stage victory crumbled and so, too, very nearly, did Guerini. He went clear with just 2km to go and Tonkov couldn't match him, but, on the flat run-in to the Arrivée, a spectator planted himself in the middle of the road, bang in front of Guerini, with a camera, then blundered into the rider as he tried to avoid him. Guerini fell; he might easily have broken a collarbone, been winded, lost the stage. Luckily, there was no injury and the adrenaline was coursing so fiercely that he scrambled back onto the bike, took a push from the imbecile who had felled him, and scampered for the line in a frenzy. He made it, lifted both arms to the sky and rolled across the line, stage winner, Tour de France. Bliss.

On the climb to l'Alpe d'Huez, Virenque took the familiar polka-dot jersey. Ostracised by some in the *peloton* and vilified by many who felt that his protestations of innocence in the Festina affair were cowardly, that he funked the issue at the start and dug himself further into a hole of defiance from which he cannot extricate himself, he retained huge loyalty from the French public. *L'Alpe d'Huez needs Virenque. Fight for your fans. We will always support you* joined the banners on the big climb. Other fans, incensed at his sneaking back into the race, daubed the route of the Prologue with his name below the needle of a huge syringe filled with EPO. He brazened it out; Leblanc finally shook his hand and, by the end of the Tour, his postbag in the count of riders' fan-mail outweighed the rest amply. His riding in the mountains in 1999 was notably less fiery than before, but he was clearing the cols with regular determination and, after the Alps, led the competition comfortably. Guerini was followed in by Armstrong's group, only 25 seconds back.

At the side of the road on the climb to l'Alpe d'Huez, an enterprising drinks vendor, advertising his al fresco bar further up the road, had posted a sign reading: *EPO 100 metres*. That is *eau*, *pastis* and *orgeat* (barley syrup flavoured with sweet and bitter almonds) mixed into a cocktail known as *mauresque*, a 'Moorish'. The Tour was probably too raw for such wisecracks.

There were already rumblings in the French press about the so-called clean race, the 'race of fresh water'. Disgruntled French riders were bitching about a two-speed *peloton* – *aux deux vitesses* – and one told an interviewer that he had been struggling to turn his lowest gear on one of the climbs whilst alongside him two riders (not French) were chatting casually as they twiddled the big chain-ring as if there were no gradient to speak of. The French fans have had to get used to foreign winners of their Tour since Fignon's second victory in 1985, but in the jaundiced climate of suspicion, the niggling bad temper hanging over from the mess in which the Tour and the sport has found itself toiling these past 12 months, the French are clearly feeling hard done by. The regulations on blood tests and dope controls imposed by their Federation are assuredly draconian. Whether these methods are more efficient is another matter, but given the marked inferiority of the French contingent in general, the unworthy sense is that there indeed *are* two gears available: with and without dope. The resentment was particularly fierce against the Spanish teams, regulated by a federation known for its lax attitude to controls.

This general resentment was talked up by the gutter press desperate for a story, eager to reopen the drugs scandal. Knowing nothing about bike racing, many of them, their *raison d'être* is to find and tip out any worms they can rake up. They turned on Armstrong. His strength was, by comparison with the rest, superhuman and therefore, almost by definition, drug-assisted. He was, one writer said, a Martian. (Thirty years ago, another French journalist spoke in awed terms of *la planète Merckx* and *Merckxissimo* when the Belgian crushed the Frenchman Roger Pingeon, winner in 1967, by 17m 54s in his first Tour. Such generosity is not in large supply these days.)

The best-placed French rider in the *peloton* halfway through the race was Laurent Brochard, World Champion in 1997 and already an hour lag of Armstrong. How could this be? Yet, when he won the rainbow jersey, Brochard was riding for Festina, pop-full of EPO, and actually tested positive after the Worlds. Maybe he isn't that good after all when, finally, he is riding at his natural speed.

And the speed that so many of them were riding at: it's unnaturally high, whined the journos in the non-specialist French papers. Not true, in fact. Certainly the average speed of the '99 Tour did turn out to be the highest ever – over 40kph – but one entire stage had been raced with a strong assisting wind, and Pantani's overall time was very nearly 40kph over another relatively flat course. These accusations were pretty thin straws to be clutching at. And what of the performance of their darling, the professed innocent, Virenque?

One French doctor said that there was no known case of a sportsman surviving cancer and being stronger for it. Medically this may well be true, but so what? The exception neither proves the rule nor limits the possibility of exception. And, I should say, that anyone with a grain of insight into the psyche of a top-level athlete who has picked himself up off his death-bed, fought back to fitness and then into the highest level of competition of a sport which he loves and once excelled in, would not find the new intensification in will, commitment or even resistance to physical suffering at all astonishing. Statistics cannot disprove what is self-evident. It is a truism that the difference between amateurs and professionals is in preparation; and between the very best pros and the also-rans even more preparation. Champions win because they work harder, all the time.

The press had an ally. A young pro, Christophe Bassons, formerly a junior rider with Festina and now riding his first Tour with the French team sponsored by their lottery, La Française des Jeux, was trumpeting himself as Mr Clean in a *peloton* composed largely of dope-heads. This was not helpful. In articles about his experience of the Tour commissioned by *Le Parisien*, Bassons was blowing the whistle on the hypocrisy, cheating and double standards of the sport. He openly attacked his fellow riders, in swingeing language, for keeping their traps shut, not owning up to the fact that no one, *no one*, could win a Tour stage just by turning the pedals. This last charge he made even before the Tour started. He had, he said, always refused drugs and been mocked and reviled by the other riders for his purist stand. The *peloton* put up with him for a while but finally had enough and he became a leper in the ranks. He finally quit because he was mentally – not physically – drained. Armstrong himself had ridden up alongside him to advise him that his sermonising had no place in the Tour; that it was unprofessional to bleat about what he imagined to be going on in the pro ranks he had only just joined and that if he wouldn't stop the rant he ought to leave. Bernard Hinault commented that it was the duty of a rider to ride the Tour not to moonlight as a journalist and, besides, for all his holier-than-thou opinionation, Bassons habitually slept in a hypobaric tent to boost the count of red cells in his blood. He was overdosing on oxygen.

The press seized on the story, naturally: the yellow jersey putting the frighteners on the young small fry as proof of a general complicity amongst the members of the *peloton* to maintain *omertá* – the vow of silence.

To cap it, in the last week of the race, the French heavyweight journal *Le Monde* broke the story that traces of corticoids had been found in Armstrong's urine after a dope test on 4 July, Independence Day; how they love a bit of synchronicity. Corticoids are cortisone derivatives which hasten relief from swelling and skin ailments, notably, but which can also aid recovery from fatigue. The article in *Le Monde* followed a denial by Armstrong at a special press conference, that he had taken any corticoids which, in this immediate post-EPO era, are the most topical doping agencies. It was nauseatingly apparent that some pompous asses of the non-sporting press were desperate to gather themselves up in their prophetic mantle and scream *J'accuse!*

Armstrong was an enigma, said *Le Monde*, not so much because he had survived one of the most virulent forms of cancer (neglecting to add that if caught early it is also one of the cancers more amenable to cure) but because he had achieved the remarkable feat of producing traces in his urine of a banned substance which he claimed never to have taken. The French National Laboratory for the Fight Against Doping states: either the body contains banned substances or it does not; that is the sole question to answer. In Armstrong's case the test showed a level of 0.2; normal levels,without doping, lie between 1 and 6. However, *Armstrong had without shadow of doubt taken corticoids.*

This kind of rationale is veering towards the kind of nasty legalistic petty-fogging on which Robespierre and company based their Revolutionary law – you are either for the Republic or against it; neutrality is a crime – and McCarthy his disgusting witch-hunt of communists, party members or sympathisers.

In answer to the question put in French by the *Le Monde* journalist 'have you taken corticoids?', Armstrong said he had not *taken* corticoids, thinking that *taken* must refer either to pills or injections. In fact he had used a cream commonly used by bike riders to ease a saddle sore; the cream contained tiny amounts of corticoid and some of this must have seeped into his system. The attacks took some time to peter out. Armstrong, with admirable composure, remarked that one thing he would certainly advise any cancer sufferer not to do would be to wear the yellow jersey in the Tour de France, stress being a prime factor in susceptibility to the disease. Eddy Merckx, surely mindful of the agonies he endured after being banished from the Giro in 1969, visited him to give him encouragement at this difficult time. It is worth pointing out that Armstrong lives in France, races in France and is subject, therefore, to the same constraints imposed on all French riders. If he does go on to sue *Le Monde*, the action may compel a more measured approach to fact and unsubstantiated and irrelevant information among journalists. For all their harrying of medication in cycling, they would do well to examine their own addiction to sensational gossip as the unvarnished truth. But, ignorance has become a stock-in-trade. One British writer, the France correspondent for a broadsheet, indeed, said that of course the modern Tour is much tougher than the pre-war Tour which was a leisurely affair, averaging around 25kph . . . blah blah blah. 25 kph on those roads up those mountains? That is *fast*. And on what did he base this absurd statement? A photograph of the 1920 *peloton* dawdling along at the beginning of another 300-plus kilometres of riding on dirt tracks, as two riders light up cigarettes (see p.164).

In the Pyrenees, Armstrong's fellow US Postal riders – Tyler Hamilton and Kevin Livingston in particular – gave a sterling display of team riding. They rode themselves into the ground over Peyresourde, Aspin, Portillon, Tourmalet, Soulor and Aubisque to protect their leader; no effort was spared to keep the speed high at the front of the leading group until, spent, they could peel off and leave the day to Armstrong himself. This was classic Tour sacrifice of the lesser ambition to the greater, achieving precious advantage by total dedication to final victory rather than intermediate gains. Armstrong himself had worked as *domestique* for Jonathan Vaughters in the Dauphiné Libéré earlier in the season, driving the race up Mont Ventoux with his team-mate on his wheel. The loss of Vaughters in the pile-up on the Passage du Gois was a heavy one; but Livingston and Hamilton earned their share of the prize money by some magnificent support riding. This always puzzles those uninitiated in the protocols of bike-racing, but the work of the *domestique*, who is not capable of winning the race, in devotion to the cause of a leader who *is*, can be simply explained. They are doing for him what the pacemaker is employed to do for the record-breaking track athlete. Bike racing demands many varied strengths and talents; the best riders must have a broad talent but even they cannot do everything, and every Tour victory is a combined effort to which every contribution, however humble, is vital.

The drug hounds did make one paltry scoop: the Belgian Ludo

Dierckxsens, breakaway winner of the eleventh stage into the hotbed of French cycling, St Etienne, reported to the dope control and handed over a doctor's prescription for a banned corticoid – Synacthen – which he'd used to cure tendinitis in his knee. Unhappily, though he tested negative, he had not informed his team doctor about the medication. The doctor said he almost certainly would not have prescribed the drug, and, applying the strictest rules of team ethics, the manager sent Dierckxsens, 'honest but a bit silly', home.

The flat stages between the mountain ranges and after them towards Paris are traditionally where lesser riders can sometimes steal a victory; it takes cheek and a willingness to bury yourself in the handlebars, hoping that the rest of the bunch will be happy enough to let other idiots cane themselves through the heat and exhaustion of the latter part of the race. Dierckxsens had his day, briefly; so, too, Comasso, the Italian champion riding for Saeco, a sweet reward for all the selfless work he had done for Cipollini (out after a crash in the first mountain stage).

Tom Steels clocked his third victory, in the sprinters' home-from-home, Bordeaux, two days before the final time-trial, but a few riders at the back of the bunch had the grim experience of riding into a cloud of tear gas (or mace?) sprayed on them by a delinquent who darted out of the crowd with a canister and let rip. Laurent Madouas spoke for them: 'Coming off a bend, I saw a man in the crowd holding a spray can; he squirted it over us: I thought it was water. But quite soon I felt my eyes burning . . . it was terrible. I called out for the doctor; I thought I was going to fall off. For ten seconds I couldn't breathe. What if it had been poisonous?' Even after the race they were all feeling groggy, with irritation in their eyes, throat and lungs.

Time trial. Stage 19. 57km, Paris Futuroscope
This science-fiction business park south-west of Paris hosted the Départ of the 1990 Tour and a stage finish in 1994, when the victor, Jan Svorada, was in his pomp. Armstrong won it, to be sure, but only by nine seconds from Zülle and, for all the talk of the American's massive superiority, it must be recalled that, dis-counting the calamitous loss he suffered on stage 2, Zülle was

second by only one minute 24 seconds. That Zülle rode on after the disaster on Stage 2 and raced with such tenacity and class was the mark of a true professional; effacing the miseries of the past year, he showed great courage. By winning all the Tour's time-trials on his way to overall victory, Armstrong joined an élite trio: Merckx, Hinault, Indurain.

Champs-Elysées, 25 July

The crowds gather early; the sun is broiling; the big screens show pallid images of the progress of the race, 143.5km from Arpajon up through the outlying suburbs of the city. They are due to erupt onto the grand avenue at around half past three in the afternoon but they are late. Policemen patrol the piste beyond the double line of barriers, one per ten metres or so. More people arrive and swell the numbers close to the smooth *pavé* of the road. Up to the left, caught in the haze above the avenue of trees, we see the Arc de Triomphe, the route either side hung with pendant flags: French tricolour and the red and blue of the city of Paris. The mood is good-humoured; this is the city *en fête populaire*. Earlier that morning I had done some shopping and the man in the wine shop, down from Les Arts et Métiers where I am staying, voiced his opinion about the Tour de France: 'They should have two Tours: one with drugs and one without. Then you could choose which one to ride in.' He said it with a smile but the scepticism was weary. Nice man, intelligent, good on wine, but, evidently, no bike fan. The race – oh, just a bike race, for heavens' sake – didn't excite him, and the drugs scandal sickened him. Not sport. Unworthy of the French people. Fair enough. I didn't argue the case: he may be right. I feel differently and want to believe in the renewal; without trust and a determined attempt to remove suspicion, what chance have the cyclists, ever, of riding on fresh water?

At last we can see from snatched glimpses of the big screen – some Swiss patriot is waving his flag across the line of vision, damn – the city outskirts. And soon they will see what every Tour rider who has completed the race has seen: the Eiffel Tower. How wonderful it will look to Boardman, no pretensions this year other than to grab a stage win at the outside, if he could, but above all to finish the ride, only his second finish in six starts.

Our view of the road is piecemeal, too many heads in front of us, but when the procession does come in, heralded by the publicity caravan, on a spree of driving, blonde girls hanging out of cars, and the crumpled race organisers slumped in overheated saloons making the final lap, motorbike police outriders, suddenly, there is the long line of gaudy lycra, polished enamel and the bronzed legs and arms of the riders, the men going for home. A shiver of speed, muscular grace, choreographed it looks, says my companion, a dancer, beautiful, rhythmic, supple, *exciting*. And, for the flash of time's open eye as they shoot by on the far side of the carriageway from us, it is *exciting* and the crowd cheers and whistles and settles, nerves akimbo, into the short wait, two minutes or so, for them to round the U-turn at the top of the avenue by the Place de l'Etoile and so back down past us, in a whirr of spokes and alloy mechs. And out of sight to make the laps, ten of them.

Next time round, a stab at a break, but it's quickly swallowed up by the bunch, which seems to be generating a sort of combined speed, like a multi-celled dynamo. Another circuit and another break goes further ahead; two men gain a minute, but it's not long before that advance is being chewed away like a leaf in a locust's jaw: not so much because the bunch is exerting itself as that the two escapees have had it, done what they could, a bit of viewing time, publicity for the French lottery and then it's gone, the day we rode the Champs-Elysées at the head of the Tour de France.

The Telekom team had this last chance to get Zabel onto the winner's podium. He has the green Points jersey secure enough, but no stage victory. In truth, though, however consistent he has been at the finishes and in the intermediate sprints – where guile is quite as important as raw speed – he hasn't looked the sharp sprinter he was; a few metres lacking in pace, a hint of caution in his handling of the hurly-burly, maybe. He misses out again, and the Australian McEwen rides into his own page of history with a dazzling rush to the front past the big hitters. Joy.

And as we go, we hear the strains of the Star-Spangled Banner drifting across the road. Armstrong: the greatest come-back of the century, *L'Equipe* called it. *Chapeau bas.*

.

CHAPTER TEN

2000

Answering the Cynics

Some French fans have grown cynical about the Tour de France. *Les Bleus* have carried off football's World Cup and Euro 2000. Mary Pierce has won the French Open tennis. Their rugby team reached the final of the World Cup. But the French cyclists? *Rien.* Altogether fishy.

When the American Lance Armstrong sealed his 1999 win with an emphatic ride in the final time trial into the Futuroscope theme park in the Vienne region, large sections of the French press were incredulous. Armstrong was from another planet: so utterly superior to the other riders. What was he taking? Were the French riders really so markedly inferior? Impossible. Virtual reality had taken over and, as if in wry amusement at the notion or else determined to scotch it, the Tour organisers announced the opening of the 2000 Tour back in this centre of the world of virtual reality: a first stage time trial over 16.5km back into Futuroscope. Perhaps the hope was that the symbolism of quitting fantasy land for the hard roads of truth would signal a return to a clean Tour, an honest race, a genuine contest.

Armstrong faced much tougher opposition than in 1999. The German Ullrich started in the rainbow jersey of reigning world time-trial champion, but, if the pressure on him to repeat his '97 victory was intense, the same could not be said of his preparation for the race. Overweight during the winter months, he had renounced or abandoned a clutch of early season races through illness or lack of training. The Tour is not a race in which a rider can improvise: lack of racing miles cannot be hidden and it says a lot for the patience of the Telekom management that they are prepared to keep faith with a rider who has, so far, delivered much less than his talent promises.

The Italian Pantani, booted out of the 1999 Giro d'Italia, came to the Tour after a miserable year. He had done very little racing and a deep crisis of confidence and chronic depression had reduced an explosive attacking spirit to extreme diffidence, muddled up with vague talk of return or retirement. No one knew what he was going to do; least, perhaps, Il Pirata himself. However, with a week of flat stages to ride himself in, Pantani might well be a real threat.

Of the other major contenders, none, in my view, had a genuine chance of overall victory. Despite his class and early promise – yellow jersey in his first Tour – Zülle never really looked like a Tour winner. The Frenchman Laurent Jalabert affronted home opinion when he climbed off his bike and quit the race in '98 in protest against the rough-handling of riders by police investigating the Festina affair (see chapter 8). He refused to ride in France for two years and his motivations were suspect. His Spanish ONCE team is not subject to the Draconian anti-doping routines of the French federation and he was accused of dodging the crack-down that, so many domestic riders claimed, had unfairly crippled French cycling.

French riders aren't winning the one-day Belgian and Italian classic races, say the home riders. But, says Jalabert, they never have. There is no cause to question his motives on this. Without question the most complete pro cyclist in the *peloton*, he sacrificed his place as number one in the World rankings by not riding several rated races to concentrate on preparing for his return to the Tour – almost certainly his last – with a view to a podium place.

The darling of the French fans, the ace climber Richard Virenque, five times winner of the King of the Mountains prize, is always touted – not least by himself – as a potential winner of the Tour. Very few specialist climbers have won the Tour but, when they do, they transcend themselves. Virenque is a commanding man in the mountains; elsewhere, he is ordinary.

Mario Cipollini crashed while training in Tuscany a few weeks before the Tour, broke two ribs and was out. In the past few years, the 'red train' of the Saeco team, driving the chase of escapees or winding up the speed for the final sprint, had controlled the *peloton* with imperious power: all to get Cipo into the frame for the last 100 metres to the *Arrivée*. His absence from the Tour meant that, for the first time in a few years, the role of chief pursuit was open to takers. In the event, no team consistently took it on.

Almost inevitably, the doping scandal hung round the Tour before the off like an old has-been. Routine blood tests eliminated three riders – Rossano Brasi, Andrej Hauptman and the Russian champion, Serguei Ivanov – from the Tour for high haemocrit levels of over 50 (i.e. the proportion of red oxygen-carrying cells in the blood). Ivanov was sacked by his Dutch Farm Frites team a few days later and Brasi – labelled a 'moron' by his Polti manager – was immediately suspended by his team until he could explain himself. The Tour director, Jean-Marie Leblanc, said that 'this shows that the Tour de France is not prepared to tolerate cheats.'

Lance Armstrong has always declared forthrightly against drugs; his fight-back from cancer is, he says, proof enough that the very idea that he is taking dope to enhance his performance is absurd. Asked what he is on he replies: 'I am on my bike.'

The first stage featured a slight climb around halfway, a minor ascent to 109m, which the Tour organisers had given a fourth category ranking in the mountains prize. On it, the German sprinter Marcel Wüst, stole a media coup for his Festina team. Wüst mounted a light road-racing bike, rather than a slightly heavier time-trialling machine, rode steadily to the foot of the one km climb, then gave it all he had. This won him the polka dot jersey of the King of the Mountains prize and four subsequent appearances on the winner's podium.

The stage was won by the only Briton riding: David Millar, at 23 of the age that many of the greats have actually won the race – Anquetil, Fignon, Ullrich – but nurtured over four seasons of professional cycle racing to enter the race, not as a contender but a future prospect. He took the time trial by two seconds from the reigning champion, 14 seconds over Ullrich, 15 seconds over Jalabert. It was a superlative performance: into yellow on his first day in the Tour. It might prove to be a shirt of fire. This was only the beginning of a three-week ordeal. Nothing can detract from the glory of that moment; but the Tour exacts a far higher price than any other race.

Millar was, from the very start, up against things which would either harden his resolve or, possibly, reduce him from a potential winner to a catch-up man, and there are plenty of those around. That night he could not sleep, wondering if it was a dream. *Golden Fleece? Me?*

The Belgian fast man Tom Steels won stage two and brief ownership of the green points jersey after the Dutchman Erik Dekker, silver medallist in the '94 Olympics, launched an early attack and was joined by the renowned *baroudeur* – the man who will attack for honour's sake alone – Jacky Durand. This was to become the pattern of the race: with the big men slogging it out for the high placings, the rest were animating the day's action, day after day, in the only way open to them: attack. And here, the pathos inherent in bike racing, where the men who have been out on their own, up to 250km in the attempt to take a stage win, are caught within metres of the finish by a pack driven to crazy speeds to overhaul them. At the moment of junction, there is not even a sideways glance: there is no mercy, whatever sympathy the individuals in that great train of overtakers may harbour. That is the race. No room for sentiment. Dekker paid heavily for his failed bid: he came in with two other riders nearly 15 minutes down.

Here is an interesting insight into team tactics, however. When the *peloton* split in the run-in, with Laurent Jalabert in the front group, his fellow ONCE rider, the Spaniard Abraham Olano, fourth in 1997 and a noted time-trialler, headed the chasing bunch. Olano could see no yellow jersey, nor Lance Armstrong in the lead group and, knowing that the time gap between the front group and his chasing group – which must, therefore, include Armstrong and Millar – would be that which elapsed from the time the winner crossed the line to when the chasing leader crossed, he slowed the pursuit. Although the distance between the two bunches at the finish was only a few metres, the time gap was nine seconds, which moved his leader Jalabert into third place – a mere six seconds down on the yellow jersey.

Steels also took stage three after Jens Voigt of Germany and the Dane Michael Blaudzun broke clear for 124km. Since Voigt had a deficit of only 46 seconds on Millar, the Briton's Cofidis team felt obliged to lead the chase: always a gruelling expense of effort, since the other teams are content to sit back and slipstream the pursuit. In the final kilometre and a half of the run-in, Millar rode into a pile-up when Jean-Patrick Nazon – of whom more later – and Markus Zberg crashed and Millar, some way back, swerved adroitly past the heap of bodies and bikes and somersaulted over the barriers of straw bales. In the tumble his chain went adrift and he had trouble relocating it. But, the sole team rider who was there pushed him back to speed and Millar saved the yellow jersey by seconds. 'It scared me,' he said 'but I'm not hurt.' Whatever volcanic emotions they feel, these guys have an entirely charming way with understatement.

Millar lost the golden fleece two days later in what many regard as a grossly unfair element of racing: the team time trial, where the talent of the individual is squashed into the best that the weakest member of a team can do. It is the severest test of any team's strength, cohesion, organisation and collective will; it exposes any frailty. It's unrelenting; quite horrible, even if you're strong. The time is registered on that of the fifth man over the line.

Jalabert's ONCE outfit took the stage by 46 seconds over Armstrong's US Postal team, despite the attempt of a disgruntled night-club owner – anti-Jaja – to sabotage their ride by lobbing five straw bales into the road near the start. Armstrong made a tactical error on the final climb, across the bridge over the Loire into St-Nazaire, 3.3km long, 60m high and buffeted by fierce winds off the Atlantic, by forcing the pace too hard and dropping the rest of his team. Nervy moments – time lost regrouping. However Ullrich's Telekom team lost one minute 26 seconds on the day, Pantani's Mercatone Uno three minutes 34 seconds, Zülle's Banestos four minutes 23 seconds. Zülle was furious with his team: he said he had to do so much work on his own to keep the momentum going that, finally, he was exhausted and got dropped. They had to wait for him. A bad case of disarray.

The ONCE victory was significant in time gains and psychological dominance. Millar's French Cofidis team lost nearly three minutes on the day and Jalabert, on this American Independence Day, took the yellow jersey for the first time since 1995. It was, he said, a symbol of his comeback, heralding, he hoped, a new start.

The fifth stage witnessed another cruel act of highway robbery: Jens Voigt and Sebastian Demarbaix shaped what turned into a long breakaway and were joined by five others, including the restless Dekker. Twenty km from the Finish, Voigt and Dekker jumped from the rest of the escapers to try for the win. The *peloton* had timed their effort to perfection, alas: Dekker and Voigt were engulfed by the chasing pack a tantalising 400m from the line. King of the mountains, sprinter Marcel Wüst took the stage edging out his fellow German on a rival team, Zabel, who had not won a stage since 1997.

Generally riders accord the yellow jersey a certain respect, until the racing gets serious. However when Jalabert stopped at the side of the road for a pee a few miles from the Départ in Vitré on stage six, the French firebrand Jacky Durand – last year's *lanterne rouge* and winner of the Combativity prize – launched an attack. He almost certainly hadn't seen Jaja by the side of the road, but the *maillot jaune* was furious: this was a mild form of treason. 'Next time, I'll piss in the hotel,' he said.

Durand was joined by Zabel's 36-year-old Italian team mate Alberto Elli and 10 other riders; the attack succeeded, by seven minutes 49 seconds over the bunch. The Dutch champion Leon Van Bon took the sprint and Elli, who had been only two minutes 15 seconds down on Jalabert, took yellow. Jalabert's ambitions were higher than interim possession of the jersey, but he was understandably miffed at the shabby way in which he had lost it. As to why his ONCE team did not organise a chase, he offered the excuse of tired legs; also, that since there were 12 men in the break working well together, the eight men plus one leader of any other team would be hard put to match the effort.

Durand is a famous stirrer. Himself a former yellow jersey, after winning the '95 Prologue, and French National Champion ('94), his swashbuckling attitude may be unsettling – '*doucement, Jacky,* steady on,' ran the cartoons – but it makes for lively action. He doesn't often win, but he is always ready to deliver some punch.

He was last years *lanterne rouge* – traditionally the last man in the race – and winner of the overall Combativity prize (points are awarded daily for the attacking spirit) and Durand typifies the breed who win it. Better, too, the *lanterne rouge* than the anonymity of a place in the middle order.

The lanterne rouge that day, Jean-Patrick Nazon, in his first Tour, typifies another breed of rider. The Australian sprinter Stuart O'Grady was brought down by another rider 80km from the Finish in Tours. He was badly hurt – X-rays later revealed that his shoulder had been broken in three places – but he rode on. The hope always persists that there is nothing but heavy bruising; few of them quit the Tour without the most pressing cause. O'Grady draped the useless arm over the handlebars and caught three riders, including the man who had crashed into him. On every small climb he faltered; as he faltered, Nazon, honouring the code of mutual help in distress, came behind to push him. Meanwhile, the man who'd crashed into him was griping that O'Grady wasn't doing any work to help the *grupetto*, the last men on the road, escape elimination on time. O'Grady, of course, had to abandon that evening. And Nazon went later, completely exhausted in the mountains.

France won not a single stage in the '99 Tour so, when the unlikely sounding Frenchman Christophe Agnolutto hoisted the tricolour again after a lone break of 79 miles on stage seven, France rejoiced. Agnolutto held off the chasing bunch which timed its effort poorly and Wüst spoiled Zabel's charge for second place. It was Zabel's birthday but there were no presents on offer.

Next day, Erik Dekker, riding his seventh Tour without a win, timed his effort more sagely and went with a mere 30km to go. Victory at last. There followed the last flat stage before the climbing, final chance for a while for the opportunists. This time Paolo Bettini outsprinted his fellow escapee, the Belgian Geert Verheyen, after 180km miles away to add a Tour win to his victory in the Belgian Classic Liège–Bastogne–Liège. But the race was about to explode.

Stage 10 ran 205km over three severe climbs – one first category, two *hors catégorie* – to the mountain top Finish at Lourdes Hautacam.

Monday 10 July. Dax. Heavy rain; driving wind; cold. The conditions were appalling: as if the Pyrenees were unleashing a foul bout of bad temper because the Tour had spared them but one measly day this year. Lance Armstrong, who likes the bad weather as much as the rest loathe it, was in chipper mood.

A few abortive attacks after the start, but, at 33km, the irrepressible Durand went and was joined by the Belgian Nico Mattan and the Basque Javier Otxoa. The trio cut loose. Durand was dropped on the first category col de Marie Blanque, a nasty 10km climb. Over the top, the *peloton* behind by 15 minutes, Otxoa and Mattan pounded on down into the valley towards the col d'Aubisque, a steadier ascent than the Marie Blanque but much longer. When the main pack reached the foot of the mountain, the attacks began and the field split. Armstrong's team went hell for leather trying to contain the action but, one by one, fell off the pace and Armstrong found himself unsupported, in company with his main rivals, Ullrich and Pantani. Virenque attacked and crossed the summit one minute ahead of them; two class climbers – Jose Maria Jimenez and Fernando Escartin – at 35 seconds.

Jalabert, like many of the others, was suffering and way back: the cold and wet had eaten into his bones, his muscles were inert, he could not, as he put it, get into the red, i.e. push himself over the limit of comfort. This is the harsh reality of the mountains: riders crack or lose all force. They hear voices in the crowd, some urging them on – *Tiens bon! Courage!* Hold on, courage – others, probably drunken and big-bellied, taunting them: 'You're 10 minutes down. Weakling. Washed up.' Is it surprising they lose heart? Even the best find themselves demented with fatigue, reduced to the *grupetto*, which normally contains the sprinters, struggling to scramble in under the guillotine. This is the Calvary: the high road to suffering and mere survival.

Armstrong rode onto the final 13km climb with Pantani, Ullrich, Zülle, 10 minutes 30 seconds behind a group containing Virenque, Escartin and Jimenez. One kilometre in, Pantani attacked and was instantly checked by Armstrong and Zülle. Ullrich couldn't answer. The pace was ferocious; Zülle fell away, Pantani held for a while but Armstrong, who had come to the

Pyrenees and ridden this particularly hard ascent several times, was pedalling with the rapid fluency of a born climber and aggressive sustained power. His acceleration took him up to and past Virenque. Only Jimenez could hold his wheel. Five kilometres from the summit, Otxoa's lead had shrunk to four minutes 58 seconds. In 8km the American had gained over five minutes on the lone escapee. At 3km Jimenez was done for and Armstrong, out of the saddle still, was hunting down Otxoa, by now clinging onto his lead by willpower and the hectic dream of victory. He made it, by a mere 42 seconds, and Armstrong took yellow. He had distanced Ullrich, now in second place, by four minutes one second, and Pantani, hitherto the best climber in the *peloton*, by almost six minutes. The Frenchman Christophe Moreau, riding for the reborn Festina team, claimed third position at five minutes 10 seconds. Armstrong's resistance to cold and wet, coupled with an exceptional focus, an instinct for the kill that marks out all the best, had simply stunned them all. Pantani confessed that, whatever hopes he'd cherished of an early resurgence, reality had hit him on that climb.

On the relative flat next day, Dekker took his second win; in 10 days of the Tour he had spent no fewer than 592km off the front in breakaways.

After a rest day, the riders set out for Mont Ventoux, the first time in 13 years the Tour had finished at the col. It was Thursday 13 July, 23 years to the day after Tommy Simpson's death on the mountain. The mistral was in full career; temperatures on top of the bald mountain were not much above freezing. David Millar's ambition to win the white jersey, for best young rider, had died in the wind and rain up to Hautacam when he conceded nearly seven minutes to the Spaniard Francisco Mancebo. Now his aim was limited to reaching Paris. Shortly after the start for Ventoux in Carpentras, he got caught in a pile-up; contused ribs and a bad tyre burn (from a spinning rear wheel) made riding very uncomfortable but he bravely continued.

Pantani and Armstrong fought the victory on the mountain to the last. Pantani, who had ridden himself into something approaching his true explosive form, unleashed the kind of attack on the bare slopes for which he is celebrated. Armstrong was dropped and, for a while, made no move to follow; however, he rejoined and rode elbow to elbow with the Pirate up the last cruel three km. It was clear that the American had the legs of the Italian but, in a gesture as gauche and naïve as it was intended to be generous, he allowed Pantani to cross the line ahead. The misunderstanding which sprang from this clumsy attempt to reward Pantani's courage in his comeback led to an undignified spat. Pantani interpreted the gift as patronising. Armstrong insinuated a lack of gratitude; the strongest should win on Ventoux and everyone knew who was the strongest. In which case, why did the American yield to a sentimental whimsy and not show himself superior?

The American showed a distinct lack of grace, referring to Pantani as Elefantino, Dumbo (his old nickname), as having shown his true colours. Ullrich was a gentleman – and the most talented of them all, Pantani behaved without honour. While the Italian said he was not insulted by the use of the nickname, Armstrong plainly meant the gibe. The gathering spat, conducted through press conferences, was unseemly; Pantani's reaction – on the road – was to prove far more eloquent. If Armstrong thought the Tour was finished, he was wrong: there was, said Pantani, still Pantani to deal with.

Ullrich lost a further 29 seconds on Ventoux; Moreau one minute 31 seconds and his third place to the young Spanish climber Joseba Beloki who could, it is said, hardly believe he was in the Tour, let alone riding third overall. After the stage, David Millar, in an interview, summed up his feelings about being in the race and surviving the mountain despite excruciating pain: 'I've always thought of cycling as having an epic, romantic scale. It's a beautiful sport, a great sport. I've always like the epic nature of all that suffering. That appeals to me a lot.' Two days later, having traversed three mighty Alps over 2,000m, and 249km, he was saying: 'That's ridiculous. Eight and a half hours on the bike. That's not sport. That's sado-masochism on a major scale. It's ridiculous.' But, he added: 'You have to hang on and never give up.' Plainly he does not lack courage.

The stage went to the Colombian climber of the Kelme team, Santiago Botero, who wrested the King of the Mountains jersey from his team mate Otxoa. Pantani, at two minutes 46 seconds, just spurted clear of Armstrong to take third place and no favours.

In the second alpine stage the day after – Galibier 2,645m, Madeleine 2,000m, mountain top finish at Courchevel 2,004m, 63.6km of climbing all told – Pantani applied real pressure in something like his old style. Armstrong began to look vulnerable; so, too, Ullrich, who had neither the legs nor the will to take advantage. Fifteen kilometres from the finish, Pantani attacked. Armstrong's team mate, the climber Kevin Livingston, relayed his leader painfully back to the Italian but then faded. Pantani spotted this and surged again, Armstrong had no answer. Pantani was flying. Up ahead Jimenez was clinging to the possibility of a lone victory, but he was out of luck. Pantani caught him and, riding into and out of a tunnel in the closing kilometre, emerged in bright sunshine to take a stupendous victory. Armstrong limited his loss to 50 seconds; Ullrich went down by 3 minutes 21 seconds, but Pantani had, most brilliantly, announced himself back. The American, lacking humour as well as *politesse*, said that, after the gift of the Ventoux stage, for Pantani to attack on Courchevel was ungentlemanly. A charmless comment which betrays his ignorance of the *mœurs* of continental bike racing.

If, barring accident, overall victory did seem decided, the game was not yet played. After a second rest day, the race took in a dreadful 196km across four more alpine monsters with virtually no valley links between for recuperation. The climbing started at 67km, on the col de Saisies, and Pantani attacked, a move calculated to hurt Armstrong. The American's team had no option but to chase; the effort wore them thin and left the *maillot jaune* badly exposed. Pantani persisted and opened a clear gap, in wary company with three others: Virenque's team mate Pascal Hervé and two men from the Kelme team – Fernando Escartin and Pascual Llorente. Over the second climb, the second category Aravis, Llorente lost contact. Armstrong, in a group of some 30 riders, was containing the deficit to around a minute as the leaders crossed the third climb of the day, the col de la Colombière. On the descent, Virenque counter-attacked with Moreau, Botero of Kelme, the current King of the Mountains, and his team-mate Otxoa; they rejoined Pantani. The yellow jersey group came up to them shortly after; with the lead group reassembled, it was all left to do.

Pantani, though, was spent. He had been suffering bad stomach cramps and had received no help from his fellow escapers, but he had blown the race to bits.

Moreau fell away, the Spanish climber Roberto Heras attacked and was quickly joined by Virenque. Ullrich found his legs and began to test Armstrong who was having a desperate time. He had made the elementary – amateurish – mistake of not eating properly and became a victim of *une fringale*: the bonk, hypoglaecemia, radical loss of energy. Riders with the *fringale* can black out. It was, he said afterwards, the worst day he had ever spent on a bike. He felt light-headed, he ached with hunger, was scared that he was going to lose the Tour. (He might have done, had Ullrich been in riper condition, and primed for the kill. Pantani lost 13 minutes 44 seconds on the day.)

Virenque and Heras hurtled into Morzine in tandem; the unfortunate Spaniard overshot a bend, crashed into the barriers and trashed his front wheel. The four-times winner of the Mountains prize Virenque, due to face criminal trial on charges of drug-taking in November, took his first win since 1997. It was the most beautiful of his career, he said – revenge for the exclusion in 1998. Ullrich took second and two minutes out of Armstrong, who showed enormous fortitude and courage in battling through the horrors of that calvaire on the mountain.

But, his reaction to Pantani's audacious riding was telling. 'It was,' he said 'a waste of time and energy. I provoked him and Il Pirata walked the plank and I almost lost the Tour.' But that is exactly the point, and Armstrong missed it, spectacularly.

His strategy for the Tour had been, quite clearly, decided in advance: to paralyse the opposition early on Hautacam and then sit on the lead. Like many riders, he wears a two-way radio and is in constant communication with his *directeur sportif* in the following car. Pantani, by contrast, does not wear an earphone. He rides on his own gut feelings. Armstrong, once nicknamed headstrong, *had* a similar wilful quality, if less astutely deployed. Now he is almost *too* controlled by the voice from the team car. His victories, accordingly, have a rather clinical look. Pantani, having shelled himself out, succumbed, that night, to a bout of dysentery and abandoned.

The race was, effectively, over. Armstrong had been forced to hang onto his lead with every ounce of strength he had left. Ullrich was paying for yet another cavalier winter off and on the bike. Pantani had returned to the highest level, but too late. Who knows what an epic there may be should both those former winners come to next year's Tour, fully prepared.

Armstrong had, nonetheless, shown himself worthy; just. He is the ultimate professional. He prepares harder and with greater industry than anyone else – he shrugs off extremes of weather, and, as he puts it, nothing the road throws at him by way of suffering gets close by comparison to the miseries of chemotherapy. Surviving what might have been a mortal cancer has imbued him with a supernatural capacity to absorb punishment and this saved his Tour. But, he built this win, as his first, on a single killer strike and, for all his perceived superiority in this Tour, his win owed as much to the default of Pantani and Ullrich as to his own enforcement throughout.

In the final time trial, however, 58.5km from the German town of Fribourg-en-Brisgau to Mulhouse in Alsace, he achieved the stage victory which gave gloss to the overall win. Only four riders since the war – Walkowiak 1956, Nencini 1960, Aimar 1966 and Lemond 1990 – have taken overall victory without winning a single stage. Armstrong salvaged that honour by beating Ullrich by 25 seconds. This was, in moral terms, a decisive margin.

The interest of this Tour lies both in what it promised for the next race and in the intrinsic merits of the victory that crowned it; memorable more for what might have happened. The first week was certainly the best of the flat stage openers for years: the absence of the Saeco 'red train' encouraged a flurry of quixotic attacks. Erik Dekker's three stage wins born of lone enterprise marked a welcome return to a buccaneering spirit amongst the lesser lights of the *peloton*. Zabel took a record fifth green points jersey. No fewer than nine team leaders did not finish, including poor Zülle, second in 1999.

The young Basque Joseba Beloki held onto the third place he took on the stage to Ventoux and joined Ullrich – second for a second time – on the podium. Beloki and his team-mate Moreau – fourth and first Frenchman respectively – restored the image of the Festina team so besmirched in the doping scandal of 1998. Happily, the drugs controversy hardly resurfaced. Cycle sport has taken the issue on in a way that no other sport has. There is no room for complacency: the problem had been radical and endemic. However, a bold start has been made; except that Giorgio Squinzi, the boss of the Italian Mapei team, (which had a bad Tour), said that it was simply not possible for any cyclist to lead a race like the Tour de France without the use of a performance-enhancing drug. There may be proof, or rebuttal of this claim in the offing. The Tour organisers have kept riders' urine specimens to be submitted to a test for EPO as soon as it is approved as scientifically accurate.

The Tour was scarred by a tragedy. A 12-year-old boy was hit by one of the following cars as it overtook down the line of the caravan and later died of his injuries. Before the start out of Morzine, the riders observed a minute's silence in his memory, a silence shamefully broken by a hovering television helicopter. The Tour de France stopped out of respect for an innocent casualty of its remorseless progress. Whatever cynics say about the race, it is as true now as it ever was that it is prepared to stop, look hard at itself and renew. There is an extraordinary humanity at its heart, a humanity forged in what may seem like a strange crucible – of suffering and overcoming self-imposed pain – but one that is probably unique in sport.

CHAPTER ELEVEN

2001

Armstrong v Ullrich

Rules for selection of teams for the Tour de France, based on Union de Cyclisme Internationale (UCI) rankings and Tour organisation conventions, seemed clear enough: the top 12, plus the reigning champion's team and any French teams within the top 20. However, in January 2001 the Tour director, Jean-Marie Leblanc, changed the rules with apparent caprice. He picked the top ten, added one Belgian and five French (including two Second Division) and reserved four wild-card entries to be named later. This provoked dismay. Wild-card entries are almost always suspect: grace and favour above true worth, although when Greg Lemond won the Tour in 1989, it was as the leader of a wild-card team. He was now spokesman of the American Mercury-Viatel team who, by results, certainly merited selection for the Tour. They, like several highly rated Italian teams, had to sweat out a long wait.

The professional cycling world and the Tour de France – its great showcase – in particular, has been under enormous pressure since the Festina affair in 1998. The willingness of the Tour organisers to enforce draconian measures to eliminate the scourge of drugs has been energetic and laudable. Yet, international cooperation has not been solid; the French Cycling Federation, following the lead of the Minister of Youth and Sports, Madame Buffet, has imposed fierce discipline; other authorities have been less prompt. Leblanc not only wants the Tour to be rid of the suspicions which cling to the race, to all cycling – and what other sport has been so vigorous in its efforts to purge itself of doping? – he is adamant that the new strictures which apply to French riders must and should apply to all foreign riders who enter the Tour, whatever less stringent rules apply to them on their home turf. This is controversial and, when the four wild-card entries were announced, the controversy looked wilful. No Mercury, no Mercatone Uno – led by Marco Pantani, the 1998 winner – no Saeco, home of the flamboyant sprinter Mario Cipollini. Instead, a ragbag of three more Second Division French teams and one obscure Basque outfit.

Leblanc might well plead that Pantani was not welcome because he still faces criminal charges of drug-taking, yet a French judge is pursuing a judicial inquiry into Lance Armstrong's US Postal team on similar suspicion, after bags containing unspecified medical supplies were dumped in litter bins in the autumn of 2000. Leblanc told *Le Figaro*: 'The sword of Damocles that hangs over riders who dope is heavier than ever. We wanted to turn the page and put our trust in the younger generation of riders.' Fair enough. But if Pantani and the Italians were being snubbed because of suspicion what of the wild-card French CSC-Tiscali team, one of whose riders tested positive in the Giro d'Italia? This was chauvinism, surely, and blatant favouritism; the greatest bike race in the world sadly reduced for partisan reasons. French cyclists – acknowledged by Laurent Fignon, winner of the Tour in 1983–84, to be second-rate – were being given an undeserved leg-up. But Fignon, now director of the first major stage race of the season, the Paris–Nice, had included several Second Division French teams to expose them to top-flight competition: sink or swim.

Leblanc shrugged off the outcry. The race would make its own decisions, just as the road decides the winner. As to the favourites, the exclusion of Pantani – a fiery climber of real threat in the mountains – effectively meant that the Tour would be a duel between Armstrong and his runner-up in 2000, winner in 1997, Jan Ullrich. He had been ill-prepared in 2000 but seemed to have concentrated harder, physically and mentally, before the 2001 race. He chose to ride the Giro d'Italia, always Eddy Merckx's favoured preparation for the Tour, whereas the Texan Armstrong chose to ride – and win – the lesser Tour de Suisse (which included a mountain time trial). Hounded by the smart French press who have always doubted his honesty, he had renounced all racing in

France before the start of the season and was even quoted in an American paper as regretting the fact that the greatest bike race in the world had to be in France. Texans are notoriously insular, even within the USA. His prickly attitude came over as arrogance; his brashness as Francophobia; his exaggerated smarting at criticism, direct and implied, as guilty protest. However, he softened; diplomacy both ways. He added a French stage race to his calendar – the Circuit de la Sarthe. It was a welcome gesture, a signal that he was prepared to understand and manage French reactions to him rather than bite back and, like Achilles, sulk in his tent. Yet, just before the Tour, it transpired that he had been working since 1995 with the infamous Italian doctor Michele Ferrari who had once described a dose of EPO as no more dangerous than a litre of orange juice and is now under investigation for drug abuse. Rather naively, Armstrong said he couldn't see what the fuss was about; Ferrari was an essential part of his team, they'd been concentrating on altitude training and, until proved guilty, the man was innocent, wasn't he? Armstrong said: 'My personal experience leads me to say that I have never had to question his ethics or standards of care.' His personal manager added: 'Ferrari is a brilliant scientist and physiologist with a chequered past but he's an essential part of Lance's support team,' which seemed to beg more questions than it answered.

One of the men who had given him trouble in the 2000 Tour, the Colombian climber Roberto Heras, had been neutralised: made an offer he could not refuse, he had joined Armstrong's team, to help the Texan in the mountains, in return for support in the Vuelta a España. One of Armstrong's closest allies, his boyhood friend Kevin Livingston, had left the team to ride for Ullrich, a move which Armstrong likened to high treason. This gives some measure of his egotism. The Frenchman, Christophe Moreau, was the only local man likely to have any impact, but whatever encouragement his victory in another Tour warm-up race, the Dauphiné Libéré, might hint at, the hope far outweighed the possibility.

The Circuit de la Sarthe was won by David Millar, who came to the Tour burdened with a huge weight of expectation, expectation not much justified by miserable early season results. Could he repeat his victory in the 2000 Tour first stage and win the yellow jersey?

He'd talked a lot since, but hadn't done much. The pressure on him – internal and external – was intense.

Prologue. Dunkerque. 7 July.

Not since the summer of 1940 can have there been so many British crowded into the nondescript Channel Port. Millar defined the 8.2km Prologue as 'one of my biggest objectives of the season' although surviving the whole Tour 'and learning a lot more' was far more important. He is realistic; at 24, he is three years off the age when most riders think seriously about doing well in the Tour. US Postal have approached him, but he remains faithful – for the moment – to the French Cofidis team who have nurtured him for nearly four years. 'When I was suffering early this spring, they would tell me just not to worry. I really appreciate that.' Agreeable modesty on the eve of the Tour. Then he distributed invitations to his post-Tour party, an act of hubris if ever there was one. About 1km from the finish, he went into a tight bend too fast and tried to correct his line, the back wheel locked and he went down heavily on his left side. The friction of the crash burst his back tyre and he lost nearly a minute on the bike change; he struggled in with a badly bruised kneecap and a lacerated thigh and arm.

Moreau, of the formerly disgraced Festinas, won the Prologue and gave France the first yellow jersey of the Tour. On Stage 1, two other French riders set out as if to prove that if overall honours were beyond them, individual panache was not. Two Second Division riders, Christophe Oriol and the irrepressible Jacky Durand – who once won the Tour's Combativity Prize as well as holding the *lanterne rouge* (for last man in the race) into Paris – attacked after about 56km and built a lead of 8 minutes, only to be held up by a level-crossing barrier. (In 1935, the unknown Romain Maes ducked under such a barrier and sped into Lille minutes ahead of the fretting *peloton*, a lead he held all the way back to Paris.) Durand and Oriol whiled away the wait jocularly signing autographs for a crowd of bystanders until Leblanc pulled up and ruled this undignified. When the goods train finally rumbled through, the escapees had lost 3 minutes 20 seconds of their lead and though race regulations should have detained the *peloton* for a similar time, they were reined in for only two minutes. Durand and Oriol were caught 14km from the finish. Erik Zabel, chasing a record sixth green jersey, took the stage but he was riding the Tour without a lead-out man. The team managers had opted to back Ullrich for overall victory; there'd been no room for a man to serve Zabel and as he crossed the line he eschewed the traditional raised arms salute in mute protest. For Millar 'this was the worst day of all – I've been bleeding down my leg all day'. Yo-yoing off the back all day, he came in 5 minutes 45 seconds down and though he was facing the task bravely – ' if I got through today I can get to Paris' – the humped uphills on the cliff-top road to Cap Gris Nez over which he'd just struggled, are nothing by comparison with the massive climbs of the Alps and Pyrenees which lay ahead.

Racing into Antwerp on Stage 2, a break of 16 riders went clear, including 4 from Stuart O'Grady's Credit Agricole team. The plan was to get him into yellow but Marc Wauters, watched by the Belgian royal family, did his patriotic duty, jumped clear across the line, took the 20-second time bonus and became the first Belgian to wear the yellow jersey since Johann Bruyneel, now *directeur sportif* of US Postal, in 1995. However, O'Grady's points gains boosted his longer objective of the green jersey. For Millar there was another session of torture, another pile-up at the back of the main field near the finish. 'I've never been in so much pain in my life. God knows how I'll get through the next few days.'

Stage 3 finished at a hectic speed over the flatlands of Flanders, home territory of the beefy Belgian sprinters, the *flahutes*, 'flat-outs', brought up on local *kermesses*, mill-race round-the-town wallops that breed three essentials for close-quarter bunch breaks: bike-handling, nerve and feverish out-of-the-saddle dives for the line. Zabel can mix it with the best and keep a cool head; he took the sprint out of the stampede. Marc Wauters was nowhere. O'Grady put on yellow. Millar reported some improvement: he'd managed to sleep better and even suggested that 'later I could even make a show on a stage'. If this sounded more like self-convincing than a genuine possibility, it is a tribute to the depths of mental toughness and physical resilience that these bike-racers have to take for granted.

Next day the race went back into France. Laurent Jalabert, 'Jaja', the former world number one, back in a fairly new team (Danish-sponsored CSC-Tiscali) after falling out with the Spanish ONCEs for whom he'd ridden for many years, has been out of favour with the French public since he retired from the 1998 Tour in protest. He went into exile in Geneva and rode no French races. In February, he fell off a ladder doing some DIY, fractured three vertebrae and might well have missed the Tour. On Stage 4 the ONCE-Eroski team made a concerted attack at a feed station, in flagrant violation of the Tour's code of ethics. The US Postals reacted swiftly and chased furiously for around 80km to reel them in, the pace so hot that the *peloton* split into five bunches. Jalabert, like many others, was caught napping and missed the first split. Furious that he had been dropped, *and* by the ONCE team he'd quit in some dudgeon, he and two others immediately counter-attacked, as soon as the leaders were caught. They came in just clear of the chase and wily 32-year-old Jalabert, who hadn't won a race since the previous June but was now revitalised and keen to make a point, matched Belgian Ludo Dierckxsens' surge to take his third Tour stage win. Any disaffection the French public had felt towards the absentee Jalabert vanished. He was winning for them again. They smiled with him. French riders were, it seems, determined to repay local support. Leblanc's controversial selections may have been shrewd after all. Signs near the Arrivee underlined the riders' half of the bargain: '*Dôpage . . . Dégagé*' (Dope . . . Nope).

The well-drilled ONCEs, even without their ace time-trialler Abraham Olano, started as favourites for the Stage 5 Team time-trial; they had won in 2000 when the event was reintroduced for the first time since 1996 and may even have used the compact team attack on Stage 4 as a warm-up. Continental racing calls the time trial 'the race of truth' but regards it as a minor delicacy in the larger feast. Not all riders can be bothered to devote extra training to solo clock-beating: it can be soul-destroying. From that perspective, the team time-trial counts for absolute self-destruction; the slowest men stretched on the rack of the fastest. Time for the stage is taken on the fifth rider across the line. Cohesion is vital. Losing weaker men intensifies the strain on those left in the hunt. O'Grady's Crédit Agricoles had dropped two of their nine men long before the finish of the 67km course and the survivors were looking ragged. However, the *directeur sportif* Roger Legeay (who rode seven Tours), a man deeply imbued with *fougue*, fire in the belly, drove up alongside in the team car and gave them the sort of rousing talk – a mélange of bollocking and '*die for the country*' – which Napoleon appreciated in his generals. They rallied, took the fastest time in the intermediate time check and were inspired to an unexpected show of aggressive team spirit. They won the stage and O'Grady kept the yellow jersey.

Armstrong's US Postal team suffered. He, a time-trial specialist, bore much of the hard work at the front. Normally, the teams ride in two parallel lines: one line brings men up to the front; as each successive man reaches the head of the first line he usually relays for only as long as it takes him to peel off and onto the front of the second line. Meanwhile, the rider at the back of this line will be swinging onto the back of the other line, thus making his way back up to the front. Armstrong was holding the front far longer than the rest – relays lasting up to a minute, sheltering the weaker men in his slipstream but distancing them with sudden accelerations. Suddenly, around the 45km mark, Christian Vandevelde skidded on the central white line, which was wet with rain, and went down, taking Heras with him. Vandevelde wounded his arm; Heras was unhurt. Armstrong generously (or prudently?) pulled up and waited and the team lost about 45 seconds, the margin by which the ONCEs, with one of his rivals, Joseba Beloki (3rd overall in 2000) beat them. The Deutsche Telekoms split to pieces; Ullrich and four others came in alone, 24 seconds down on US Postal. Ullrich was now 30 seconds down on Armstrong overall. Even such small cracks have to be plugged later.

Stages 6 and 7 took the riders down through the Vosges mountains into Alsace-Lorraine – Jan Kirsipuu won the bunch sprint into Strasbourg – and on through the Doubs where, on Bastille Day, with the timing of a magician, the resurgent Jalabert took his second victory of the Tour. Suddenly, euphoria turned to shock when a deranged man drove a maroon Renault 21 headlong at the Finish line. He'd heard voices telling him to go and embrace France's rehabilitated hero but been turned away from the finish enclosure because he had no pass. He was stopped only when someone smashed his windscreen. A middle-aged woman standing by the barrier was flung into the air and taken to hospital with serious injuries to her head and legs.

Jens Voigt, O'Grady's team-mate, took yellow. Millar was slogging on, his directeur talking about 'character being forged by suffering', but the rider admitted that he hadn't been able to hold on even over the small climbs. 'Any other time I would have packed it in. I honestly thought I was out of it. If I hadn't had another rider – Bart Leysen – with me, I would have been eliminated.' Vandevelde was forced out when he crashed into a metal stanchion on the descent of the Col de Fouchy mountains and aggravated his arm injury.

On Sunday 15 July, a 14-man break made Tour history. Led by Erik Dekker, the Dutchman who took three flat stages in breakaway attacks in 2000, the group were away for some 209 kilometres in miserable conditions – low cloud, 10 degrees Celsius, rain. The main *peloton* left the pursuit largely to the US Postals who eventually gave up interest. The lead group contained O'Grady but no one of real threat for the overall victory, save for two who might just give the main contenders trouble in the mountains: Kivilev and Aitor Gonzalez.

The break eventually began to split; Dekker attacked with the Paris–Roubaix winner Servais Knaven some 25 kilometres from the finish; they were joined by Dekker's team-mate Wauters and Aitor Gonzalez and in Pontarlier, Wauters led out for Dekker to sweep in, clear. The main *peloton* came in 35 minutes 54 seconds down on his time, the largest gap in post-war Tours and one which put 161 riders well outside the time guillotine – fixed at 10 per cent of Dekker's time. Strict ruling would have reduced the field to the 14 of the break. Exceptional cases allow exceptional decisions and strict regulations were waived.

At the finish, Dekker was trembling with cold but as he pointed out, at least they'd endured the foul weather half an hour less than the rest. Kivilev, a rated climber, had gained 13 minutes on the day. O'Grady profited: he took back yellow and green.

In 1998, the Russian Sergei Ivanov led a go-slow ride into Aix-les-Bains, at the foot of the Alps, in protest at the rough treatment meted out to his TVM team during the drugs scandal. Three years on, he attacked on his own 9km from the finish and crossed the line as victor of the 9th stage, to the annoyance of Tour officials, who are very sensitive to symbolic coincidence. (That same day, a court in Reims handed his ex-manager Cees Priem a suspended 18-month prison sentence, plus a fine of £7,420 for illegal distribution of drugs.) And a Spanish rider, Txema del Olmo, was expelled by his team, the Basque newcomers Euskaltel-Euskadi, for testing positive for EPO. Leblanc commented: 'This proves that the EPO test works perfectly. I am pleased about this but it confirms that we have no reason to relax vigilance: obviously some riders are incorrigible.'

It is riders who make a course hard and there is no such thing as an easy Tour de France. Race routes differ but so, too, do difficulties. The first two weeks of the 2001 Tour were ridden at fierce pace; relentless attacks tore holes in the *peloton*; the early taste of climbing sowed further fatigue. The lesser teams seemed to be set on damaging the US Postals before the real challenge of the mountains. The fighting spirit of the perennial *baroudeurs*, men like Durand and Dekker, had flared like a contagion, to the delight of the public, at least. On the eve of stage 10, first of the Alpine forays, the mood was unduly sombre. Tomorrow, for most of them, there would be little breath left nor much inclination for talking. There was 209km to go. A few minor ascents leading to three *hors* category climbs: col de la Madeleine, 2000m; col du Glandon, 1,924m, finishing atop the dreaded mountain cul de sac l'Alpe d'Huez, 1,850m. Total climbing, 60.7km. O'Grady, who admitted that the day before he had been in terrible straits and only wearing the yellow jersey had kept him up with the race, knew that he would surely lose the Golden Fleece this day, probably to second-placed François Simon whose brother, Pascal, lost it on the stage to l'Alpe d'Huez in 1983.

Nasty as the Huez stage would be, it was but the first of a block of mountain stages.

Stage 11
32km individual time trial, the final 18.7km an average 8 per cent climb to the mountain-top finish in Camrousse. (This was the first mountain time trial to be included since 1996, when Evgeni Berzin won in the yellow jersey.)

Rest Day. Transfer by plane to Perpignan

Stage 12. Pyrenees. Perpignan–Ax- les-Thermes.
Distance: 166.5km. Total climbing: 53.1km. Col de Jau 1,506m, col de Coudons 883m, col des Sept-Frères 1,253m, col du Chioula 1,431m, Ax 1,375m.

Stage 13.* Foix –St-Lary-Soulan.
Distance: 194km. Total climbing: 68.4km. Col de Portet d'Aspet 1,069m, col de Menté 1,349m, col du Portillon 1,320m, col de Peyresourde 1,569m, col de Val-Louron-Aspet 1,580m (St. Lary) Pla d'Adet 1,680m
   * The stage was originally scheduled to cross the col de Port (1,249m) too but a local speculator, a politician, *persuaded* the Tour organisation to re-route the race past his new golfing and leisure complex.

Stage 14. Tarbes–Luz-Ardiden.
Distance: 144km Total climbing 47.1km. Col du Haut de la Côte 645m, col de Mauvezin 520m, col d'Aspin 1,489m, col du Tourmalet 2115m, Luz-Ardiden 1,715m.
   Rest Day.

Statistics are of limited value. Selective facts and figures tell only the story you choose to tell. The statistics quoted here tell only one story and are stark enough to dispense with superlatives – no extremely, no very, no anything, just five *hors catégorie* hard days.
   And a word about rest days. All riders hate transfers by plane. Their work is rooted in rhythm and anything that disrupts that rhythm is stressful. The break from racing may be welcome, but that rhythm has to be sustained: an hour and a half ride to keep the muscles loose and to bypass the body's immediate impulse to begin to wind down. A tricky balance between relaxation and routine stress.

On the first major climb of stage 10, the col de la Madeleine, Millar knew he was finished. The appalling physical effort merely to hang on at the back like a tin can tied to a car bumper, the wasting effect of scratching up the strength and willpower to stay in the race had drained his morale dry with the force of a turkey-farm eviscerating suction pump. But, with enormous courage, he made the col – nothing, he said, would have induced him to abandon on the climb, the shame of it – and cruised to a stop on the descent. The dread of giving up was at last overwhelmed by the terrible certainty of not being able to go on any longer.

The col du Glandon is reckoned one of the worst climbs in the Alps by many, including Bernard Thévenet who virtually wasted himself towing a chase group up it in 1977, the year of his second victory. He was riding to save his yellow jersey. The others had their own agenda and left him to the work. Dead in the saddle at the summit of l'Alpe d'Huez, unable to walk or eat, he had nonetheless held onto his lead over the day's winner, Hennie Kuiper, by 55 seconds. It seemed quite possible that Armstrong was in similar straits this year. Ullrich's Telekoms were driving a fierce pace and Armstrong's team had fallen away, save his climbers, Heras and Jose-Luis Ribiera. Armstrong appeared to be suffering – roiling at the back, eyes sunk. The Basque climber from the wild-card Euskaltel team, Roberto Laiseka, 32 years old in his first Tour, even reached out at one point to pat him on the back in encouragement, so grim did he look. Perhaps he would crack – he nearly had in the Alps the previous year. Ullrich piled on the pressure down the long valley descent and out onto the approach road to the final beastly 14km up l'Alpe d'Huez. Ahead of them, Laurent Roux, who had escaped with two others at 6km and went clear solo on the Glandon, was tantalisingly close to a miraculous victory.

A right-hand bend and there it is, the first slab of the massive wall, a horror. The Armstrong/Ullrich group contained a clutch of ace climbers. This was their terrain, but suddenly, the hitherto resolute line of Telekoms wavered, as if they were unsure whose turn it was at the front. Ribiera and Heras charged through and, fast as you like in their slipstream, Armstrong. He sped past and, with one withering look at Ullrich as if to say: ' Here's my hand. Time to see you,' he was out of the saddle, accelerating on low gears; 39x21, 3.95m for every full turn of the pedals and turning those pedals at around 85/90 rpm. It was breathtaking; a show of irresistible force. No one could follow.

Some 4km up he had established a gap of 2 minutes; at around 7km he went past the luckless Roux with nary a glance. The speed of his pedalling – chainwheel a blur like a *moulinette*, a child's hand-held windmill – has drawn comparison with legendary pure climbers such as Charly Gaul, Federico Bahamontes, Lucien Van Impe. Gaul notably first adopted low-gear 'twiddling' though he stayed in the saddle. Others preferred the dancing style, out of the saddle, which requires huge stamina and lung-power. In the rarefied thin air of the mountains, most big men prefer higher gears which take more strength to turn but less toll on breathing. Ullrich has tried to adapt to faster pedalling but admits it simply doesn't suit him. Armstrong has, from the first, pedalled at high revs; having lost some 5 kilos of body weight in his fight against cancer, he now has a leaner frame which responds to specialist preparation for tremendous accelerations on the climbs.

At the finish, there was no evident jubilation. Armstrong gritted his teeth and jabbed the air; a gesture of spite, it seemed, an *I told you so . . . get off my back.* Perhaps he felt overjoyed; the perception at the time was different. Later he confessed that he might have expended too much energy; he had ridden himself to the limit and though Ullrich, grinding away, had lost 1 minute 59 seconds, there was still a long way to go. Incidentally, he pulled out his earpiece at about halfway: no advice he was being given could possibly help. He rode the climb at 21kph (Armstrong at 22kph) more than 1 minute slower than when he took overall victory in 1997.

Armstrong had become only the second American to win on the alp – after Andy Hampsten in 1992. Lemond, the eventual victor, and Bernard Hinault crossed the line together in 1986, though the Frenchman is credited (in French records) with the win. That case apart, only Fausto Coppi had won on the alp (the first time it featured in the Tour, 1952) and in Paris. Armstrong was clearly moved and had, at last, begun to reveal some sense of the history of this race; that it is not simply the greatest bike race in the world, but possessed of a legendary status, a mythology which sets it apart as a sporting event. You don't just turn up, win and go home. The reach of merely riding it is far longer and deserves a greater respect than he has demonstrated, being too preoccupied with his own concerns. This apparent indifference to the unquantifiable mystique of the Tour de France has alienated Armstrong. He has, if tardily, begun to evince a welcome sensitivity to the peculiar hold the race has on the

French. It is rooted in their national tradition. Armstrong, surely prompted by his Frenchwoman PR advisor, has softened and begun to open up to the impact of his deeds, *and* to talk in less hesitant French: 'L'Alpe d'Huez is a classic climb, a very special stage and it means a lot to everyone in cycling. It's probably the most famous climb in the sport and that motivated me today. I wanted to win on the Alpe and it's not something that many people have done, so it's an honour to win the stage. [Earlier on] I continued to 'suffer' a little, I played poker, because I assumed that if I bluffed then they would ride harder.' His time for the ascent, 38 minutes, was only just slower than Pantani's 1997 record of 37 minutes 35 seconds.

(A 60-year old cyclist, attempting the ride before the race collapsed with a heart attack and died.)

François Simon took yellow – his brother Pascal had phoned him to tell him to get the jersey for the family – but he had no illusions about his 20-minute lead over Armstrong who, if he had overcooked it showed no sign next day to Chamrousse. During the winter, he had come down to train on these alpine stages and, when the big cols were closed by snow, he rode the mountain time trial several times. That is where his Tours are won: in the freezing cold of February, Bruyneel videoing him as he rides, producing a monitored profile of how to ride each and every climb. Work, work, work; you prepare best for something by doing it. He took the stage – the route forms part of the col de Luitel, scene of one of Gaul's epic stage wins in 1958 – having led at every time check, by 1 minute over Ullrich whom he now led by over 3 minutes. Kivilev lost over 6 minutes: his potential threat had had no real substance.

It was the first time anyone had taken consecutive alpine stages since Pyotr Ugrumov (another of Dr Ferrari's consultees) in 1994. The last defending Tour winner to do so had been Merckx in 1972.

2km from the finish on the climb up to Plateau de Bonsacre above Ax-les-Thermes, Armstrong once more turned coolly to stare into the grimacing face of Ullrich, his mouth agape with punishing effort, before racing away; never was the phrase 'putting down the hammer' more expressive. Ullrich had led all the way, punishing himself to tire the American, but Armstrong showed no fatigue, even seemed to be smiling before he overtook the German champion. The Colombian Felix Cardenas beat his fellow breakaway Laiseka by 13 seconds, and Armstrong by 15 seconds.

Stage 14.

The 1971 Tour crossed the same climbs they face today. The ridges are steeped in history – Allied airmen and soldiers escaped from Occupied France into neutral Spain guided by local mountain men, at considerable risk to themselves; many of them were smugglers well-used to dodging the revenue patrols on the cols. In the Middle Ages, Jews fled the Spanish *pogroms* over the same passes, and when Franco's Falangists took Barcelona, the roads filled with Republicans straggling into exile, many of them with no more than a suitcase. One such refugee traipsed over the col du Portillon and 35 years later his son, Luis Oçana, racing towards that same mountain, crashed out of the Tour. In 1995, Fabio Casartelli died on the Portet d'Aspet and the day before at the signing on in Perpignan, Lance Armstrong was presented with a small replica of the memorial to his friend. We could only guess at how he would feel, how they would all feel, when they rode past. Nearing the end of the stage, the race would pass through a village called Garin, the name of the winner of the first Tour de France. History was crowding in on us that day.

I rode up to the col to wait for the race across a graffito scrawled on the tarmac: *Dieu Armstrong . . . Jaja dans le Baba* (marginally less crude than 'up your arse'). 'God Armstrong . . . Jaja's kidding himself.' Back down to my station at a hairpin.

The break went through and, five minutes later, the main bunch. The overriding impression, especially if you've recently crawled up the climb, is of the sheer force, the power, the ruthless focus; this drive is already wilting in two guys off the back – Steffen Wesemann and *lanterne rouge* Bart Leysen, caught up in the following traffic of cars and petrol fumes, haggard, suffering, both due to abandon later that day, cast adrift like the empty bidons, food bags and wrappers that litter the route. Spectators are asked to chuck their refuse in official Tour de France waste bags attached to small wooden stakes.

The buccaneering Durand got a big cheer – 'Ja-cky ! Ja-cky !' Armstrong, a few riders off the front, looked impassive, though arriving at the Casartelli monument in training not long before he had wept like a child; this is the hidden face of these men. All the suffering in training, the cold dark days of winter etch the pain; once the race is on, they wear the mask of apparent indifference.

The rest of the escapees wilted, Jalabert rode himself into a lone lead, 162km out in front, over five of the six cols and took the mountains jersey from Roux. The chase behind him crossed the Peyresourde and down. Ullrich, never a very handy descender, carried the fight on, risk be damned. He took one corner too sharply, shot off the road, only just short of a metal barrier – which might well have crippled him – turned a somersault over the bike and disappeared from view. A few seconds later, he scrambled out of the undergrowth, passed up his undamaged bike and remounted. Armstrong had waited. The respect for his rival was plain.

Jalabert was eventually caught on the last climb of the day, his legs gone, by Armstrong, riding with magnificent ease. Armstrong actually offered Jalabert his wheel but, as the Frenchman said, he'd have needed a motorbike to stay with him. But what a marvellous show of professional dedication that day out in the blistering Pyrenean sun had been. *'Allez Jaja!'* they cried. Leblanc called it *'grandiose'*. Jaja had reclaimed French hearts, as well as the mountains jersey *and* overall in the Combativity prize. This had not been the only day he'd shown aggression and tenacity.

Armstrong had sworn this victory for his dead friend Casartelli and, mirroring that day in Limoges in 1995 when he had dedicated the stage win to him, he crossed the line at the Pla d'Adet with both arms pointing to the heavens. He really had opened his heart to the race and those who honour it. Confidence had allowed him more generosity.

Jalabert took no mountain points but retained his polka dot jersey and would hold it to Paris, thus becoming the only man apart from Hinault to win both green and mountains jersey outright. (Merckx won the mountains competition in 1969, but the *maillot à pois* – a copy of one of the famous jerseys worn at the popular night racing in the Vélodrôme d'Hiver from the 1930s to '50s – was inaugurated in 1975 at the insistence of Félix Lévitain.) Kivilev was now second overall; Simon had ceded yellow to the American and Oscar Sevilla of the Kelme team, who were well ahead in the team competition, had established an unassailable lead in the young riders' (under-24, white jersey) competition. (Young rider? He looks about 15 years old.)

Ullrich had not given up. Next day he fought hard over the Aspin and the monster Tourmalet but could not shake Armstrong off. 'I tried hard to put him in trouble. I have never been so strong but there was nothing more I could do.' Laiseka rode to a glorious solo win that afternoon at Luz-Ardiden. One minute eight seconds behind him, Armstrong and Ullrich rode in together and as they crossed the line, Ullrich, just ahead, gallantly put out his right hand, conceding victory. Armstrong clasped it. Nothing symbolises this Tour better: the frayed nerves, suspicion, discourtesies and bickering of the previous year gone; a compelling rider who had matured into a great champion, with a rival of exceptional tenacity. There was unmistakable respect between them. A race worthy of the Tour's legend. Asked when he knew he could not win the Tour, Ullrich replied: 'On Luz-Ardiden.'

Armstrong even addressed his unpopularity. Speaking of the *prix citron*, the mock prize journalists award to the least cooperative rider, he said: 'I don't like small talk or posing for photos doing stupid pointless things. I give them intensity in the race and I'll go on doing so; isn't that enough?' He had a point and speaking candidly about it was immeasurably more convincing than the bristling of previous years. Another regular *prix citron*, double winner Laurent Fignon supported him. Some people find Armstrong cold but that is nothing to reproach him for. Maybe when so many people want a piece of you there is no other way to be. On the other hand, Armstrong had hired a bodyguard. He had, he admitted, been very nervous at the start of the Tour. Fignon with a hint of irony remarked: 'Maybe that's a sign of the times.' Nonetheless, at a press conference he himself called in Pau on the Rest Day, Armstrong appeared relaxed, ready to field questions with genuine concern, to help and inform. In the bilious climate of relations a year ago this would have seemed ingratiating, sheer politicking. Now, it had the feel of a rider who had overcome a number of personal gripes and emerged into a clearer frame of mind.

There were other, less seemly events to report. Italian riders complained that the *lanterne rouge*, Jimmy Casper (more French panache, if at the back of the race) had been shamelessly taking tows up the mountains, a practice well-established in Italy, but then as shamelessly popping up at the front of the race to contest the intermediate sprints next day. This was not fair play. On the second Rest Day someone stole the Départ bell and Leblanc had to borrow one from the director of the *Dauphine Libere*. Jonathan Vaughters was stung by a wasp; his right eye puffed up so badly that he was compelled to take anti-inflammatory corticoids (a banned substance), which meant that he had to withdraw from the race early in the next stage. The French Minister, who followed the race that day, agreed that there are occasions when medical treatment ought to be permissible, clear of any charge of doping. And as Ullrich decelerated across the line on Stage 16, a spectator made a grab for his hat and nearly decked him. The yellow jersey decided, there remained the duel for the green jersey between O'Grady and Zabel.

Stage 16 was won by Jens Voigt from the Australian Bradley McGee, two survivors of a long break. McGee was so exhausted that he could do nothing at the finish. Descending into Tulle, a bunch of 30 riders took a left-hand bend too fast and piled up. Five riders were evacuated to hospital, their season finished, with three broken collarbones, one fractured wrist and a serious facial wound amongst their injuries.

Next day, Voigt punctured 5km from the line and rode like the devil to get back into the bunch to help his team mate O'Grady contest the sprint with Zabel, but the lead was shrinking.

The 18th stage, a 61km individual flat time trial, was won by Armstrong in matchless style. So laid back on the starting platform as to be signing an autograph – he had done his warm-up in the company of his wife and son, a domestic intrusion of the kind once distinctly alien to the Tour's ambiance – he took 1 minute 24 seconds out of Gonzalez de Galdeano, one of the ONCE domestiques, and 1 minute 39 seconds from Ullrich. The big gain of the day was the 2 minute 8 second margin Beloki got over Kivilev, which hoisted him into third overall, so that the order at the head of the leader board stood exactly as it had a year before.

In the tussle for the green points jersey, Zabel was reeling O'Grady in: another win on the penultimate Stage 19 and 45 more points amassed brought him to within two points of the Australian's total. On the final run-in to Paris, the Telekoms – organised by their *directeur*, former fast-man Walter Godefroot – backed Zabel with impressive efficiency and cropped all the intermediate sprint bonuses on offer; the Crédit Agricoles, unable to revive the cohesion they had displayed in winning the team time trial, seemed to have given up. Zabel took the lead by four points, his lieutenant, Alexandre Vinokourov, who had already worked so tirelessly for Ullrich in the montains, sprang his lead-out efforts with faultless timing and still had energy for a solo break on the last lap of the Champs Elysées. He very nearly made it; what a reward that would have been for surely the most industrious domestique of the Tour. But the pack was on him, the Czech sprinter Jan Svorada led in, with Zabel and O'Grady on his shoulder.

Armstrong, Ullrich, Beloki: the same three on the podium as in 2000, but what a change in the shape of the Tour, in the atmosphere. There is an enduring image of Zabel and O'Grady smiling together after the race, arms about each other's shoulders, the accord of friendship after a tough duel clean fought. The hitherto taut American confessed '*C'est le Tour où j'ai pris le plus de plaisir*': it is the Tour that has given him most *pleasure*. Leblanc suggested that there was indeed a fresh optimism abroad. 'I have the feeling that most of the riders have turned the page. It has been a good Tour. We have regained vigour, oxygen, we have put the smile back.' Such a smile as Rik Verbrugghe's when he was heading for the line on Stage 15, Marco Pinolti on his wheel; he even had time to adjust his glasses as they plopped off his nose *twice*. What's he *doing?* we thought. On a stage victory and he's worried about his bins? He made it.

It was undoubtedly an unusually taxing race. The Banesto doctor, Jesús Hoyo, said that of all the five Tours he had followed, it was by far the hardest on the riders' powers of recovery. But, despite the domination of Armstrong, it was no procession. The attacking spirit animated it from start to finish and, as Fignon said, 'either at the side of the road or in front of the television, people want to see riders at their limit, some going well, others not so well. The Tour resembles life: there are heroes and there are losers. I think this time, the public has been well served'.

TWELVE

2002

Armstrong's Four-Square Triumph

The shape of the 2002 race had a decidedly lopsided look: ten flat stages, a week's worth of mountains – twenty-one in a lump interspersed by one flattish stage and a rest day – leaving a bare three-day run-in to Paris. Lance Armstrong, going for a fourth consecutive win, predicted that this would be his hardest Tour yet, but that was no more than self insurance against what he calls the suicide of projecting victory. However, although the opposition was talked up, there was nobody of real challenge to the reigning champion who makes no secret of his obsession with the yellow jersey. 'When I stop riding the Tour de France, I stop riding.' He can afford to. There is no commercial pressure on him to race elsewhere. His sponsors – the US Postal Service – have no particular interest in anything other than the most prestigious victory and if Armstrong and the team delivers that, the rest of the racing calendar is of very limited publicity appeal. It's an emphatically self-serving attitude with which those more deeply imbued with the traditions of cycle sport do not have much sympathy. But, while Armstrong's passion drives him, there is unlikely to be a halt in his wins.

It was Greg Lemond who began this trend of concentrating solely on the Tour win, although Lucien Van Impe, in his day, framed his entire season round the hunt for the mountains prize.

The biggest threat, Jan Ullrich, was out with a damaged knee. The Italian opposition was depleted and in disgrace: Marco Pantani was under investigation for doping, but, after a dreadful ride in the Giro d'Italia, his career is almost certainly finished; Gilberto Simoni, winner of the 2001 Giro, had been bragging that he could give the Americans trouble, but tested positive for cocaine after a short Italian stage race and he and his Saeco team were banned; Stefano Garzelli received a fine of £45,000 – 100,000 Swiss francs – and 9 months suspension for the use of probenecid, a masking agent, during the Tour; and Dario Frigo had only just returned after his suspension. The police raid on the Giro d'Italia, 6 June 2002, caught him in possession of pots of dope which, he protested, he had no intention of using, they were 'for inspiration' . . . by some mystic purpose, presumably. (Bought through the Internet, delivered at Milan Linate airport on the hush hush, one bottle, which cost him £500, turned out to contain salt water. If it had contained Hemassist, he'd have had to keep it at -6°. Dope? Dupe.) Of other riders in the race, only two looked close to being dangerous: the Spaniard Joseba Beloki, third in 2001 and the Columbian Santiago Botero, an all-rounder – King of the Mountains in 2000 – who can race against the clock. Botero had even had the effrontery to beat the specialist Armstrong in a time-trial in a warm-up race before the Tour. The French clung forlornly to their only overall contender, Christophe Moreau, whose win in the 2001 Prologue was as close as he had come, and would be likely to come, to any challenge. But, as Armstrong never tires of saying, the Tour is unlike any other race: a bad day in the mountains, such as he suffered in 2000, can wreak havoc. Luckily for him both Pantani and Ullrich failed to capitalise on that occasion, but there is no such thing as a safe margin. In 1972, Eddy Merckx, riding for his fourth victory, lost 10 minutes to Luis Ocaña and only took the race back after the Spaniard had to abandon after a dreadful crash. But, Ocaña was a potent rival: Armstrong has none.

That said, this year's Tour was full of wonderful racing and quite a few upsets and surprises which make it the great event it is. Jacky Durand, the man who loves to go out alone, darling of the Combativity competition, was booted out for a silly infraction. The Norwegian Thor Hushovd, was nearly eliminated by missing the time barrier on Stage 2, but stuck to his job and took the win on Stage 18. David Millar was blown out of contention for Best Young Rider – his stated aim for the race – after the very first mountain stage but, two days later, managed to win a stage. As to the battle for the Green Jersey, Erik Zabel aiming for a seventh win in a row, it became the story of the Tour: settled with a majestic flourish on the Champs Elysées.

The Tour began in Luxembourg. The last time it had started here, in 1989, Pedro Delgado, the reigning champion, got lost in town on a warm-up ride and missed his Prologue start by over two minutes. This year, the US Postal's local man, Joachim Benoît, the only Luxemburger in the race, gave his team an in-depth guided tour of the route – 7km of fast descents, sharp corners, cobbles and a wicked uphill drag – only to fall off on his own ride the next day. Armstrong, riding in team colours – he said he needed the motivation, the incentive, of chasing yellow – won by two seconds from the amazing, evergreen Laurent Jalabert, a former World time-trial champion. Millar, who admits that his concentration on training in the mountains had cost him some speed, nonetheless came fifth and was full of ambition. He had been making all the sacrifices essential to a good ride. He was, it seemed, beginning to let the bike do the talking for him.

The race spent two days in the tiny Duchy which has produced three Tour winners and four victories: François Faber, 1909; Nicolas Frantz, 1927 and 1928; and Charly Gaul, 1958. On the first stage, the young Swiss rider Rubens Bertogliati made a do-or-die break on the last climb to take the win and, by virtue of a time bonus, the yellow jersey – the first Swiss to take a stage since Alex Zülle in 1996. Robbie McEwen, one of three Australian fast men in the race nurtured on track racing – with Bradley McGee and Stuart O'Grady – was riding in some pain from a pinched nerve, but made no secret of his intention to battle with Zabel for green. Back in Germany, Zabel's team-mate Ullrich, who two months earlier had been booked for drink-driving, had now been caught taking amphetamines in a disco at three in the morning. His manager, Walter Godefroot, close to exasperation with the froward rider of more promise than returns, said he didn't know whether Ullrich would have the willpower, now, to return at this level: 'He's been saying all the right things but he hasn't backed that up with actions. We need to know what he's going to do.

Maybe he'll just go and live off his money,' he said wearily, 'he's got enough of it.' (The six months suspension imposed on him subsequently means that he won't be able to race until March 2003.)

The last rider to win a Tour stage wearing the rainbow jersey of World champion was Bernard Hinault who took three in his third overall victory in 1981. The Spaniard Oscar Freire, the current rainbow jersey, has twice jumped the pack to win the World's Road Race, and did the same on Stage 2, pipping Zabel and revenging his loss to the German in his home-town, Torrelavega, during the 2001 Vuelta a España. Hushovd limped in 19m 22s later weaving unsteadily through crowds who thought all the riders had already finished. Stricken with severe cramp, he had struggled on and was applauded for his heroic effort at the line by the Tour organiser, Jean-Marie Leblanc. In view of his courage, the time rule was waived and he stayed in the race.

Next day, it was McEwen who relegated Zabel with an irresistible turn of speed down the barriers, though Zabel's time bonus put him into yellow as well as green. The Australian said afterwards that no sprinter can claim to be the best in the world, only to be the best on the day. As to the reason for his startling speed – specific muscle-toughening and high-rev pedalling developed through track racing – he said, of himself and the other Ozzies, with professional bluntness: 'We try harder.' Example? O'Grady, who had taken up the fight with Zabel in 2001, suffered a bout of tachycardia during the stage: his heart-rate went up to 225, way beyond his racing maximum of 184. He received medical attention in the saddle, and not only recovered, but even raced up to the front to contest the sprint.

The team time-trial, won by Beloki's Spanish ONCEs, caused ructions in Jalabert's Danish CSC Tiscali team, managed by the 1996 winner Bjarne Rijs. The stated plan before the ride was to dump any rider who punctured apart from Jalabert, Tyler Hamilton and Carlos Sastre. With 20km to the finish, the Danish champion Michael Sandstöd punctured. Rijs said wait, the radio in the mechanics' car wasn't working – they drove on. Rijs dithered, then ordered them to get going, but in the muddle they had lost 53 seconds and Jalabert an almost certain yellow jersey. A terrible disappointment but, as he put it when tempers had cooled, no cause for bad feeling; the Tour goes on, so must they.

Two days later, Jalabert, 'Jaja', was signing autographs when a bell rang but locals assured him it was for Mass. It *was* in fact, for the start of the stage. Somewhat stressed, he chased on, reflecting that he had good legs and . . . maybe a chance of doing something. The ONCE rider Gonzalez de Galdeano took over the lead and became the first Spaniard to wear the yellow jersey since quintuple winner Miguel Indurain.

Idle in Italy, the great speed merchant Mario Cipollini, whose new team Acqua e Sapone were not ranked high enough to ride the Tour, announced his retirement. 'I feel bitter at not being able to ride the Tour and have a chance to win a stage. The sponsors do not recognise my value.' He's said as much before. Another fit of petulance? Italian cycling being under such a cloud of suspicion, it badly needs Cipo's crowd-pleasing, dope-free image and, given that this autumn's World's Road Race over a flat course should be ideal for him, he soon reversed his decision.

Back in the Tour, Christophe Moreau, riding with a fractured vertebra, was having a wretched time, heading straight for every crash going, it seemed, and there were plenty – Millar was caught up in several but, luckily, shrugged off the bruises. However, crashes put paid to Tom Steels, Freire and, in a 70kph pile-up, Marco Pinotti (nose split open) and Rik Verbrugghe (broken collarbone), although the Belgian somehow made it to the stage finish, one handed. On the same day, the Estonian sprinter and former yellow jersey Jan Kirsipuu took the honours riding for the second-division French Ag2R team, in the Tour as the last wild card selection in May. 'We ought to congratulate the Tour for letting us ride,' he said, with a dig at the often arcane selection criteria applied by the organisation.

Zabel got his win on Stage 6. Dutchman Karsten Kroon, a Tour rookie, grabbed the win of his life on Bastille Day, having only one previous victory in an obscure Swiss one-day race – in his palmarès. However, the big news at the start of the second week was Botero's victory in the individual 52km time-trial in Britanny. It was the first time in four years that Armstrong had lost such a stage and suddenly there was talk of a loss of form, a vulnerability, a chance that he might wilt under attack. He admitted that he hadn't felt good and was expecting to come 22nd not 2nd. Claiming not to be making excuses, he said: 'When you start at different times, the conditions can change and in the last 5km I was suffering.' Conditions can change, for sure, to help or hinder – Merckx himself lost a couple of races of truth in the Tour – but really, the loss of 11 seconds was not going to worry Armstrong, even if Botero's directeur sportif was saying: 'So Armstrong is human, after all.' Later, US Postal directeur Johann Bruyneel let slip that they had chosen the wrong gearing and deprived the American of the necessary power – a curiously elementary mistake, given their scrupulous attention to every last detail. However, Armstrong positively welcomed the bullish commentary. 'It's attack until they crack, or I do', which is about as succinct a definition of the will to win as you could get. He was, though, still sounding off like the po-faced Yank he is, and made an unworthy side-swipe at the ONCE boss: 'I think Manolo [Saíz] has a problem with the fact that one of his ex-riders [the US Postal director Johan Bruyneel] has been far more successful as a manager in this race than he has.'

Millar, who had had to 'hang on for grim death at the end' pulled on the white jersey of Best Young Rider and professed himself happy: he didn't even feel on his best form and yet there he was, close to the top guys. Alas, not for long.

On the rest day before the Pyrenees, Jaja announced that he would be retiring at the end of the season, but this old-school rider, complete professional, competitive at all times and in all disciplines, had more surprises to pull yet. After 14 years it would be time to end 'the story of a young kid who rode bikes with his friends and dreamt of becoming a professional rider and riding the Tour de France'.

Close to the village of Poteaux, 26km into Stage 10, a 7-year-old boy, Melvin Pompele, who may have had the same dream, ran across the road to rejoin his grandparents, straight into the path of one of the publicity caravan Land-Rovers and died instantly. It is a mark of the mannerly police handling of the bystanders out in the country that the roadside atmosphere is relaxed and good-humoured. One can only hope that such a tragedy – the second in three years – will stiffen vigilance rather than crowd control.

Col d'Aubisque, Stage 11, was the first Pyrenean col traversed by the Tour in 1910 and continues to the climb that concludes the day, the Tourmalet, but only to 6km below the summit at the ugly ski-station, La Mongie. The US Postals had a simple plan: to ride for the win and race as if they already had yellow. The heat was intense, the expected attacks on the Aubisque did not come, the lead group arrived at the foot of the last 14km climb intact and the Postals opened up. First George Hincapie blasted off the front at a cruel pace, José Luis Rubiera relayed and then the specialist climber, Roberto Heras went to the front, Armstrong on his wheel, and suddenly upped the pace so high that only Beloki stayed with them over the last 5km. Even Armstrong was at his limit, telling Heras to slow down; he could barely keep the pace, no thought of attacking and, though it would have been seemly to allow Heras the stage win, Beloki was close, they could take no risks. There were time bonuses on offer – 20, 12 and 8 seconds. This might suggest a lapse of moral strength. Armstrong could surely afford a handful of seconds? More likely, he and Heras were required to abide by team orders – as Rubens Barricchello, bidden cede victory to Michael Schumacher in the Austrian Grand Prix. The sponsors make a huge financial investment: minor details of sportsmanship, moral power versus naked force, cut no ice with them. The man they have enriched by hiring them has the no-frills responsibility to win the big race for them. End of story.

Some metres from the line, Armstrong dropped behind the Basque rider, then, to the dismay of the crowds of Basques cheering their man on, jumped past both him and his team-mate to pocket the 20 seconds time bonus on offer; his weary wave did for a victory salute. At the close, he was once more in yellow with Beloki at 1 minute 12 seconds, Botero at 4 minutes 13 seconds and Millar, perhaps reassessing his 'curiosity about the mountains' for which he had prepared hard, losing 7 minutes 23 seconds to the lead and any realistic hope of the white jersey in Paris. Jalabert, plainly driven by tireless professional enthusiasm, had spent 120km out on his own in a bid for the stage win and accumulating points in the mountains competition, which he'd won in 2001, entirely against expectation and by similar opportunistic forays.

Three kilometres from the line, riding on empty, he watched the leaders flash by. Only 4 minutes down overall, he had known they would have to chase him. Armstrong, he said, bestowed a wry look of sympathy.

There was no sympathy next day on the hard road to Plateau de Beille, crossing the col de Menté where Ocaña crashed out of the 1972 Tour, the col de Portet d'Aspet, where, in 1995, Armstrong's team-mate and friend Fabio Casertelli crashed and died, the col de la Core and the col de Port, whereon a series of punctures drove Charlie Holland, the first Briton to compete, out of the 1937 race.

Jalabert attacked early once more, amassing points in the mountains *and* the Combativity prize – worth 200,000 francs in Paris – awarded daily to the rider who shows most aggression. Past signs pleading 'Don't go Jaja' and 'Jaja in peas' (i.e. the red polka dots of the mountains jersey) he rode another 143km in a breakaway, expressly to get ahead in the mountains competition, but after a while, as he said, beginning to enjoy himself. The former specialist sprinter (green jersey 1992 and '95) wanted to finish his last Tour on a high. The Plateau de Beille proved just too high: 16.5km of 8 per cent average gradient to a summit at 1,780 metres. Once again, Rubiera then Heras led the onslaught and the rest, save Beloki, dropped away. Nine kilometres from the top, Jalabert, unheeded, watched them go. He ended the day 11 minutes 36 seconds down but in the peas . . . the jersey of *panache*, he calls it. Another 5km and Armstrong struck for home, up the climb he had trained on in May, using his familiar high-revving style, out of the saddle. This sudden burst of his strength may be unanswerable; so far, for sure, it remains unanswered. That dizzy whirring of the pedals, devouring a kilometre virtually every two minutes of uphill, is the hallmark of his superiority, and it derives from the exhaustive training methods and analysis which he and his support team apply to winning this race.

He experimented at two different rates: 75rpm and 100rpm. Both produced similar power output, heart-rate and speed – around 30kph on the climbs – however, the faster rate on a lower-gear ratio is ultimately less taxing on the muscles if more demanding of the lungs and so that is what they plumped for. In winter, accompanied by Bruyneel in the car, he comes to the Alps to ride and *learn* the climbs. At the end of one 8-hour session, to the top of la Plagne, back down, up again – all this come rain or snow – he was actually turned back by a heavy fall of snow which made the col unpassable. The American Jonathan Vaughters, former medical student riding for the Crédit Agricole team, has drawn sharp contrast between what he terms Armstrong's modern scientific preparation and the old-school methods. Armstrong leaves nothing to chance, to the extent of doing special work on his middle body to sustain the heavy strain of holding an extreme crouch position in time-trials. He weighs pasta and checks what difference the greater or lesser intake produces on the bike. He scouts the ground, he rides it at race speed: there is no terrain for which he has not readied himself psychologically and that is where he gains so much over his rivals. The deliberate absence from the extended demands of racing which most teams feel obliged to answer, leaves him mentally fresh anyway; the specific reconnaissance means that he has all but eliminated the chance of being surprised at any part of the route. Such meticulous provision added to a natural athleticism which he has honed to supreme physical efficiency is at the root of his supremacy . . . in this race. True, he won both the Midi Libre and the Dauphiné Libéré, two of the shorter mountainous-stage races, traditional leg-stretchers for the Tour, (as did Merckx in 1971 and Indurain in 1995), but he rarely makes much of a showing anywhere else. It is a moot point, of course, but many argue that Armstrong gave more to professional cycling before he became obsessed with the Tour de France. Until another rider of equal talent, mind and body, adopts similar demonic methods to winning one race per year, Armstrong is likely to stay 'up there' as Gonzalez de Galdeano (yellow jersey for 7 days) put it, gesticulating at the sky. He is not a great climber, he does not stun the field with massive gains; his victories are built on accumulated small gains and his own impregnability to attack.

The French call his swift cadence 'the coffee grinder'; it might more aptly be called the mincer through which he shreds the hopes, and strength, of anyone who tries to stay with him.

Looking back for Heras on the climb to Plateau de Beille, he was clearly ready to hand over the win if he could, due reward for his Spaniard lieutenant's sterling work, but Heras had not the legs and came in 1 minute 4 seconds adrift, just ahead of Beloki. Like all the other climbers, Beloki can maintain a steady pace – he never lost much more than a minute on the climbs; it is the abrupt surge of speed which he cannot counter. To put some perspective on the impact of his crushing attacks, Rubiera, having mounted the first assault with frantic acceleration, fell away when his turn was done and finished nowhere. That is the cost. Armstrong holds the wheel and saves energy but, on a mountain, not nearly so much as on the flat. Thus, from nearly the same effort as his front man, he then turns on the irresistible force and they all fall away behind him. One who had crumpled the day before was poor Vaughters; things had not been going well. The Crédit Agricoles, prime players in recent Tours, were having a dreadful time of it and Vaughters having climbed off after a crash – the fourth year in succession he has had to abandon – declared that he had done with the race and the sport altogether. He was in profound distress and may change his mind.

The stage did for Durand, too. The inveterate chancer of the solo break chanced the beady eye of the race commissaries, hitched a tow from his second team car, was spotted and, after he trailed into the finish 40 minutes down, protesting innocence, was kicked off the race, the car too. Sad end.

Routinely, Armstrong batted away any hint at complacency – he had no great time advantage yet, there was still a long way to go, anything could happen. Truth was, he had built an unassailable lead. What's more, his team, a very shaky outfit during his inaugural win in 1999, has become a well-drilled, solid, immensely strong unit dedicated absolutely to their leader's victory. And, not even Merckx ever won the first two mountain stages of a Tour back to back two years running as Armstrong has now done.

Millar trailed in over 50 minutes down which bodes ill for any notions about one day going for the overall victory. The bout of glandular fever early in the season which allowed him to come fresher to the race than might otherwise have been possible, may have tapped deeper into his physical resources than he'd thought. And yet, the white jersey already forfeited and his ribs bruised after a tumble in Alençon, he'd saved energy on the Plateau de Beille and took to the road next day determined to win. He felt good all day and 'it's easy to be cunning when you feel good'. He had written a note: *Today I win*, which is almost formulaic in French cycling parlance, a favourite dictum of the great Hinault, and 8km from the start in Lavelanet, he joined a break on the first climb in company with his idol, Laurent Jalabert, patiently consolidating his rather cheeky lead in the mountains competition, and two others. Another seven riders jumped across the gap to them and when Jaja botched an attack some 18km from the finish in Béziers, Millar and four others, including the notably fast men – David Extebarria, Laurent Brochard, Michael Boogerd – went clear. The last kilometres were hard on the nerves and the legs but Millar outwitted and outsprinted the rest with a fine show of *attitude* as much as anything. It was, he said, 'a sublime race today' and declared that professionally, it was his best moment. The last Briton to win a Tour road stage had been Max Sciandri into St-Etienne, in 1995. Millar's winning streaks are certainly bold; for the time being they are short-lived. Jalabert had now ridden 429km in breakaways over three days.

All the riders dread Mont Ventoux: the bald mountain thrusting up like a gazebo of the gods to survey the distant encirclement of alpine chains and Cévennes catches every caprice of wind and weather, and the final 6km of road up to its summit is as ugly a stretch of metalled concrete as can be found. In 2000 Armstrong made the crass error of gifting the win to his rival Pantani: he was surely bent on making that good this 14th stage, the second longest of the 2002 race, 220km from the old cloth-working town of Lodéve and source of most of France's uranium to the col at 1912m, the forbidding high place which the novelist Antoine Blondin christened 'the despot of cyclists'. Blondin lived in the St Germain quarter of Paris, neighbour to Jean-Paul Sartre and the rest, and refused to stray beyond its pavements except once a year for the Tour de France, which he followed 28 times. This does not explain the grip the race continues to hold on the French, but it does give some hint at the potency of the dream which stirred the young Jalabert and countless others.

Ten escapees, including the five-times King of the Mountains Richard Virenque, left the main *peloton* early, stayed ahead and reached the lower slopes of the Domaine of the Angels with 21km to ride in 35°C heat, some 10 minutes up on the chasing yellow jersey group. Virenque, suspended for eight months after finally admitting to taking EPO as a member of the disgraced Festina squad and shunned by all the French teams, had taken a lowly-paid contract with the Belgian Domo-Farm Frites team. He announced his comeback with a bold 242km break to win the sprinters' classic Paris-Tours, by *two seconds* over the chasing bunch – a race not even Merckx won. (One Belgian rider quipped: 'Merckx and I won everything between us: I won Paris-Tours and he won everything else.') Reviled by some, yet still the darling of many, Virenque, a slave to camera lens and column inches, looked dead in the saddle as the first steepness began to bite. He said later that some of the breakaways had done no work; perhaps his fatigue was an act; what followed was certainly an amazing performance. One by one the others fell away and he was alone, in the lead. Behind him, Armstrong was isolated in company with Beloki and his team-mate Mikel Pradera. Heras was having a miserable time this day; as Armstrong put it, in defence of his champion domestique, Ventoux does strange things to people. Botero slumped by over 15 minutes, Millar by 18 and the oven-baked slopes were littered with stragglers of considerable class.

Some 6.5km from the top, with Virenque hanging onto a four-minute lead, Beloki attacked, if you can call it that. It took Armstrong no more than a second or two to catch his wheel and go past at such velocity that the impression was of royalty spurning the vulgar. Within 3km, the American had opened a three-minute gap but he had let slip the chance to catch Virenque. Had he gone no more than a kilometre earlier, he would probably have nobbled him; as it was he was 2 minutes 20 seconds behind, but another 1 minute 45 seconds up on Beloki who consigned any hope of overtaking Armstrong to dust: 'We've been on the moon today and we've seen what the astronaut is capable of.' Armstrong, whose time to the col, 58 minutes, beat Pantani's 2000 record by 53 seconds, was stung by the chants and boos of a small number of beer-swillers at the roadside: 'Dopé Dopé' which is not French for one of the Seven Dwarfs, but nor is it anything other than the tattle of a moronic few more interested in ring-pulls than bike-racing. The American ignores the vast number of genuine fans cheering him on and instead he pillories the abusive idiots who shout louder. It's a pity, but rage is one of his prime motivators, apparently. Even in speaking of popularity he reveals how thin his crust of self-belief is: 'It's sometimes frustrating. You see the guys they [the fans] accept and cherish and really love and cuddle and it's the guys that in the group you say "I don't *ever* want to be like that guy". I want to be the guy that keeps his mouth shut...' Pardon? Dwelling on the matter of popularity in his book, *It's Not About the Bike*, he says that he is indifferent to being liked in general because 'my wife likes me, my son *will like me*' – my italics, but a telling point. No one could possibly doubt Armstrong's passion; but it is, in many ways, very two-dimensional.

The French have never warmed to the hauteur of winners; there is something inhuman about the aloofness of the men apart and the one aspect of the Tour de France which is possibly unique in all sport is the very stark human dimension of the race between man on his bike and the hard road, the rivals, the weather, the crushing psychological combat. Any rider who appears impervious to all that becomes something of an ogre. It was not until Merckx had been trounced in 1972 and then fought back with such patent courage that his true stature was recognised by the French public, and not till their man Thévenet beat him in 1975 that they *liked* him. He emerged as a man who could live past frailty and sublimate the effect of harsh adversity by sheer character and determination. Armstrong has not yet had to show such qualities, save in the loneliness of the cancer ward.

As for Virenque, who lives nearby Ventoux, it was a gallant victory, a real gain for his morale and, be it said, his image. It also confirms how much he owed to the performance-enhancing power of EPO: evidently he can still climb a mountain with panache, but not day after day as hitherto. He cannot challenge for the overall mountains prize now that he rides on his own legs.

Hushovd had put the agony of the cramps behind him and won the last sprint of the day at Châteauneuf-du-Pape – prize, a hundred bottles of the vintage.

The 30-year-old Lithuanian Raimondas Rumsas, riding in his first Tour for the Italian Lamprei-Daikin team, had been plugging away and now moved up to third overall.

The emergence of one rider who dominates the Tour, even for a number of years – and several have – does not reduce the race. The tussle for overall victory may be decided long before the arrival in Paris, but that does not stifle the competitive spirit in genuine men of the Tour, the riders devoted to the nobility of their profession as well as the routine obligations. When it becomes pointless even to imagine a rider like Armstrong having a bad day – 'a day without' as the French put it graphically – there are yet still laurels to be won and on stage 15, Botero seized his chance. With a rest day in which to reflect, he turned the calvary of Ventoux into a Sacred Way of victory on the longest haul of the race – 226.5km over seven climbs to the first category finishing ascent to Les Deux Alpes.

He'd decided to forget about the overall classification after the Pyrenean ordeal. Although a former mountains prize-winner, he is not a natural climber, more dependent on raw strength and, as the final kilometres to the day's win showed, of pretty uncooked style, too. Leading a break containing six others, he reached the foot of the last climb with 9½ minutes on the chasers. Mario Aerts was the first to stick his neck out, Botero ground after him, Axel Merckx countered, but steadily Botero pulled himself clear, clamped awkwardly to the bike, shoulders rolling with the strain, head lolling, mouth agape, a picture of desperate, in extremis, effort, but strong enough to hold clear by 1 minute 51 seconds on Aerts. The yellow jersey stuck close to Beloki and gave away nearly 7 minutes from an ample chest of spare time.

On the last climb, Beloki actually attacked and, though Armstrong was on his wheel at the time he didn't react for some time. When he did go, it took some ten seconds or so – uncharacteristically long – to put the dampeners on the insolent Basque. In an interview later he explained that he *hadn't known Beloki was attacking*. Since these riders can detect trouble at the hiss of an opponents accelerating tyre, this is very odd; except that, of course, he was, mechanically, awaiting orders from the earpiece.

In another interview Botero was saying that a stage win was more important than coming 4th or 5th on general classification, that he'd had one day and come back and 'like the rest, I'm a human being, not a machine'.

On the day when Moreau finally had had enough – another crash and a badly cut lip – and climbed off, Botero, joining Luis Herrera as only the second Colombian to win two stages in the Tour, had hoisted himself back to 7th from 18th, taken a glorious stage win and shown that any serious rider can – and should – take his chance.

Next day it was Michael Boogerd who showed the requisite audacity, and, after a 127km solo break, became the first Dutchman to win atop a mountain in the Tour since Gert-Jan Theunisse won on the 'Dutch' mountain (because always crowded with Dutch fans) l'Alpe d'Huez in 1989. Boogerd's only other stage win had been at Aix-les-Bains on a cold wet July day in 1996, at the end of which Armstrong, riding his fourth Tour, abandoned, feeling 'blocked'. Three months later, he was diagnosed as having testicular cancer. To complete the vignette, Armstrong has twice narrowly lost the Amstel Gold Dutch classic one-day race, once to Boogerd in a two-up sprint.

Boogerd mounted his attack at crazy speed on the twisting descent of the Galibier – Giant of the Alps, first included in 1911 and, at 2645m, the roof of this Tour – and shook off his pursuers at the foot of the climb to the col de la Madeleine. From there, the plunge into the valley and finally up to la Plagne, where in 1987 Stephen Roche rode himself into oxygen debt to claw back time on the yellow jersey Pedro Delgado, an act of sheer will unconnected to heart-rate monitors which brought him overall victory.

At 3km to go, Armstrong launched his attack, without response from any of those on his shoulder. Once again, he, or rather Bruyneel in the team car at the other end of the radio to Armstrong's earpiece, mistimed his move – half a kilometre earlier would have sufficed to take the stage victory – and, whereas two years back Armstrong was rather naively dismissing the idea of potting stage victories as beneath the dignity and professional status of a Tour winner, he has since matured. Stage victories, especially on the open road, whether on mountains or flat, are the stamp of enduring class. His Prologue win gave him 12 such – level with Zabel and Cipollini – and he added three more to put him level with Freddie Maertens, one behind Jacques Anquetil (5 times overall winner), René le Grèves and Charles Pélissier, neither of whom won the race. Merckx has the record with 34; Hinault 27.

Both the Frenchman Laurent Dufaux and the Spaniard Oscar Sevilla, best young rider and 7th overall in 2001, abandoned with stomach upsets. Jalabert stretched his lead in the mountains prize over Botero and saw Virenque buckle on the climb to the Galibier. Perhaps he was working the extraordinary magic of his number in the race: the 51 that Merckx carried on his first ride and victory and Ocaña in his 1973 win, that Thévenet was given in 1975 when he beat Merckx, that Hinault bore to victory in his first ride, 1978.

Boogerd, 'Boogie' to his flatland friends, relied for his luck on a necklace medallion containing his first tooth, his girlfriend's first tooth and a four-leaf clover he'd been carrying that day in Aix. Such jewellery is not always a good idea. Towards the end of one stage, O'Grady's neck chain got caught in the computer attached to his handlebars; he had to break the chain to rip it free and found the bits tangled up in his jersey later.

Frigo escaped on the final long downhill of the Tour, third day in the Alps, a tricky descent from the col de la Colombière with his fellow Italian Giuseppe Guerini and the Belgian Aerts. They had held off a chasing group of 13, animated by Jalabert, grabbing mountains points with relish, and on the sprint into Cluses, home of a National School of Watchmaking, Frigo timed his jump perfectly and saved Italy from a second barren year in the Tour. Reflecting on the more disagreeable events of the recent past, Frigo said: 'I prefer to think of beautiful moments like today; what's happened before is forgotten', although the point about the drive to eradicate doping from the sport is that it must *not* be forgotten.

Next day gave any small fry, keen to work, their last chance for a win before Saturday's individual time-trial and the procession into Paris. There were still mountain points on offer so Jaja had a full day's employment ahead of him and the battle for the green jersey points was hot. McEwen and Zabel had been swapping the lead during this final week, but were now level, McEwen wearing the jersey because of higher placings overall. McEwen suspected the US Postals of an agreement to help Zabel; he had some cause. Eighteen months before, at a small early season race, he'd launched an attack, unaware that Armstrong was taking a pee. There is an unspoken rule of gallantry in the *peloton* about such calls of nature – witness Jalabert's rage in the 2000 Tour (see p. 232). Armstrong raced to rejoin McEwen and gave him such an earful that the redoubtable Ozzie, who might have been inclined to apologise, was riled and told him to let it drop. Armstrong, not one to let things go on past showing, had been taunting McEwen sarcastically with that one lapse of manners from halfway through the Tour. Finally, McEwen had exploded and spat back (the French verb is 'lancer' . . . touché): 'Shut it or I'll stick my fist in your mouth.'

On this stage 18, McEwen took the lead by one point and, there being no points awarded in the time-trial, there would be a showdown on the Champs Elysées for the second year running. Introduced in 1953 to give the riders with no hope of winning overall another competition to ride for, the green jersey had been won by many illustrious Tour men, but never by an Australian. McEwen was in bullish mood. If Zabel wanted to send his men up ahead to collar the hot-spot sprints, that was fine by him – he was denying himself as well as McEwen and the Australian had shown himself to be faster than the German. Besides, he knew what it was to win on the Champs – in 1999 – which Zabel, four times second there, did not.

The last Norwegian to win a stage had been Dag Otto Lauritzen in the Pyrenees, 1987. Today, Hushovd, the former under-23 world time-trial champion, now 24, theoretically eliminated on day two, beat two fellow escapees, although the former Danish champion Jakob Piil had the misfortune to pull his foot out of the pedal in the final metres and, even worse, to land full crutch on the crossbar as Hushovd snatched the win by a tyre.

Zabel's Telekoms, this year devoted to his cause in the absence of Ullrich, cannot have been cheered when news broke that the former Tour winner had been suspended without pay but not – yet – sacked from the team.

On the first occasion that Macon hosted a time-trial, in 1991, Indurain beat Gianni Bugno by 27 seconds over 57km. Armstrong, launching into the leg-sapping roller-coaster 50km with the zeal of a man determined to show why he was wearing the yellow jersey, delivered the coup de grâce. Rumsas, runner-up, conceded 52 seconds and Beloki, 9th, lost a further 2 minutes 11 seconds. Millar rode superbly to take 4th place at 1 minute 14 seconds.

The Australians had had a great Tour. Baden Cooke and O'Grady – disappointed of the green jersey but still full of fight – were rarely far from the action in the sprints, McGee had taken a stage win and so too McEwen, who now had the chance of the big prize. There were two intermediate sprints on offer in the final stage: McEwen, bursting with confidence, took the first at a gallop, charging past the group of pink-jerseyed Telekoms trying to squeeze him out, and put himself a further three points ahead of Zabel. The second hot spot disappeared under a small swarm of blue-jerseyed US Postals. Conspiracy theory proven. In fact McEwen says he overheard Armstrong in conversation with Zabel: that in Zabel's place he wouldn't contest the sprint because if he lost it he'd be handing a big advantage to McEwen. A very negative attitude.

And so onto the final circuits of the Champs Elysées, paradise fields indeed for the 153 weary survivors of the original band of 189.

The usual flurry of attacks went off and were trawled back, Rumsas, in the thick of the forlorn attempts to deny the sprinters their last flourish on the uphill of the famous paved avenue to glory and blessed relief of no more bike for a few hours.

The field came together and McEwen and Zabel's Telekoms started the run-in.

On the final corner, Zabel missed his line, took it too fast, checked and lost precious ground. By the kind of sharklike killer instinct that marks out the best fast men, McEwen virtually sniffed the mistake and went pell mell for the line, thrusting off the challenge of his fellow countryman Cooke to cross the line, second-stage win, this the more illustrious, and crowned with the marvellous prize of winner: Points Competition, green jersey on the podium, where Armstrong shook him by the hand and said: 'Nice work'.

This victory McEwen dedicated to his baby boy. The first win on the Champs he'd given to a close boyhood friend, a fellow racer, killed by a truck whilst out training after the Olympic Games in Barcelona. That is another very particular aspect of cyclists: the passion of their friendships.

It was the first time since 1996, their third contention of the Tour, when Rijs took the overall win and Zabel his first points prize, that Telekom had no man on the finishing podium, but Zabel was already saying that he could not quit the race with this bitter taste of defeat and that he would be back.

Jalabert, by contrast, made a sweet farewell to the race he has ridden with such ardour: King of the Mountains and Combativity prize, both by emphatic margins and the deserved applause of a benevolent crowd as he rode the final stage on a specialised polka-dot bike given to him by the manufacturers, the legend 'Thank you Jaja' on the down tube.

Armstrong, having nearly lost his life to cancer has dedicated the win to the Tour. Giancarlo Ferreti, manager of the Fassa Bortolo team whose Ivan Basso won the white jersey as best young rider, does not approve of this narrow focus. He raced with Anquetil at the end of his career and Merckx at the start of his, and says: 'In 10 or 15 years time, Armstrong will be remembered only as a rider who won the Tour de France. Merckx and Hinault won everything – one-day classics and other Tours and Indurain won the Giro and Tour double, twice. Armstrong's focus is bad for cycling in general – it distorts the calendar but he has no commercial need to ride in other races.' There's the rub: the *commercial* need. The world has changed and the big corporations control the race, not the ambitions of individuals riding it. Ferreti has a point, but to an extent, Armstrong is in hock to his employers and there can be no denying that, paid to do a job – win the Tour – he does it with professional, with ruthless efficiency and he is, simply, without peer. In the Tour de France. He will not stifle interest in the race. Anquetil didn't. Merckx didn't. Not even the metronomic Indurain could do that. The race is and will always be larger than the life of all those who ride it and so long as the dream is vivid, so the race will endure.

Miguel Martinez told a reporter in the French press: 'I come out of my first Tour with immense souvenirs. I crossed the Galibier in the lead group as my father did when he won that stage [Mariano, 17th stage 1980]. I lived something huge that day and I am already impatient for next year.' The baton handed on, the tradition maintained, the continuum of the Tour.

Next year, the centenary race will start with a Prologue time-trial round the Stade de France and depart next day from outside the Café de Reveil in Montgeron, from where the first riders set out on the début Grande Boucle.

NOTE: Driving away from Chamonix in the French Alps on the last day of the Tour, Rumsas' wife was stopped by French police. Her car was loaded with testosterone, corticoids, EPO, growth hormones and anabolic steroids, enough to supply the entire team for the length of the Tour. Whether the fact that she was still ferrying them about suggests none was used remains to be seen. She was immediately incarcerated in a Lyon gaol; Rumsas himself missed the plane back to Italy and, at the time of writing, the case is still *sub judice*. Doubts had been expressed about Rumsas and, though riders *do* occasionally come from nowhere, they rarely can do so nowadays without incurring suspicion. Jean-Marie Leblanc confessed himself mightily surprised at Rumsas' third place on the podium but, in the light of the sorry mess in which Italian cycle racing finds itself – riddled with dark secrets, it seems, if not entirely manned by dope fiends – the cause of the Italian Lamprei-Daikin team, who dumped Rumsas instanter, is nevertheless in some peril.

CHAPTER THIRTEEN

THE CENTENARY

In planning the route of the centenary race, the organisers took full account of the Tour's great history and the epic nature of its enduring appeal. Stage 1 of the 1963 race began in Paris (the last time) but there had never been a Prologue in Paris. The riders launched down a ramp in the loom of the famous landmark that greets their arrival back in the capital, the Eiffel Tower; official start of the first stage, next day, after a neutralised parade through the eastern arrondissements, the heart of revolutionary Paris, past the place de la Bastille, out to the Café Reveil (now a Tex-Mex bar/restaurant) where the first race had begun. The six finish towns of the inaugural Tour – Lyon, Marseille, Toulouse, Bordeaux, Nantes and back to Paris – were on the itinerary, for sure, and a special competition for the rider with the accumulated lowest finishing position into each. To emphasise the heroic stature of the great race since its inception, the core of its appeal, the beauty, the folly, three days in the Alps, followed by a couple of flattish stages, an individual time trial and, without pause, a gruelling three days in the Pyrenees; three mountain top finishes all-told, before a second rest day and one final ordeal of climbing.

With Armstrong bidding for a record-equalling five straight wins, his opponents were eager for their own bit of history and staking verbal claim, at least. Gilberto Simoni, recent winner of the Giro d'Italia, who missed much of last year under suspension for doping and hadn't ridden the Tour for six years, said he was ready to take on the American without being frightened of him: 'I don't think he has ever confronted an adversary like me in the mountains.' The Basque leader of the ONCE team, Joseba Beloki, three times on the podium in Paris, second in 2002, promised a more aggressive ride than in previous years when, to the dismay of many, he appeared content to lurk in Armstrong's shadow but could mount little more than token attacks which were ferociously quashed by the American. Another Basque climber, Iban Mayo, came second to Armstrong in the Dauphiné Libéré and gave him a hard time in the Alpine stages. He was eager to stir things up in the mountains, especially the Pyrenees, where the home support would be fanatical. Santiago Botero, now riding as leader of the Telekom team, winner of the Mountains prize in 2002 and current World time trial champion, had matured into a more balanced rider but, on his own admission, was prone to at least one off-day in the mountains: not a good basis for other than an intermittent challenge. His teammate, the Kazakh Alexandre Vinokourov, was enjoying a record season: winner (for the second year running) of the early season stage race Paris–Nice and the Amstel Gold classic, he had been hard hit by the death, in a crash, of his great boyhood friend Andrei Kivilev. Those victories he said he owed to Kivilev whose strength he felt riding in him.

Of the other heavyweights in the peloton, Jan Ullrich was the rider whom Armstrong admitted he feared most. However, after 14 months out of competition because of injury and a ban for (recreational) drug-taking, it seemed unlikely that his form would be sufficiently strong to realise any potent threat. Team Coast, for which he had signed after leaving Telekom, had folded for lack of funds only months before the Tour and Ullrich was rescued only by the return to sponsorship of a classic marque: Bianchi, the legendary Italian bike manufacturers whose sky blue colours were most famously worn by the great Fausto Coppi and Felice Gimondi. On the Friday before the race, Gimondi, winner of the 1965 Tour, appeared at the presentation of Team Bianchi to the press and made Ullrich a gift of one of his jerseys from the 1960s. A poignant historic moment entirely apt in the context of this centenary. Ullrich was, nonetheless, diffident about his chances of doing much more than, maybe, taking a stage victory. To pose Armstrong any real problems was, he suggested, beyond his slowly recuperating powers and morale.

Marco Pantani, depressed and distrait, languished in a rehabilitation clinic, but perhaps the most colourful, if not, in terms of long-term ambition, the most notable, absentee from the line up was Mario Cippolini, the World road race champion. How could the Tour de France not invite the fastest man on two wheels, resplendent in his rainbow jersey? Jean-Marie Leblanc was adamant: the Lion King roared a good race in the first week but where would he be when the gradients began to bite? He'd been excluded from the 2002 edition and, after the unveiling of the 2003 race route, Cipo said, rashly: 'If invited, I will race there for the first week as far as the Alps.' Leblanc took him at his word and, against considerable opposition and the decided opinion of many, including some of Cipo's sprinter rivals and a lobby of French journalists, said bluntly: 'We weren't convinced he deserved our total confidence. The Tour de France is a competition, not a show.' To Cipo's further chagrin, the wild card he felt due to his team was awarded to the relatively humble French outfit, Jean Delatour, a very obvious chauvinism, in the view of the volatile Italian who manages to crawl over the mountains in his own national tour but has never shown the same commitment – or regard for its tradition – in the older race.

A similar failure of respect – whether real or perceived – had, hitherto, alienated Armstrong from the French press and it seemed that his ignorance of, or disregard for, Tour custom would, once again, raise their hackles and his bile. The centenary yellow jersey reverted to a tradition which blanket logo advertising snuffed out in the mid-80s: it would bear the initials HD, commemorating the father of the Tour, Desgrange. Armstrong, as reigning victor, ought to wear the jersey in the Prologue. At first, he demurred; he 'preferred to earn the right to wear it'. This apparently trivial insensitivity to time-honoured protocols actually amounted to a weighty failure to observe Tour tradition and Leblanc prevailed upon him to bow to it.

Suffering from a stomach bug – a bad reaction to antibiotics – may have contributed to a departure from his habitual custom: he did not reconnoitre the Prologue route, a 6.5km loop from the Eiffel Tower, across the river and back to the south end of the park at whose head the Tower stands.

David Millar had ridden a strong Dauphiné Libéré and gave signs of hardening into a fully committed professional. He had firm ambitions: to win the Prologue and 'have a crack at the overall if I'm well-placed after the Alps'. He admitted that turning pro so young and staying with the same team had rather cocooned him. He'd at last realised that serious preparation for the Tour cost rather more than he had hitherto been willing to pay; that riding up a mountain once wasn't enough. To be ready for what a climb was going to do to him on race day he needed to ride it once, twice, three times in succession to inure himself to the frailties that always emerge under extreme duresse. For years, he said, it was as if he'd been asleep: it was time to wake up and stretch himself to the limit.

Fully awake, then, and riding out of his skin, Millar sprinted out of the penultimate corner of the short Prologue a meaty five seconds ahead of the field, when, jarred by the cobbled surface, his chain jumped on the freewheel and then unshipped from the chain ring. He was forced to slow and lean down in the saddle to replace it. Four other members of the team had had the same problem – mechanics usually fit a double ring whose changer acts as a guard against losing the chain. Millar raced back to speed with venom but the advantage had gone and he lost the first yellow jersey to the Australian sprinter, Bradley McGee, by 0.08 of a second. No words can or should intrude on disappointment of that order.

Having thrown his bike at the mechanic's feet in an access of fury, Millar rounded on the Cofidis team boss. He demanded, and got, the demotion of Alain Bondue, with whom he has long had a testy relationship, from head honcho to domestic organiser and declared himself not only ready to lead the team from the front but, more pertinently, determined to match words with actions.

Stage 1 into Meaux ended in a catastrophic pile-up. In the final 400 metres the peloton en masse, sprinters like barracudas scenting blood, charged into a sharp right hand bend at about 75kph, José Enrique Gutteriez, perhaps shunted out of what may have been an uncertain line by another rider, lost balance, one foot sprang out of the pedal and he went down and took many others with him including Armstrong, who rode over the line on a replacement machine. Samuel Sanchez bunny-hopped over two stricken riders but Tyler Hamilton, a strong contender for the podium, rode into a sprawling Jimmy Casper and sustained two hairline fractures in his collarbone; Casper had to be helped away wearing a neck brace and Levi Leipheimer, the American who, as a rookie, came eighth in 2002, fractured his pelvis. Amazingly, only Leipheimer and a teammate Marc Lotz, did not make the start next day. The stage was taken by the Italian Alessandro Petacchi, winner of six stages in the Giro: he's quick, clever, nerveless and certainly aware of home expectations that he would fill in for Cipollini and fill in with style.

Robbie McEwen, overall winner of the green jersey in 2002, pulled it on again; the Points competition was going to be a fierce tussle – a quartet of feisty Australians, among a record seven riding the Tour, McEwen, McGee, Stuart O'Grady and Baden Cooke, prominent among the contenders.

Hamilton's decision to ride on – 'I'm not doing this for the team, I'm doing it for me,' he said – is typical of the man who learnt how to suffer when, as a young downhill skier, he bore up through long freezing stretches on ski lifts. During the 2002 Giro, he somersaulted into a tree at 60kph and broke a bone in his left shoulder. However, he kept quiet about the injury, rode on for another 16 days, 3 of them over the Dolomites, and finished 2nd in Milan, having ground the enamel off 12 of his teeth because of the pain. His CSC team osteopath, a charismatic Dane, Ole Kaare, is something of a wizard: he works on not just the injury but the response, mental and physical, of the patient to the trauma. He was sanguine about Hamilton's capacity to survive, his shoulder firmly bandaged to reduce jarring, so long as he could make it through the first 20km of the next stage. The team mechanic bound his handlebars with three rolls of tape, further padded with strips of gel, and raised them to make braking and changing gear easier, as well as lowering the pressure in his tyres. He finished Stage 2 'as white as linen' having got through five hours of excruciating pain partly by going through every song he could think of in his head. Casper also suffered horribly but brushed aside the misery: 'That's cycling for you . . . you block out the pain.'

(On the 9th stage of the 1920 race, Honoré Barthélémy crashed, broke a bone in his shoulder, one wrist and lost an eye, but battled on through six more stages to come 8th in Paris.)

An audacious 197km break by the young Frenchman, Frédéric Finot, was ridden down in a searing attack by David Millar but the peloton mowed them both down just before the finish in the old fortress town of Sedan where Cooke beat Jean-Patrick Nazon, Jaan Kirsipuu and Erik Zabel, celebrating his 33rd birthday. Now three Australians commanded the race: McGee in the yellow jersey, McEwen in green and Cooke in the white of best young rider. Next day, Nazon, from the Delatour outsiders, missed out again but having moved up the order thanks to the 12-second time bonus for second place in Sedan, garnered enough intermediate sprint points to become the first Frenchman to pull on the leader's jersey since François Simon in 2001. Born in Epinal he had the added prestige – perhaps inexplicable to anyone who does not appreciate how passionately the French feel about the Tour – of winning yellow as a boy of the region, a local hero. Petacchi, whom the French press had dubbed 'the gentleman sprinter', took the stage, and wrested the green jersey from Cooke, despite narrowly missing the Austrian Rene Haselbacher who lost control of his bike some 200 metres from the line. Haselbacher wobbled, leaned on McEwen who leaned on Cooke who stayed upright and leaned back and Haselbacher careered into the barriers. Petacchi swerved, stamped on the pedals and made a long run for the finish. Earlier he had been saying that his form wasn't good enough to get him through the Tour but this win, he thought, at the end of a stage ridden at a average speed of over 48kmh, had boosted his confidence for the long haul. Four days and two more stage wins later he rode 52km of Stage 7 onto the second category col de Portes, first uphill of the Tour, and climbed off 'having run out of energy'. He had not only emulated Cipo's speed during the first week of the Tour but his predictable rapidity of departure at the end of it. (Another of his teammates also abandoned and, the following day, four more which reduced the team to three riders, one of them Ivan Basso, best young rider in 2002.)

The 69km team time trial into Saint-Dizier, 'a flourishing industrial centre better by-passed,' says the *Blue Guide*, won by Armstrong's US Postal put his teammate Victor Hugo Peña into yellow – by one second – the first Colombian rider ever to wear it. Peña started his athletic career as a swimmer but, inspired by radio reports of the exploits of Luis Herrera, winner of the Alpe d'Huez stage in 1984, saved his earnings from giving swimming lessons to buy his first bike. Uncharacteristic of most of the cyclists who have come from the high Andes to dominate in the European mountains, particularly Herrera and Fabio Parra (3rd overall in 1988), whose brother Ivan was riding the Tour with the Kelme team, Peña is no climber, but the taking of yellow was a huge personal honour and an affirmation of the team's overall strength. Top riders in weaker (poorer) teams suffered – unfairly, it may be argued. Beloki and Ullrich lost over half a minute to Armstrong, Botero and Vinokourov 1 minute 31 seconds, and Mayo a demoralising 3 minutes 33 seconds. Given Armstrong's strength in the mountains, such a deficit effectively put Mayo out of serious contention. The team time-trial is spectacular and it exposes those teams – Millar's Cofidis, for instance – who are not well organised, but I am not convinced that it has a true place in this race. The winner owes much to his team; the victory is never his alone, but the proof of a team's strength in depth is, perhaps, better left to the vicissitudes of battle on the open road.

Peña's temporary status as race leader was not allowed to hamper his role as domestique for Armstrong: how often do we see the yellow jersey going back to the team car to load up with water for his boss up the road with the peloton?

From Lyon, the race headed for the Alps: a couple of introductory climbs before the first category col de la Ramaz, 1,000m of height gained in 15km before the rundown into Morzine. Two riders attacked from the start; two more, including one of Virenque's team men, Paolo Bettini, joined them and, at one point, had a lead of over seven minutes on the main bunch. At the foot of the col de Portes, Virenque set off in pursuit. 138km from the finish, he caught the escapees and rode up the slopes of the col de Ramaz on his own. A similar lone attack had carried him to victory in Morzine in 2000. He was also aiming to match the six-times Mountains prize winners, Bahamontes and Van Impe. From the summit, 22km, a short 3rd category climb, a jubilant descent to his sixth Tour stage victory and, 11 years after he first wore the yellow jersey, in his début Tour (after a break of 235km), he pulled it on again. Laurent Jalabert, now riding motorbike pillion as a television commentator, praised Virenque's audacity. 'Too many cyclists weigh what they might lose before considering any possible gain. Virenque doesn't bother to ask that kind of question. He attacks to win, he is not afraid of blowing up. If that happens, so be it, at least he's tried.' The yellow jersey was certainly on loan but he had also won the polka dots.

They say that a rider can lose the race in the mountains but cannot win it there. On this day, when Armstrong and most of the main contenders rode in together, Simoni and Botero were fried, 6 minutes 15 seconds down; not so much an off day as a long weekend.

Leading Armstrong by 2 minutes 37 seconds, Virenque must have believed he could stay in yellow until Bastille Day but the long solo ride had taken its toll. Fortified with EPO he could sustain prolonged effort day after day. Now, in the savage long haul over the Galibier and on to l'Alpe d'Huez, his bruised frame wilted and he trailed in 9minutes 29 seconds down.

Armstrong set up his 2001 win with a scorching attack on the first ramp of the Alpe. Nothing like that, this day. At the base of the climb, two escapees, Mikel Astarloza and the French champion, Didier Rous, held a lead of 2 minutes 10 seconds. Manuel Beltran and José Luis Rubiera of US Postal upped the tempo so high that it blew the chase group to bits. Virenque was dropped, so, too, Ullrich. Armstrong looked as if he was doing no more than hang on; he admitted as much later – Beltran, a newcomer to the team, had revved too quickly, from lack of experience. 'A fast tempo is good but this was supersonic . . . not good.' Ullrich fought his way back but when Beloki attacked, 10.5km from the summit, no one answered. He passed Rous and Astarloza but was himself reeled in after 3km. Mayo broke clear 500 metres on, followed by Hamilton and Beloki. This time Armstrong countered but, 4.5km from the summit, the astonishing Hamilton, scarce able to get out of the saddle because of his injury – every time he did he lost 50% of his power and 'it hurt like hell' – launched another attack. Beloki, with the fortitude of a rider intent on burying his reputation as a wheel-sucker, also went again. They could not get clear, but Beloki's assaults on Armstrong, six in all, (Hamilton tried five times) were evidence of a welcome new vigour and spirit. Vinokourov did get clear and clawed back 39 seconds of his deficit on Armstrong – 27 seconds on the road plus 12 seconds bonus for second place behind

Mayo who took the stage and a gain of 2 minutes 32 seconds. Millar faltered but, driven on by pride, limited his losses to 4m on Armstrong. For Simoni, who arrived in a state of near collapse, nearly 13 minutes down on Mayo, and Botero, a massive 42 minutes 19 seconds, it was a humiliating end to their pretensions. Botero, who'd ridden only the Tour de Catalonia and Germany in preparation for the Tour, attributed his lame showing to 'lack of vice, the spirit of competition'. Other Colombians came to racing hungry – he had grown up with food in his belly. As for Simoni, his powers of recuperation had gone. Armstrong, now in yellow, was harsh: 'It's easy to talk before the battle and Simoni is a big mouth. He underestimated the Tour de France – it's not the Giro. He needs to come back to earth.'

Of his own form he was surprisingly candid: '. . . what's important are my sensations and they're not good. I'm not as strong as I have been in other years. I actually felt worse at the start of the stage and on the Alpe I was slightly better, but even so Beloki's attacks were really hard to answer.' This boded well for Beloki's promise to be on the attack in the Basque Pyrenees.

In blistering heat, on the final descent into Gap the next day, Vinokourov away on his own, Beloki led the perilous high-speed chase, Armstrong on his wheel. The tarmac had melted; wheel rims and brake blocks smouldered. Apparently Beloki felt his front wheel puncture; he applied the rear brake and the blocks seized on the carbon rim. (A risk with carbon.) The back wheel locked, flicked one way then the other, ripping the tubular tyre out of its seating and poor Beloki went down, a sickening fall onto his right side. Behind him, Armstrong steered left in a near panic, off the road, past a gendarme and into a stubble field. He kept going, cross-country, across the neck of the hairpin, dismounted, shouldered the bike over a ditch and back onto the road to rejoin the small chasing group.

In a terrible strife of pain, Beloki lay on the road, his right wrist and elbow broken, the top of his femur fractured. (A second fracture was reported some days later.) It was a sickening end to the brave race he was riding.

Vinokourov took this Bastille Day stage – the first Frenchman home was Rous in 12th spot – and a further 56 seconds on Armstrong to move into second place, 21 seconds behind the lead.

He was clearly prepared to act on his promise: to isolate and disrupt Armstrong by persistent aggression.

Through temperatures of up to 52 °C, the riders sweated down to Marseille where Jakob Piil took the stage in a two-up sprint with another member of a long breakaway, the first escape of the Tour to succeed in staying away. Nearing the line, Fabio Sacchi reached out to shake the Dane's hand and muttered something in Italian. 'May the best man win?' Piil took that as a good omen and, allowing the Italian to jump for the finish, coolly rounded him and took the win. It was some recompense for losing out in a similar sprint with Hushovd the year before when his shoe came adrift from the pedal metres from the line.

When the pack came in, Millar made a surprise appearance at the front to lead out his pals McGee and Cooke 'for fun'.

From there, on another broiling day of Languedoc sun, to Toulouse in readiness for the first individual time trial, 47km from Gaillac to a new outdoor pursuits park built in a disused open-cast mine at Cap'Découverte.

It was stifling hot: 38 °C in the air, 61 °C on the road. We walked into Gaillac past the bike shop which the Bianchi team had rented for their warm-up – a sweet coup for a local enterprise and a smart move by the team to permit their riders to prepare in an air-conditioned interior to reduce sweat loss. Armstrong, by contrast, prepared outside the team bus, under a canopy of plane trees, for sure, but in the airless heat, earphones clamped over his head, eyes fixed on the ground, spinning the turbo trainer.

In these two vignettes the circumstances which swung the day: Ullrich came to the start cool, Armstrong hot and dehydrated.

Ullrich took the stage – 47km across the exposed rolling landscape of the Tarn flayed by the Dog Day sun – and beat Armstrong by 1 minute 36 seconds. It was a triumphant return to the top level, a resonant drubbing of the American, a time-trial specialist. Ullrich, now a mere 34 seconds off the lead, (what he'd lost in the team time-trial), was always brimful of talent but, as his former boss Walter Godefroot put it, he takes some shaking out of his torpor. 'You constantly think he's going to drown but he doesn't get moving till the water is up to his nose.'

After the rest day, David Millar had succumbed to a lung infection, could hardly breathe at night and was convulsed with coughing fits. This made his effort in the time trial – 7th at 3 minutes 55 seconds on Ullrich – the more commendable.

Ullrich himself had only just recovered from gastritis, having to peel off the back of the peloton to relieve himself: taken short and given the speed at which they were riding, he had to make it short.

Stage 13. Toulouse–Ax Trois Domaines.
I rode up the grisly final 9km climb ahead of the race (though not the wicked 14km Port de Pailhères which immediately precedes it) under a torrid sun, frequently compelled to weave through the crowds lounging across the road. This reinforced the impression of just how taxing it must be for riders at the limit of endurance faced with a mêlée of fans jinking about ahead of them. It's unnerving. On the commentary box monitors I saw the bunch hit the lower slopes, the wicked gradient I had just toiled up, saw one of them take off his helmet and ditch it into the verge – a nice souvenir for one fan. Following the death of Kivilev, the UCI imposed a rule that riders must wear helmets at all times except on a mountain top finish so long as the climb is longer than 5km.

Ahead of the field, Hamilton's CSC teammate Carlos Sastre rode clear for victory from his fellow breakaways 7km from the finish. CSC, managed by former Tour winner Bjarne Rijs, assisted by Sean Yates, now led the overall team competition.

Back down the climb, Armstrong, in a small group of six riders, was suffering. 3.5km from the line, the Basque climber Haimar Zubeldia attacked, Ullrich and Vinokourov caught him but the American couldn't reply. Another kilometre and Vinokourov jumped away, Ullrich caught his wheel and the two of them accelerated, ticking off seconds, precious seconds, of their deficit on the yellow jersey.

Zubeldia recovered and overhauled them, Vinokourov faltered and could only watch as Armstrong, mustering a desperate effort, went by. I watched them cross the line, each one of them, head sunk with fatigue, drained. Ullrich was now only 15 seconds adrift.

Armstrong had so far shown no flash of the dominance of the previous four years. There were signs of hesitation, an involuntary flinching, almost, from the extremes of pain.

Jalabert commented that it was clear, now, that Armstrong was vulnerable and 'in the peloton any sign of weakness is public enemy number one'. However, I talked to Paul Sherwen, who knows the American well, and he said he'd never seen him so calm, so unperturbed, despite this unwonted frailty. Asked whether he was having trouble with his back after an 80kph crash in the Dauphiné Libéré, Armstrong said 'No' and smiled. A specialist osteopath had recently flown in to give him some treatment but there was no pain or incapacity. Sherwen reckoned that Armstrong would make his move on the climb to Luz-Ardiden on Monday. 'It's a climb he knows well, the last mountain-top finish and he's done it there before.'

I cycled back down the climb and was held up by a policeman to make way for a line of team cars speeding off to beat the traffic. Seconds after I meekly dismounted, a French cyclist rode up, brushed the admonishing hand of the gendarme aside brusquely and continued down the road, civil disobedience being something of a national tradition in France.

Stage 14. Saint-Girons–Loudenvielle.
Distance: 191.5km. Col de Latrape 1,110m, Col de la Core 1,395m Col du Portet d'Aspet 1,069m, Col de Menté 1,349m, Col du Portillon 1,320m (and 10km of Spanish road to Luchon), Col de Peyresourde 1,563m, followed by a nice gentle 3km cruise down into the valley.

We rode up to the Portet d'Aspet and stopped in Orgibet, a small roadside village, what must have been most of the population gathered in knots to watch the race go through. A gaggle of little girls perched on a window ledge. National policeman assigned to patrol this tiny sector of the millions-strong audience across the country reproving the kids who darted across the road, heedless of any danger. But . . . beware. The publicity caravan is on its raucous way, tearing past, filling the road, a klaxon-blowing cavalcade of motorised water bottles, coffee pots, advertising billboards, Camembert cheeses, carnival floats, hurling out sweets, yellow musettes, card games, picture magazines, baseball caps, key rings (*lots* of key rings) and so on, disco music blaring, young girls the French call '*les miss*' waving from the open-top cars, the bare-flesh glossy smiling fanfara of commerce and come-on.

An hour or so later, the race approaches. A break: 4km from the start in Saint-Girons, 17 riders, including Virenque and, keen to reahabilitate himself, Simoni, went clear and they swish past, too concentrated to be bothered with the food bags they've collected at the feed station just down the road. However, when the main field comes through, about 15 minutes later, riders are sitting up going through the musettes, flinging out stuff they don't want – energy bars, mostly – another random largesse for the straggle of spectators. And suddenly, there's Armstrong rummaging through his lunch. He tosses out a round object wrapped in silver foil more or less at the feet of one of my companions, Karen from Rhode Island. When the race has gone through and calm returned, we repair to the bar up the road for lunch. What's she going to do with what turns out to be 'Lance's muffin'? This is kinda like the Eucharist, ain't it ? She reflects, decides, takes a nibble. We lean forward. So, what's it taste like?

'It's terrible,' she says.

At the foot of the Peyresourde, the breakaway group, thinned out on the Menté, held a lead of nearly 8 minutes on the yellow jersey group which contained all the favourites. Mayo and Christophe Moreau laid down the gauntlet, Vinokourov picked it up, Armstrong stuck to Ullrich and let them go.

All the way to the summit, Mayo sat on Vinokourov's wheel, doing nothing to support the attack. On the far side, down in the valley, the survivors of the escape group were battling for position and Simoni, another rider who did little but follow this day, jumped to the line just ahead of Virenque and Laurent Dufaux. Simoni had struggled the day before and been told to abandon by his director but refused. 'Fighters always overcome,' he said.

Vinokourov gained 43 seconds on Armstrong who came in with Ullrich and was now a mere 18 seconds behind him. Next morning, Simoni went to the US Postal team bus to call on a rather startled Armstrong. Given the acrimony of earlier exchanges, it was a conciliatory gesture on Simoni's part. Knowing that Simoni has a child, Armstrong made him a gift of one of his yellow jersey Crédit Lyonnais toy lions.

On the lower slopes of the Tourmalet, I passed a trio of Gallic cross-dressers – dimity frocks, splash lipstick and five o'clock shadows – sporting a banner: 'What we most admire about the bike is the pedal', *pédale* being the French for 'pansyland'. The approaches to the summit were densely packed, caravans and motor homes which had been up there for several days – picnics and parties – and the swathes of orange, the Basque colour, spread like beds of French marigolds. They say that the Basque language is so unfathomable that when the Devil tried to learn it he could master only seven words though what they were he wouldn't disclose – possibly the Deadly Sins, in which he has a vested interest. Halfway up the climb I'd passed a bunch of grinning men sporting orange favours who'd taken prisoner the Dutch nutter who follows the bike race dressed as Beelzebub, possibly to pummel some specialist vocabulary, if not rude sense, into him. 3km from the col, another party, some 30 strong, sat on one side of the road, three abreast, laughing and shouting as they rowed themselves up some imaginary stream of their own exuberance. Suddenly, I feel the bike pitched sideways and turn round to swear at the idiot who has lumbered into me, but it's a jovial bearded man in a tangerine cloak smiling at me, all teeth, as he gives me a hefty push up ten or so metres of gradient. Thanks, mate, whatever the Basque for that is. I wave, anyway, and reach the summit just as the police move across the line to close the road ahead of the publicity juggernaut.

From the hot sun at the col, back down to the cool overcast drizzly grey of a light Pyrenean mountain mist in La Mongie. Standing outside a café, the road no wider than 10 metres, we see the young Frenchman Sylvain Chavanel race past, giving his lowly Brioches-La Boulangère team spectacular air time. He broke from an early escape and has dropped Botero. Chavanel has 4km of this 2114m climb to do, a long drop to the base of the last climb of the day, 17km up to Luz Ardiden at 1,715m. It's a tall order but he looks strong. When Botero comes through, a different story: ashen, grim-visaged, he looks near cooked.

A lull, expectation hangs heavy, and suddenly in a rush of speed that makes your stomach clench, the main field is on us and past, up that unforgiving tarmac which cost our heart so dear, but each one of them looks drawn, the muscles of the face pinched as if – and it is surely true – every fibre of their frame is stretched taut with effort. The small men and the titans alike race at these climbs like demons of the chase. We learn that 4km lower down the climb, Ullrich attacked and Armstrong didn't respond. He said later: 'It was a trenchant attack but I said straight away it wasn't the time to move. The Tourmalet is a long climb and there's a long descent towards Luz-Ardiden . . . I decided to keep my rhythm and come back steadily. But Ullrich was super strong and I said to myself, "If he continues at that rhythm he's going to win the Tour".' He did reel him in. Ullrich's failed attack was censured by many – he went too soon. But, his ardour for the fight was showing and he felt good, he was doing his job.

Further up, responding to team orders, Botero waits for Vinokourov who had been dropped in the Ullrich tentative and is already 5 minutes off the pace. Botero began the Tour as team leader; now he is just another domestique. Had he managed to stay with Chavanel he might have been allowed to go for stage victory; as it is, his job reverts to that of support for the main man.

And, in the quiet after they have gone by, we observe the very wretched misery of the men who haven't been able to stay with them, who have been dropped, even by the grupetto, the group which sticks together in mutual self-help to beat elimination on time, isolated broken riders facing a lonely trek to almost certain disqualification but refusing to give in. Jean-Patrick Nazon, wearer of the yellow jersey for five days, had dropped out of the grupetto. He was afraid, he pushed on the pedals, but without force – it's like trying to walk in wet concrete – then saw the tail-enders and breathed once more: he was safe. No such luck for Axel Merckx, another victim of stomach upset, shelled out early on. He toils past us, gaunt with dismay, his body slumping, eyes hollow, eyes that will flood with tears when he trails in way past the time limit. Merckx was one of only eight Belgians riding the Tour and no Belgian rider has won a Tour stage for two years. It marks a sorry decline for a nation with such a vibrant history in the race.

At the foot of Luz-Ardiden, Chavanel had 5 minutes lead on the 18 riders of the yellow jersey group, to which Vinokourov had gutsily fought his way back. Chavanel, it appears, had cracked mentally on the morale-sapping stage to Ax Trois Domaines and nearly quit. This was his way of repaying himself for that close call.

In each of his four victories in the Tour, Armstrong had delivered one withering hammer blow on a mountain top finish to pulverise his rivals: in 1999, 6km from Sestrières, 2000, 3km from Lourdes Hautacam, 2001, 13km from l'Alpe d'Huez, 2002, 3.5km from La Mongie. It was, surely, now or never.

10.5km from the top Mayo attacked. Armstrong answered with Ullrich close behind. But, Armstrong, rounding a corner too close to the spectators (his own fault, he said) clipped one of them, his right brake hood caught in a musette and he fell heavily on his left side, taking Mayo with him. Ullrich swerved to avoid them. They remounted and Rubiera relayed his leader back. Suddenly, Armstrong's right shoe slipped out of the pedal (his gears, jarred in the fall, had jumped), he wobbled and fell onto the cross bar but somehow stayed upright and regained poise. An attack might have won him the tour but Ullrich very decently slowed and Hamilton curbed the rest. The lead group reined in and waited for Armstrong to rejoin.

At the 9km board, Mayo attacked again and Armstrong pounced. It was, he said, a desperate move and the very fact that he said that suggests that he was not ready to go or thinking of it, beforehand. Evidence of an unwonted shakiness of will? He said he'd had a number of problems during the Tour, even discounting the incident before the race when a pigeon had shit on Bruyneel's suit and the Czech rider Pavel Padrnos had muttered 'bad omen'. Pretty bad jitters, to be bothered about a bit of stray birdlime. After the fall he had sensed a great rush of adrenaline and said to himself: 'Lance, you want to win the Tour ? OK, you attack.' Would he have gone further up? Would he have waited on Ullrich's move ?

But he went; not perhaps with the fluency of previous years but with a concentrated ferocity which swallowed Mayo and spat him out, left Ullrich with the pursuers and, 4.5km from the finish, brought him alongside Chavanel, who had been out at the front for 123km. Passing the luckless winner of this year's Tour du Haut Var, he slowed to pat him on his back, a consolation much appreciated, not only because it demonstrated an overt expansiveness of spirit for which he has not been conspicuous but a due homage to the ethos of the Tour. In showing respect, this year Armstrong won it.

He crossed the line having gained, with the 20-second bonus time, 52 seconds on Ullrich. Mayo, in an obstinate show of pusillanimous self-interest, nipped past the German – who had done all the work of chasing – to snaffle the 12 seconds bonus.

Vinokourov, the big loser of the day, came in 2 minutes 7 seconds down.

Millar was in a pitiable state. Racked with chest pains and coughing fits he had been dropped and fought his way back, without help, only to vomit violently from the strain. The prospect of a rest day comforted him but 'in view of my condition, I'm not optimistic'. His team doctor said: 'He's at the limit of what a cyclist can stand . . . in any other race I would have sent him home. The Tour is a race of excess.' Indeed, Millar had rounded on the doctor and, in his distress, shouted: 'When are you going to tell me to stop? I can't get better on this fucking bike.'

There remained one more day of climbing, in the Basque Pyrenees, but the stage finished with a long run downhill into Bayonne. Millar, who lives in adjacent Biarritz, naturally wanted to cut something of a dash on his home turf, even against the odds of his poor shape. He attacked 15km from the start in Pau, chasing a small group that had flown off at the gun. Anything, he said, not to have to crawl into his home town with the tailenders. In this last week of the Tour when the climbing is all but done, many riders are content to bowl along, stay out of trouble, getting to Paris intact their only objective. Some while ago, Millar himself was lambasting the 'idiots' who hit the front at crazy speeds when everyone was exhausted. But, this day, ill or not, he was showing a similar fiery enthusiasm for madcap and ultimately fruitless attacks.

As the escape fragmented on the first of the climbs, the first category col de Soudet 1,540m, it was the amazing Hamilton who, leading the descent to the base of the col Bagarguy, a horribly steep ascent to 1,327m, attacked and passed over the col with an advance of 2 minutes 10 seconds on the pursuit. He faced 95km of solo riding. Rijs, his manager, spoke of the exceptionally strong team spirit of CSC. 'Our strength is in our motivation. Tyler Hamilton is the proof of that.' As a result, they held an unassailable lead in the team competition which could earn them automatic selection for next year's Tour.

It was a quite remarkable ride. Hamilton held off the peloton with a display of sheer determination, digging for every scrap of force and energy in his body, his mind set on getting to the haven of the white line drawn across the road, alone, first. And, as he drove the excruciating weight of his bike and body, the seeming tons of it by now, towards the line he sat up, turned round and beckoned to Rijs, driving the car which had shadowed him all the way. The team cars have to turn off before the finishing strait but Hamilton wanted to thank the man, his friend, who had given him such support, not just this day, but throughout, to thank him publicly. Rijs drove up and the men shook hands.

Another story lay behind the victory. Hamilton, through lack of vigilance, had got caught at the back of the peloton near the start and his team had been obliged to work very hard to relay him back. It was for them, he said, that he wanted to win the stage.

Virenque was now assured of the Mountains prize but the competition for the green jersey seemed likely, as last year, to be decided in Paris. Cooke led McEwen by 8 points and Zabel by 13.

Bordeaux, the cradle of French cycling, has hosted more Tour stage finishes than any other city, bar Paris – 78 in 90 editions – and, because of its position in the flat coastal plain of the Landes, it has traditionally offered a big arena for the sprinters. The great sprinter André Darrigade, born near Dax from which today's stage began, took 22 stage victories in the Tour, the last of them in Bordeaux – surprisingly the first time he had won there.

Just as the Tour evolves, so is tradition thwarted. A bunch of spoilers hit the road out of Dax. By 68km – and away to their right near Labastide d'Armagnac, a small country church dedicated to Nôtre-Dame des Cyclistes – they had built a lead of over 16 minutes. 25km from the finish it was still over 10 minutes. With 18km to go, the surprise winner of the 2002 Paris–Roubaix, the Dutchman Servais Knaven, went off on his own. None of the others seemed inclined to mount a challenge and Knaven rode into the heart of Bordeaux in lone state more than 8 minutes ahead of McEwen who outsprinted Cooke and Zabel at the head of the jostling pack.

There followed another flat stage, another long break and, at an intermediate sprint, Ullrich accelerated behind McEwen to take the 4 bonus seconds on offer ahead of Armstrong, who took 2. Cooke missed out and his lapse meant that he surrendered his green jersey to McEwen. The tension between them was palpable – McEwen sitting on Cooke's wheel all day to unsettle him. The younger man was beginning to show signs of self-doubt and McEwen is a bullish individual who, having won the competition once, must have an edge in these final nervy days.

Individual time-trial, Pornic–Nantes 49km.
It was all to play for: Ullrich a mere 1 minute 5 seconds lag of Armstrong, substantially less than he had taken on the earlier ride against the clock. In 1989, Lemond beat Fignon by 58 seconds over 24.5km to win the Tour on the last day. However, on the morning of the penultimate day of this Tour, a chilly rain swept across the Atlantic coast of the Vendée and Armstrong smiled.

He reconnoitred the course by car, knowing that the weather conditions were going to make it a highly technical ride – ultra-light bikes prey to any buffet of wind, slick tyres very prone to slip on the raised gloss paint of the white line and, the cause of his crash in the Dauphiné Libéré, metal manhole covers. Inexplicably, Ullrich did not recce the course – perhaps it's a superstition with him. More puzzling, he opted to ride a bike he had never ridden before on a five-spoked front wheel which all the experts pronounced extremely difficult to control in strong winds. He also took the considerable risk of fitting a huge gearing, 56 x 11, which would make cornering very dicey. If he could turn it with consistent rhythm, it would develop a rapacious velocity; if not . . .

In 2001, Millar lost the World time-trial championship to Ullrich, having established a faster time till near the end of Ullrich's ride. However, when the German caught the rider who started ahead of him, the man rallied and fought back. This resistance gave Ullrich the needed spur and Millar saw his winning lead eaten away. He has since re-jigged his time-trial position and technique on the Manchester vélodrome.

When he woke up in Pornic his cough had gone; he felt well again, *pleasure* had come back. After a sketchy warm-up, he rode the course at an average of 54.36kph, despite a fall 6km from the end which cost him around 20 seconds. The bike was upright, the tyre simply hit a patch of oil and went from under him. Even as the mechanic fumbled to reset the chain, Millar stayed cool – it is, he says, one of his traits never to panic.

Second to last down the ramp: Ullrich. Three minutes later, Armstrong. At the 35km time check, Armstrong was only 6 seconds down. Then, calamity: Ullrich took a bend too sharp, fell and skittered into the barrier of hay bales. He remounted, but the Tour was gone, out of reach. Watching him on television, Millar said he knew from the chancey way he was riding that he'd fall. Bruyneel told Armstrong the news and the American at once relaxed. He could afford to ride safely and Millar took the stage (his third win level with Robert Millar and Boardman) by 9 seconds over Hamilton who leap-frogged the two Basques Mayo and Zubeldia into fourth overall: what a reward for a truly heroic ride in this truly stirring Centenary race.

The last stage onto the Champs Elysées set out from Ville d'Avray, (site of the Parc des Princes vélodrome, built 1936) where earlier Tours, including the first, always finished. The US Postals turned out in an ugly battleship grey strip and were fined £3,100 for 'equipment that did not conform with the rules'. What you wear at the start you have to wear at the finish. Not quite as draconian as the early days of HD (see p.85) but a timely reminder that his crotchety spirit lives on.

Jean-Patrick Nazon's Jean Delatour had announced that it would be withdrawing from sponsorship at the end of the season. There was no more cogent way of making fools of his bosses than to win on the Champs Elysées and this he did, with great éclat, ahead of the two Australians battling for green. At the first intermediate sprint, Cooke beat McEwen and was level with him. At the next, McEwen regained the advantage: 2 points. Into the final sprint, very close, McEwen's elbows out, Cooke on his wheel, alongside, McEwen bristling, Cooke barges up, their shoulders touch, overt spoiling or routine rough-house? There was no disqualification, Cooke made it and took green by two points. (McEwen was asked by officials immediately after the finish to view a tape of the incident. He had made no objection, watched the replay for form and said nothing. Uncompromising on the course, he is honest and uncomplaining in defeat – what they call 'correct', in the best tradition of the peloton.) O'Grady, to his surprise, won the Centenary prize for best showing in the six original finish cities –

compensation for the frustration of being caught after a long break a mere 500 metres from the line in Lyon.

L'Equipe's assessment of Tour winners as cyclists for all time, placed Armstrong 7th, behind Coppi who won only two, even though the American has now joined the élite club of quintuple winners. Well, other times, other ways of doing things. He has never been so popular in France as when he was having a hard time. (The French journalists, who award the least helpful rider their lemon prize, this year gave Armstrong an orange for his benign manner. He is not so kind to journalists whose remarks he dislikes – they are blacked from the list of members of the press to whom he is prepared to speak. He even has a journalist monitoring opinions in the Press Room.) As to his future, he faces what has so far proved to be the most intractable Tour gremlin of all: number six. This year he lacked the punch he had in the past; his power less explosive, his willingness to suffer impaired, yet, he did win. He surmounted trials and problems and, in that, took his hardest victory. It remains to be seen whether Fignon's poignant description of decline applies lastingly to Armstrong as it applies with summary force to all the other five-times men:

'You don't see it coming but there is a time when it just becomes more and more difficult to win . . . The cyclist's style grows more laboured. His attacks have less vigour about them. He controls the race a little less by waiting and thinking before reacting to something rather than responding instantly.'

Ullrich had limited ambitions for this Tour but the move to an Italian team and more flexible training methods has made him leaner, more resilient; Beloki suffered terrible luck just as he had begun to flourish; Hamilton's efforts under duresse diminished his threat. Next year? It is a juicy prospect.

Postscript
News was released was after the Tour that only one rider failed a drugs test: the Spaniard Javier Pascual Llorente of the Kelme-Costa Blanc team tested positive for EPO after the 12th stage.

AFTERWORD AND MYTHOLOGY

AFTERWORD

There used to be two types of rugby player: those who played the piano and those who shifted them. I have an idea there are two sorts of racing cyclist, too: those you'd want to spend time with and those you're happy to get no closer to than television allows. On 18 October 1997, in the tiny Pyrenean town of Oust, we're about to meet one of the former. I rode through here in July and have come back to the Ariège to ride some cols, go for walks with my daughter, Lucy, do some work and renew acquaintance with our hosts, Nick and Jan, cooks extraordinaire and cycling fans complete, who run a small guest house along the valley for cyclists and walkers keen to enjoy their special brand of support for Pyrenean Pursuits, the name of their enterprise.

Nick met us at Toulouse airport and we dropped in at Oust on the way home to enjoy half an hour of the Fête du Fan Club Frédéric Moncassin, a day of VTT (mountain bike) races on a circuit specially designed by Frédo. He's a big star, leading sprinter for the GAN team, a pal of Chris Boardman's, but a local boy, too. He lives in a hamlet below the crest of the col du Saraillé a few miles away – he couldn't imagine living anywhere else. Here he is, turning out for a day mixing it with local amateurs, semi-pros and a handful of other star names: Stéphane Barthe, Christophe Rinero, Henk Vogels – pals of his from the *peloton*, jobbed in to add frisson to the occasion. We park the car. Cyclists are everywhere, cruising idly or tinkering with the machines – a true cyclist is always tinkering, they say. Indeed, a pal of mine at school almost never had his bike, a very superior model, on the road: it was always in bits on the kitchen table, having its ballbearings massaged. Anyway, we found Moncassin changing an inner tube in his front tyre, chatting with a couple of bystanders. Nick went up – Frédo recognised him from a casual encounter a year ago – and they exchanged greetings, Moncassin autographed a couple of programmes – one for me – and we moved on.

There was nothing in it for Moncassin other than pleasing his fan club, drinking a *vin d'honneur* with the Mayor at 6 p.m. and chilling out at the dinner and knees-up with a local band later on, except for *amour du vélo* . . . love of the bike. It's what links us all, whether we're riding for fun or hitting the front of a jostling, jittery bunch at 60-plus kph, where a touch of wheels, a flailing elbow, a sideways rock of the frame can bring you down under a charge of wheels. You risk broken bones that put you out for the rest of the season, but routinely take risks for the glory of coming through ahead, winner of the stage. Moncassin missed out this year; second by four millimetres, stage four, a day of gruesome crashes, several riders out with injury, but he was there day after day. A slim-built guy, his father was a great sprinter, too: the power seems to come from the buttocks, the instinct from the family genes, the courage from somewhere under the jersey.

The Tour de France rode past Nick and Jan's house in 1997 and will do so again in 1998. The night before it passed in '97, there'd been a huge beano, of course: visiting cyclists from England, local enthusiasts, a trio of filmmakers from Liverpool Cycle Centre putting a short documentary together. Then came the big question: What were they going to paint on the road outside the house? Messages to the Wirral man, Boardman, naturally: Attack it, Chris. However, when it came to partisan advertising, Jan put her foot down: No, strictly *no,* Pyrenean Pursuits.

It is 4 a.m., dawn squeezing itself under night's black-out curtain, Nick and the graffiti team are out on the road scrawling the legends in white daub, when Simon O'Brien one of the inspirations behind the Liverpool Cycling Centre says:' 'How do you spell Pyrenean Pursuits?' Jan, fast asleep in bed, is what she terms a 'creative speller' and there was some doubt. But the legend is still there, and in the house a photo of the *peloton* ambling across it at a leisurely 32kph, the gaudy array of team strips offset by bunting in the trees, flags and miniature jerseys strung from the electricity poles. The Tour de France doing today what Desgrange's vision shaped nearly a century ago. Was he, come to think of it, inspired even a little by the imperial Persian horse-couriers of ancient times, the original Pony

Express: 'Nothing in the world travels faster than the Persian horse-couriers, and it's a Persian invention, exploiting their network of imperial roads. A relay of horses and riders is stationed along a fixed route, one man and one mount for each day of the journey. Nothing stops them: not snow, rain, heat of the sun, or night-time.' (Herodotos, *Histories*).

On our autumn visit to Biert, Lucy and I walked up to the Queire de Massat – a majestic view along the valley of the River Arac towards the ranges hiding the col de Port, and home to a tiny woodland shrine to a Saint Branda, ignored by my hagiographies. We drove up to the col de Crouzette (I cycled it first: a bit of a facer, 5km of acute angle to round it off, which make you think twice about this 'love of the bike' stuff) and for four hours rambled through sweet chestnut and dwarf oaks, birch and beech trees to the crease of the valley, across the stream and up the other side. We passed ruined stone houses, home to recluses in the last century who weathered winter and summer up there, several hours trek from any source of food to augment what the woods could not provide. There are mushrooms in abundance for a few weeks of the year, every year, except that mushroom pickers tread the mulch at their peril these days: the hunting lobby have introduced *sangliers* (wild boar, favoured nosh of Obélix and Astérix) into the high woods and, for their own safety – from flying wild buckshot rather than wild tusk – the mushroom gatherers are denied.

There were wolves and the famous black Pyrenean bears here once, but although an occasional mountain man turns up in the village and town squares hereabouts to show what twinkly toes the local bruins have, the danger in these sauvage regions comes largely from the human species.

Lucy rode her first col – the Saraillé – first the gentler way; which had a Liverpool racer squealing: he's a sprint specialist and rode up in company with a few of his team-mates and Nick and, at the first bit of identifiable gradient, was complaining. This prepared Lucy, 17 years old, veteran of one family-sponsored Tour de Holland and the one-off Calais–Cherbourg six-day ride, for the ascent from the steeper side and that feeling familiar to all serious bikies of: 'Sod this for a pot of japonica jam, I've *had* it.' Yet, for some reason best left to God and guesswork, carrying on anyway.

I rode the col de Péguère, 3.5km of one in five, a side turning after 7km of the col de Port. The first 500m or so out of the saddle I was thinking I'd definitely had it and any more of this and I'd turn into a puddle of something not quite kosher in the middle of the road. I decided I'd better sit down and give that a go. Surprisingly, it worked, and though it would be an exaggeration to say the climb was easy, it *was* short and the view from the top – reckoned to be amongst the finest in the Pyrenees – was ample reward. So, too, the valley leading up to the col d'Agnès – whose towering breastlike peak is macabre reminder of the grisly way she was martyred: punitive mastectomy – a 16km ribbon of peaceful riding to a marvellous panorama into the next valley at whose foot nestle the old Roman spa town of Aulus-les-Bains. I rode over names of riders long retired – a trio of Dutch aces: Breukink, the all-rounder, Rooks, the climber, Van Poppel the sprinter.

Did Robert Millar – the British rider with the best record in the Tour, Mountains Prize and fourth overall in 1984 – rejoice in the view when he led the Tour over in 1988? He never strikes me as a rider who really *enjoys* anything. His approach to journalists and the rest of humanity makes Fignon look like Mr Helpful; not so much love of the bike as 'sod off'. The ferruginous springs at Aulus continued to draw health-seekers in their droves till the craze waned and the splendiferous lodgements for the fashionable visitors, such as the Grand Hotel, empty, decrepit, forlorn, became grand only in destitution. The hydrotherapy is starting up again, though, and Aulus may see a kind of prosperity once more. Its original celebrity depended on the patronage of officers in the French army, home on leave from the war in Indochina, with the clap. Aulus provided chemical salt cures; they came in droves and Aulus thrived. Times have changed and the pox-ridden aristos of the French military have evanesced; the resorts clings on.

These are, without doubt, the most beautiful mountains I've ridden. The July of my earlier trip, we rode from Bayonne east, criss-crossing from France into Spain and back. The first two full days were murder: plunging off the main itineraries on to lonely cols in the inner ranges, we hit one in fours, thick mist, roads that seemed to peter out into grit-encrusted mud. On the Sunday, we tackled the col de Marie Blanque, 10km only, but in torrid heat.

I was expecting daily to hear the news of my mother's death – she'd been to the brink of death and back several times that year – and I got as close to capitulation on that climb as I have ever been. Nightmares followed by hours awake had smitten me physically; an appalling dread that she had died that very night reduced me mentally. John had warned me way back in January that – against our normal pattern of lead and follow – he'd be racing me up this ascent and when he appeared alongside me I very nearly caved in. I had not the heart nor the legs, it seemed, for competition. He drew ahead on his lower gears and I watched him go by. Gradually, I did reel him in but, as I drew level, I said: 'I'm finished in my head,' and I was. If ever I have been embroiled in what they call the Calvary of extreme physical and mental duresse it was then.

John stopped for a pee and I had not the courage, not the magnanimity, to stop and wait; had I paused I might never have started up again. I was nearly hallucinating with the effort of keeping going, however. Then something of salvation filtered into my head: the slight zigzag using whatever camber there was to ease the gradient. It didn't *look* steep but it was doing some terrible things to me. Slowly the torment lessened; I found a rhythm, precious rhythm. I even quickened and, as I did so, realised that the pain in my head had gone and I was riding free once more. Not fast but free, and suddenly I was there, the blessed sign reading 'col' popped out from behind the trees like a treat at a surprise party. Later that same day we rode most of the climb of the Aubisque, to Eaux-Bonnes (no towns offered on the far side) and the day after that over the Aubisque itself, down the corniche which skirts the adjacent range and up and over the col de Soulor, where Boardman crashed. That afternoon we crossed the Tourmalet. It was one of the experiences of my life to cycle that legendary giant of the Tour, to emerge from the long twists of the lower valley road and see that massive bulk of the first buttress ahead of me, the road cut into its flank rising steeply in the shelter of the rock to where it turned round the corner and out of sight. What beyond the bend?

You ride up and find that beyond the bend is another buttress, another long ramp of road, several kilometres, but by now you've got the experience not to be deterred; just ride on until you can see in the far distance, where the hairpins swishing like a snake's tail finally straighten into the final few hundred metres and the topside refuge which means you're there. After 18km nothing, you feel, could stop you. Locals on either side of the mountain claim that their approach is the worse for the riders; certainly the southern ascent, from Bagnères is steeper in places; the longer ride from Barèges imposes its own difficulties.

A day or two later, we rode the Port de Bonaigua. It lasts 24km, but is characteristic of these mountains: wooded valleys folded into sinuous rock walls, roads winding graciously to the ridges and down again like downhill skiers swaying their hips in a lovely slide along gravity's runway. More human in scale than the Alps, less tonsured than the Dolomites, wilder and more remote than both, the pleated green-clad Pyrenean ranges, dinted with countless valleys, are cycling perfection.

Another day of the October visit I cycled down the valley of the Arac, through Oust and up the long haul towards Guzet Neige, the ski station where Robert Millar rode in to his second solo victory (of three overall) in 1984 and where, four years later, in company with Giotti, he turned right past a traffic cop instead of left, 3km from the top, into the car park.

After a visit to the market town of St Girons, browsing round second-hand bookshops and antiquated backstreets, Jan suggested a trip to see the memorial to Fabio Casartelli, the young Italian rider killed in 1995. It was a sombre ride in the car up through the village of Portet d'Aspet, on to the col and down through the trees. I'd seen the accident – moments after it happened – on French television: Casartelli lying inert in a pool of blood, no indication whether he was still alive. Virenque, the winner that day, wasn't told what had happened until he was sitting in the caravan waiting to mount the podium. As we drove down, I was riding the descent in my mind: marking the way the camber seems to tip out towards the verge, to make the sinuous ledge you're riding on slope away from the mountain wall, so that the already sharp right-hander has an extra danger built in. And the long, open, serpentine twists of the road occasionally tighten to make rounding the bend an abrupt lesson in balance, nerve, judicious braking.

Suddenly, we saw the memorial ahead: it stands a hundred metres or so uphill from where he skidded. Is it just imagination that makes that sharp curve, like a kink in wire, look so dramatically steeper, more frightening, than the others? The stone that killed him is gone; a low wall fringes the verge and, at the spot, a makeshift shrine – plaque, flowers, ribbons. Till recently, there had been the same wrack of old tubs that I saw on Ventoux for Simpson; for ages a Motorola cap signed by every member of the team – a valuable collectable for anyone meretricious enough to purloin it. No one did. There are such people: the thief who walked into the museum of the Tolpuddle martyrs in the village of their birth (entry free) and stole Emmett's watch, a worthless *objet* on any market. A judge once sent a convicted thief to the gallows for theft of a watch: 'You snatched at Time,' he said 'and you caught Eternity.'

The memorial itself is a beautiful structure in white marble: a finely sculpted disc wheel merging at the back into wings, rough-hewn to suggest feathers; the leading rim is swathed in a banner, streaming back as if in wind, and etched with the five interlocked rings of the Olympic Games – Casartelli was Olympic Road-Race Champion in 1992. On the rock face opposite the unofficial shrine, someone has daubed, in white paint now fading from the weather: *HOMMAGE À UN CHAMPION*.

When the Tour rode up the Portet d'Aspet in 1997, the whole *peloton* stopped by this silent testimony to the panache and courage of a young rider bursting with enthusiasm for his chosen *métier*, to pay their respects. His wife was there, his father and mother. A fleeting pause, a re-echo of the terrible grief of that dreadful day, and the *peloton* rode on.

And how many heroes of this epic Tour have I not even mentioned. Homer would have found room for them, every one. The Dutchman, van Est, who, like Rivière, plunged off the road into a deep ravine and, to general astonishment, crawled back out unscathed. Iron Willem, he became. And would Anquetil have had his five victories had Rivière survived to match him? And what of André 'Dédé' Darrigade, sprinter extraordinary, winner of 22 Tour stages, five of them Prologues; first Bobet's and then Anquetil's right-hand man, particularly on the end-to-end holding of the yellow jersey; holder of the golden fleece himself, and outright winner of green. Yet, he said of himself: 'I was always thought of as a team man and I never pretended to be anything more.' A team man like Jos de Schoenmaker, Merckx's faithful lieutenant, out of that fateful '71 Tour with a broken femur sustained in the Midi Libre. What a difference he might have made; except that Merckx did it, after all. And the strong man, Van Springel, robbed of yellow in the final time-trial, 1968, by Jan Janssen, still riding at the age of 37, green jersey in 1973. How could I give so little space to Felice Gimondi, winner at his first attempt in 1965, of whom Merckx said: 'Gimondi is a complete rider: intelligent, brave. I admire his strength of character, his noble nature, his decency. He brings honour to our profession.' Or? . . . but that is a good note to end on.

MYTHOLOGY

God had just finished creating the world and, surveying His work, He saw France: such wonderful scenery, landscape of every description, food, drink, vegetation in abundance and rich variety – France had everything. No other country enjoyed half what France had in plenty and to spare. How unjust. So, to even things up, God created the French people.

It's a joke the French tell against themselves – add a dash of irony – and if trying to get to the heart of what makes the Tour de France unique ranks with analysing humour as unrewarding work, there's no doubt that France itself, herself, forms a large part of the equation. The country and the way its people think and feel about it. The French didn't invent patriotism – though Chauvin, father of chauvinism, was one of theirs – but they have cultivated it into a fine art.

'The most beautiful kingdom second only to heaven,' someone said of France, an earthly paradise of contrasts enough to fill an entire catalogue of holiday brochures *and* bags of room. Most of France is rural and a traveller can still roam most of France in the kind of tranquillity and solitude which the automobile destroyed decades past in cramped and overcrowded England where the traffic jam has become a protected species. Half of England is road and half the roads of England are up.

The modern Tour navigates the hexagon clockwise and anti-clockwise alternately, along the self-same roads covered by the early race; better surfaces, but the same roads. And, if scenery doesn't figure high on the riders' preoccupations – now as then –

stunning views of such a grand variety of landscape can make a difference, even subliminally; any distraction from sheer mileage, although the domineering character of the high mountains cannot be evaded. For the spectators, the impact of the Tour against its dramatic backdrop is, and was, stupendous. Consider the words regularly applied by French commentators to the Tour: legend, myth, epic, saga, exploit, heroic. 'The Tour passes through a truly Homeric geography. As in the *Odyssey*, this race is a voyage both of human endeavour and exploration to the far reaches of the land, every nook and corner.' Roland Barthes, *Mythologies, 1957*.

Mythology? Particularly in the early days it *seemed* unreal and yet there, before their eyes, palpable, true. In 1903, six years before Blériot's maiden flight across the Channel, bike riders whom people had only heard of, celebrated names and unknowns, emerged from the haze into remote villages in inner France, outlying hamlets, walled towns, and disappeared into the haze again; or into the darkness of night, their lamps like glow-worms in the distance. Vision or fact? 1997 and what has changed? Well, Blériot and his insect of a machine are ancient history but the Tour is still the Tour: fame on a bicycle, the heroes of the legend spinning through the provinces, the forgotten holes of regional France, the backwaters where television antennae angle for *télésport*, sweeping down the main street past the shops, the bar with the rusting publicity *affiche* on its side wall – St Raphaël, Anquetil's old team – and into the haze again, passing the black and white chequer sign on the garage – Peugeot, Merckx' first sponsor, Thévenet's, Tommy Simpson's.

It goes everywhere; they call it *La Grande Boucle*, 'the big loop' and everywhere it goes the people gather to gawp: they line the streets at siesta time, they hang over the garden gate, take picnics out to the verges of the long road meandering through the open wheatbowl, they crowd the tree-lined slopes of the narrow road snaking up one massif or another; roads the pilgrims took from Paris to Santiago across the Pyrenees, or to Rome across the Alps; roads laid by the Romans for their conquering armies; back-road circuits taken by Gauls on the run; secret roads the intrepid mountain guides took across the Pyrenean passes leading allied soldiers and airmen to neutral Spain; roads the young men with ambition tramped, to court and the cities, the cities paved with gold and walled about with fire; roads the troubadours ambled with poetry and music on their mind:

> They talked as they rode
> Towards the city
> At a fair speed,
> And beside the road
> The casual murmur
> Of a stream through rushes
> Over the gravel.
>> Jean Renart, twelfth century

And 800 years later, the song of the rider in distress: sprained ankle, dry water bottle, sun beating down, puncture, hollow stomach, sick and tired, trying to keep his spirits up:

> My God, where is the *peloton?*
> My God, where is the *peloton?*
> This Tour de France is unholy
> tour-ment
> A Tour too big
> This Tour's a pig . . .
> My God, where is the *peloton?*
> *Bon Dieu, où est ce peloton?*
>> Blaness, Fugain, Schmitt

The French passion for Le Tour has much to do with it being *their* Tour of *their* France in quest of *their* accolade. Cycling is *their* national sport, the sport they all follow in July. It was the first great bike race and still is the greatest. The first claim no one can argue about; the second only a fool would quarrel with. And it comes with passion, above all, in a country where passion is a legitimate plea against a charge of murder; passion both emotional and intellectual. It is the French way: frivolous in their amusements, serious and studied in their tastes. You enjoy wine: you find out precisely *why* you enjoy wine, because knowing adds to the pleasure and the pleasure is enhanced by discussing it.

The Absurdist playwright Ionesco remained unconvinced. He couldn't understand, 'The passionate desire of people wanting to lead a bunch of cyclists into Paris after a complete circuit of France . . . and a spectator overcome with joy because he'd spotted Poulidor's back flying past, three seconds in which to admire the lone passage of an escaped cyclist.' A very absurd opinion.

Roland Barthes, the philosopher, was fascinated by the extraordinary phenomenon of the Tour. In *Mythologies*, he suggests that in the Tour, myth and reality fuse and become indistinguishable: the combat both between rival men and men and Nature are idealised, the stuff of chivalric romance, say, but at the same time the men are flesh and blood, too, as never in any other myth. The resulting ambiguity perhaps goes some way to baring the secret of the Tour, its intrinsic fascination – super-human heroes battling with titanic adversity, in their shadow the retainers, the humble *domestiques*. And then the natural elements, hidden forces of evil and good, the magic of good and bad luck, conspiring to advance or deny victory. Not so far-fetched to think of it in terms of the knight's journey through the Wasteland, across the Mountains of Despair, into the Valley of False Comfort, through the Forest of Foreboding and on over the Plain of Desolation, to reach the promised city, Paris, thousands of miles away. They even call the leader's yellow jersey 'the golden fleece', Jason and the Argonauts's mythic prize.

We unromantic Anglo-Saxon *rosbifs* see a great bike race and that's that. We might get sentimental about our plucky losers, but that hardly consitutes passion. The French see a great bike race, too, but there's nothing they can't and won't philosophise about, nothing behind which doesn't lurk the metaphysics. Barthes said the names of the champions become like algebraic symbols standing for moral qualities: Valour, Loyalty, Treachery, Stoicism, Noble Sacrifice.

And the Tour liberates passion, they are all agreed on that; a very French passion, giving expression to what Napoleon identified as central to the French character: 'When I hear of a nation that can exist without bread, I will believe that the French

can exist without glory.' Glory, yes. And, after all the compli-
cation, the analysis, the philosophising and the intellectual passion
for comparison, symbol, mythic truth and the penetralia of
legend, the quest for the glory is simple: *La gloire . . . maillot jaune.*
Interchangeable.

INDEX